ENLIGHTENMENT A

DESCARTES TO KANT

Kant believed that true enlightenment is the use of reason freely in public. This is the first book to trace systematically the philosophical origins and development of the idea that the improvement of human understanding requires public activity.

Michael Losonsky focuses on 17th-century discussions of the problem of irresolution and the closely connected theme of the role of volition in human belief formation. This involves a discussion of the work of Descartes, Hobbes, Locke, Spinoza, and Leibniz.

Challenging the traditional views of 17th-century philosophy and written in a lucid, nontechnical language, this book will be eagerly sought out by historians of philosophy and students of the history of ideas.

Michael Losonsky is Professor of Philosophy at Colorado State University.

For Rosa and Miro, my philosophers

This Trayne of Thoughts, or Mentall Discourse, is of two sorts. The first is Unguided, without Designe, *and inconstant; Wherein there is no Passionate Thought, to govern and direct those that follow . . . In which case the thoughts are said to wander, and seem impertinent one to another, as in a Dream. Such are Commonly the thoughts of men, that are not onely without company, but also without care for anything.*

Hobbes, *Leviathan* 1.3

Contents

Preface

I had historical, philosophical, and political reasons for writing this book. My historical aim is to show that there is an evolution from Descartes to Leibniz that takes us to the threshold of Kant's conception of human enlightenment as something that requires the public exercise of reason. In tracing out this intellectual evolution, I focus on the topic of irresolution in 17th-century philosophy. Irresolution is seen as a major hindrance to enlightenment and it is in its treatment that 17th-century philosophers turn to the role of voluntary activity. For some, the cure for irresolution is to stimulate and encourage the human mind's automatic, involuntary, and inspired cognitive processes. For others, the way to overcome irresolution is to take control and do something, namely, literally to make some judgments and stick with them. What underlies these competing treatments of irresolution are competing philosophies of mind: on the one hand, philosophies according to which the mind is primarily an involuntary automaton, and on the other, philosophies that view the mind as primarily an artifact of voluntary human activity. My thesis is that it is the synthesis of these competing views on the proper treatment of irresolution and the nature of mind that leads us to Kant's view that the public exercise of reason is necessary for enlightenment.

I need to point out at the outset that the term "enlightenment" is ambiguous. As Kant points out in his famous essay, "What is Enlightenment?," the term refers to a historical period – the Age of Enlightenment – as well as a capacity of the mind, namely, the ability to use one's own reason confidently. Although in this book I trace themes that blossom in the 18th century – the proper home of the term "enlightenment" – back to their 17th-century roots, I am neutral about the proper periodization of the Age of Enlightenment. What I do defend, however, is that 17th-century philosophers were deeply concerned about how to attain enlightenment, that is, to use 17th-century terminology, how to improve the human understanding so that it is confident, careful, and knowledgeable, and that this led them, bit by bit, to focus on the public dimensions of rationality.

The authors I have chosen to discuss made, in my view, the most important contributions to this evolution. The minor figures I discuss, especially in Chapter 5 on enthusiasm, may not be significant philosophers, but they do play defining roles in an influential 17th-century movement that I gather under the label "enthusiasm." This does not entail that other philosophers of the period – such as Bacon or Malebranche – are irrelevant. However, my aim is not to capture every relevant feature of the evolution of the concept of enlightenment and the public use of reason, but rather to exhibit its major contours. Perhaps future work will be able to look at all dimensions of this intellectual development.

The historical work in this book is driven by my conviction that the conception of the mind as itself a "product of the workmanship of the understanding," to use Locke's words, plays a crucial role in the emancipation and autonomy of human beings. To deny a role to human volition in human belief formation inhibits critical and reflective control over our own understanding. Such a denial veils the powers that fix our beliefs and construct our understanding, especially the power of our own, as well as others', interests and passions.

Our conceptions of who we are, including what kinds of minds we have, serve to structure the architecture of our own minds (Dawkins 1976; Dennett 1991), and I believe that it is essential to human autonomy that individual human beings exercise some control over the conceptions that are, so to speak, implemented in them. This means that we must exercise voluntary control over the conduct of our human understanding. Although I do not deny the importance of involuntary processes in shaping our understanding, I think that these factors have been overemphasized at the expense of voluntary thought. By restoring the 17th-century images of human cognition as a product of our own individual and social workmanship, and contrasting it with its competing conception of human cognition as infused and inspired, I wish to make a small contribution to contemporary attempts to remake our minds. Designed and voluntary thought, or what Hobbes calls "passionate thought," is needed, as Hobbes suggests, if we are to avoid wandering, unguided, and dream-like thoughts, and the loss of all influence over the conduct of our own lives and the company in which we find ourselves.

While writing this book I have been helped and influenced by many people. I wish to acknowledge Kluwer Academic Publishers for letting me reprint portions of my paper "Passionate Thought: Computation, Thought and Action in Hobbes," published in *Pragmatics and Cognition*, as well as the Taylor and Francis Group (http:// www.tandf.co.uk/journals) for their permission to reprint portions of "John Locke on Passion, Will and Belief," which appeared in the *British Journal of the History of Philosophy*. These two papers form the bases of Chapters 3 and 4. I am indebted to Jan Cordova, Jeremy Duettra, Don Cox, Marcelo Dascal, Pat Francken, Heimir Geirsson, Paul Guyer, Fred Johnson, Dick Kitchener, Donna Morgan, and John Rogers, all of whom have in direct and indirect ways kept this project alive. I am also very grateful to Terence Moore, his anonymous reviewers, and Stephanie Sakson of Cambridge University Press for all their work on this book.

I owe a very deep personal and intellectual debt to Hans Aarsleff. He inspired this project more than twelve years ago in 1988 in his National Endowment for the Humanities Summer Seminar "Reflections on Language and the Nature of Man: The 17th Century Through Romanticism" at Princeton University, and he continued to sustain it over the years. I am also very indebted to Richard Popkin, whose work on skepticism and the "third force," along with Aarsleff's work on "Adamicism," liberated my study of the early modern period from major blind spots that were part of the traditional perception of this period.

Finally, I cannot thank Jane Kneller and Bernie Rollin enough for reading and commenting on this manuscript in various stages of its development. I am especially very indebted to them for their truly indefatigable encouragement. Without them this manuscript would have remained a batch of files in an ignored, and even feared, folder on my hard drive.

I dedicate this book to my children, Rosavera and Miroslav, who still had resolute minds when I started working on this book.

List of Abbreviations

Jacob Boehme

Au   *Morgenröte im Aufgang.* In Ur, vol. 1.
Bo   *Sämtliche Schriften,* 11 vols. Ed. Will-Erich Peuckert. Stuttgart: Frommann, 1956.
MM   *Mysterium Magnum.* In Bo, vols. 7 and 8.
SR   *De Signatura Rerum.* In Bo, vol. 6.
Ur   *Die Urschriften,* 2 vols. Ed. Werner Buddecke. Stuttgart: Frommann, 1963.

René Descartes

AT   *Oeuvres de Descartes.* Ed. C. Adam and P. Tannery. Paris: J. Vrin, 1964–76.
CSM   *The Philosophical Writings of Descartes.* 3 vols. Trans. and ed. J. G. Cottingham, R. Stoothoff, and D. Murdoch. Cambridge: Cambridge University Press, 1985. Vol. 3 includes A. Kenny as translator.

Thomas Hobbes

DC   *De Corpore.* In EW, vol. 1.
DM   *Critique Du De Mundo.* Ed. J. Jacquot and H. W. Jones. Paris: J. Vrin, 1973.
EL   *Elements of Law.* Ed. F. Tönnies. Cambridge: Cambridge University Press.
EW   *The English Works of Thomas Hobbes.* 11 Vols. Ed. W. Molesworth. London: John Bohn, 1839.

L   *Leviathan.* Ed. C. B. Macpherson. London: Penguin, 1985.
LW *Opera Philosophica Quae Latine Scripsit Omnia.* Ed. W. Molesworth. London: John Bohn. 1839.

Immanuel Kant

Ak *Kants gesammelte Schriften.* 29 vols. Ed. Königlich Preußische Akademie der Wissenschaften. Berlin: Walter de Gruyter, 1902–83.

Gottfried Wilhelm von Leibniz

A   *Gottfried Wilhelm Leibniz: Sämtliche Schriften und Briefe.* Ed. Deutsche Akademie der Wissenschaften zu Berlin. Darmstadt and Berlin: Akademie Verlag, 1923– .
AG *Philosophical Essays.* Ed. and trans. R. Ariew and D. Garber. Indianapolis: Hackett Publishing, 1989.
C   *Opuscles et Fragments Inédits de Leibniz.* Ed. L. Couturat. Paris: Alcan, 1903.
Du *Opera Omnia.* Ed. L. Dutens. Geneva: Fratres de Tournes, 1768.
F   *Oevres de Leibniz.* Ed. A. Foucher de Careil. Paris: Didot Frères, 1859–75.
GM *Die Mathematischen Schriften von Gottfried Wilhelm Leibniz.* 7 Vols. Ed. C. I. Gerhardt. Hildesheim: Olms, 1963.
GP *Die Philosophischen Schriften von Gottfried Wilhelm Leibniz.* 7 Vols. Ed. C. I. Gerhardt. Hildesheim: Olms, 1960.
Gr *Textes Inédits.* 2 Vols. Ed. G. Grua. Paris: Presses Universitaires de France, 1948.
Gu *Deutsche Schriften.* 2 vols. Ed. G. E. Guhrauer. Hildesheim: Olms, 1966.
Kl *Die Werke von Leibniz.* Ed. O. Klopp. Hannover: Klindworth Verlag, 1877.
L   *Philosophical Papers and Letters.* 2nd ed. Ed. Leroy Loemker. Dordrecht: Reidel, 1970.
NE *Nouveaux Essais sur l'Entendement Humain.* Ed. A. Robinet and H. Schepers. Berlin: Aladenie Verlag, 1962 (A VI.6). Trans. P. Remnant and J. Bennett. Cambridge: Cambridge University Press, 1982.

PW   *Leibniz: Political Writings.* Ed. P. Riley. Cambridge: Cambridge University Press, 1988.

Th   *Theodicy. Essays on the Goodness of God, the Freedom of Man, and the Origin of Evil.* Ed. A. Farrar, trans. E. M. Huggard. La Salle, IL: Open Court, 1985.

John Locke

DE   *Drafts for the Essay Concerning Human Understanding and Other Philosophical Writings.* Vol. I. Ed. P. Nidditch and G. A. J. Rogers. Oxford: Clarendon Press, 1990.

E   *Essay Concerning Human Understanding.* Ed. P. H. Nidditch. Oxford: Oxford University Press, 1975.

LN   *Essays on the Laws of Nature.* Ed. and trans. W. v. Leyden. Oxford: Clarendon, 1954.

LT   *Epistola de Tolerantia/A Letter on Toleration.* Ed. R. Klibansky, trans. J. W. Gough. Oxford: Clarendon Press, 1968.

WL   *The Works of John Locke.* 9 vols. London: Rivington, 1824.

Moses Mendelssohn

GSJ   *Gesammelte Schriften: Jubiläumsausgabe.* Stuttgart: Friedrich Frommann Verlag, 1972.

Henry More

AA   *An Antidote to Atheisme.* In CSP.

CC   *Conjectura Cabbalistica.* In CSP.

CL   *The Conway Letters: The Correspondence of Anne, Viscountess Conway, Henry More, and Their Friends, 1642–1684.* Ed. M. H. Nicolson, revised by S. Hutton. Oxford: Clarendon Press, 1992.

CP   *The Complete Poems of Dr. Henry More (1614–1687).* Ed. A. B. Grossart. New York: AMS Press, 1967.

CSP   *A Collection of Several Philosophical Writings of Dr Henry More.* 2nd ed. London: Flesher and Morden, 1662.

DD 1   *Divine Dialogues, Containing Sundry Disquisitions and Instructions Concerning the Attributes and Providence of God in the World.* Vol. 1: *The First Three Dialogues. . . .* London: Flesher, 1668.

DD 2   *Divine Dialogues, Containing Sundry Disquisitions and Instructions Concerning the Attributes and Providence of God in the World.* Vol. 2: *The Last Two Dialogues . . . Whereunto Is Annexed a Brief Discourse on the True Grounds of the Certainty of Faith on Points of Religion, Together with Some Few Plain Songs, or Divine Hymns on the Chief Holy Days of the Year.* London: Flesher, 1668.

ET   *Enthusiasmus Triumphatus; Or, A Brief Discourse of the Nature, Causes, Kinds and Cure of Enthusiasm.* London: Flesher and Morden, 1662. Rpt., The Augustan Reprint Society, Publication No. 118. Los Angeles: William Andrews Clark Memorial Library, 1966, and in CSP.

IS   *The Immortality of the Soul.* In CSP.

MG   *An Explanation of the Grand Mystery of Godliness.* London: Flesher and Morden, 1660.

OO   *Opera Omnia, Tum qua Latinè, tum quae Anglicè sunt.* 2 vols. London: Macock, Martyn and Kettilby, 1679. Rpt., Hildesheim: G. Olms, 1966.

Baruch de Spinoza

G   *Spinoza Opera.* 4 vols. Ed. C. Gebhardt. Heidelberg: Carl Winter, 1925.

Seth Ward

VA   *Vindiciae Academiarum: Containing Some Brief Animadversions upon Mr Websters Book, Stiled the Examination of Academies.* Oxford: Lichfield and Robinson, 1654.

John Webster

AE   *Academiarum Examen; Or, the Examination of the Academies.* London: Giles Calvert, 1654.

SG   *The Saints Guide; Or, Christ the Rule, and Ruler of Saints.* London: Giles Calvert, 1654.

SW   *The Displaying of Supposed Witchcraft.* London: J.M., 1677.

John Wilkins

RC   *An Essay Towards a Real Character, and A Philosophical Language.* London, 1668.

Christian Wolff

GW   *Gesammelte Werke.* Hildesheim: Georg Olms, 1962– .

PD   *Preliminary Discourse on Philosophy in General.* Trans. R. J. Blackwell. Indianapolis: Bobbs-Merrill, 1963.

Introduction: The Enlightened Mind

Immaturity and Public Reason

Kant's answer in 1784 to the question "What is Enlightenment?" is that it is a "human being's emergence from his self-incurred immaturity," which is the "inability to use one's own understanding without direction from another" (Ak VIII: 35). This immaturity is self-incurred when it is caused not by a lack of mental capacity, but by the "the lack of resolution [*Entschliessung*] and courage to use one's own understanding without direction from another." Thus for Kant, "*Sapere aude!* Have the courage to use your *own* understanding is the motto of the Enlightenment."

How can one overcome irresolution, commit oneself to using one's own understanding, and break away from the guidance of other people? Although "Dare to be wise!" is the motto of the Enlightenment, Kant writes, most people suffer from the effects of irresolution and are not enlightened. It is easier to remain in immaturity, and it has also been made safer by society's guardians, who treat human beings like "domestic cattle." First they ensure that "these placid creatures will not dare take a single step without the harness of the cart to which they are tethered" and then they "show them the danger which threatens if they try to walk alone" (Ak VIII: 35).

Rare individuals can manage to overcome irresolution and free themselves from self-imposed immaturity by "working on their own minds," but this is difficult. It is much easier to achieve independence of thought together with other people in public, especially when people are granted freedom. The freedom Kant has in mind is the freedom "to make *public use* of one's reason in all matters" (Ak VIII:

36). In fact, he writes that enlightenment requires that the "*public* use of one's reason must at all times be free" (Ak VIII: 37). Kant's example of the public use of reason is the activity of a "scholar before the whole reading public." Kant contrasts this with the private use of reason of someone in her role as a civil servant. As a civil servant, a person has to be a passive "part of a machine" and obey orders without reasoning on one's own (ibid.). In this role people submit their own reason to the reasoning of those they are serving. But this role as a passive piece of machinery in the larger institutional mechanism is compatible with at the same time being a part of "the whole community or society of world citizens [*Weltbürgergesellschaft*]" in which a person actively uses his own understanding and "speaks in his own person" (Ak VIII: 37–8).

There are six striking features of Kant's answer to the question "What is Enlightenment?"[1] First, reasoning is not something that is only hidden "in the head" away from public scrutiny. Human reasoning is principally a public activity, for instance, the activity of presenting one's views to an audience and defending them. Second, the public exercise of reason leads to and in most cases is required for enlightenment. Inner liberation typically needs supporting outward activity. By exercising our reason in public we learn how to use it on our own, thus overcoming the causes of immaturity. These two features are expressions of a third feature of this essay as well of Kant's whole philosophy, namely, that human enlightenment is not just a theoretical affair, but has practical dimensions. Unlike Mendelssohn (GSJ VI.1: 115–19), who argued that enlightenment was theoretical and could be separated from human practice, Kant believed that theory and practice depended on each other (Ak VIII: 275–6).

A fourth striking feature of Kant's essay is that the lack of resolution (*Entschliessung*) is a philosophical and political topic. A certain psychological state of mind is seen as a hindrance to enlightenment because it keeps the mind passive and in submission to the guidance of others, and enlightenment requires overcoming this state of mind. Fifth, Kant assigns a role to human volition in the progress toward enlightenment. While indecision can keep people from using their

---

1. Schmidt (1996) is an outstanding anthology that brings together in one convenient place historical and recent material devoted to the question, "What is Enlightenment?"

own understanding, the will to use one's understanding – either by the rare individuals "working on their own minds" or in the public use of reason – is a remedy for irresolution and encourages enlightenment. Finally, the mind when it is passive is characterized in terms of a machine or automaton, and Kant contrasts automatic reasoning with the voluntary use of one's own reason.

In Kant we find a remarkable conception of human enlightenment as the self-incurred liberation from immaturity and irresolution through the public exercise of one's reason. What are the sources of this confluence of themes about irresolution and volition, automation and mental activity, publicity and enlightenment? Obviously the factors that contributed to Kant's conception of enlightenment are complex and include facts about Kant's intellectual development as a philosopher, scholar and civil servant as well as Kant's 18th-century social and intellectual environment. In the following I wish to focus on one aspect of this complex story, namely the 17th-century European philosophical context that preceded Kant. The themes Kant brings together in his Enlightenment essay are not unique to Kant or the 18th century. As I will try to show in the remaining chapters, already in 17th-century philosophy we can find at least in a rudimentary but recognizable form the interplay of themes that culminates in Kant's conception of enlightenment.

Irresolution, Will, and Inspiration

Irresolution and its remedies play an important role in 17th-century philosophy. As Popkin has stressed on many occasions, 17th-century Europe was dealing with a pervasive crisis of skepticism, an effect of which on the individual mind is vacillation and the inability to generate conviction.[2] Descartes's *Meditations* document a path from irresolution to commitment, and the topic of irresolution is explicitly mentioned in the *Passions of the Soul.* When 17th-century thinkers treat the passions of the soul, they almost invariably discuss irresolution, including the inability to make up one's mind about truth and

---

2. See Popkin (1979: 85), and for a more recent and more qualified defense of this thesis, see Popkin (1998). One can agree with Popkin that there was a skeptical crisis in the 17th century without maintaining that this was the only or even the main problem of 17th century intellectual life. See Larmore (1998).

falsity. Hobbes, Spinoza, Locke, and Leibniz all discuss irresolution, including irresolution in our judgments, and offer various ways of overcoming lack of cognitive commitment.

While some call upon an exercise of willpower to overcome irresolution and attain commitment, others see in the denial of the will the key to greater insight and commitment. The role of volition in human belief formation divides 17th-century philosophy of mind. On the one hand, for Descartes, Hobbes, and Locke volition appears to play an immediate role in directing our thoughts and even in determining our beliefs and judgments. Human volition is a source of defects, as when we make judgments motivated by commitments to other things besides truth, but the exercise of will is also needed to overcome irresolution and acquire conviction. Since our thinking, including the acquisition of belief, can be voluntary, we can be responsible for our beliefs, doubts, and other judgments just as we are responsible for our voluntary interactions with the world around us. Consequently, 17th-century philosophy of mind comes with an ethics of belief and thinking,[3] such as John Locke's *Of the Conduct of the Understanding*, and it is our duty to follow those rules and conduct our thinking appropriately.

On the other hand, for Spinoza as well as the philosophers that belong to what has aptly been called the "third force" in 17th-century philosophy (Popkin 1983), volition is only a hindrance to cognition. For these philosophers, self-improvement is achieved when through the renunciation of will we become inspired or, in the case of Spinoza, when we are like "spiritual automatons" automatically moving from judgment to judgment according to its own laws without any special role played by human volition. In this respect, Spinoza has something important in common with 17th-century enthusiasm, which denigrated the will and elevated conduct driven by divine inspiration. A simple and radical version of this conception of the inspired mind is developed by the 17th-century religious philosophies of Jacob Boehme and Henry More.

Seventeenth-century enthusiasm is a kind of Platonism, and as much else in philosophy, the distinction between human cognition

---

3. The phrase "ethics of belief" is due to the 19th-century English philosopher W. K. Clifford, whose principle that "it is wrong always, everywhere, and for anyone, to believe anything upon insufficient evidence" (Clifford 1947: 77) was the target of William James's essay "The Will to Believe" (1956: 1–31). "Ethics of thinking" is due to Ryle (1971).

as an artifact of voluntary human activity and cognition as infused in the sense of being a product of involuntary processes has its roots in Plato. In the *Ion*, Plato distinguishes between art and knowledge on the one hand and inspiration on the other, and suggests that good poetry is not art or knowledge, but divine inspiration. While knowledge is a power of the individual, inspiration is a "power divine, impelling you like the power in the stone Euripides called the magnet" (533d). However, Plato allows for a kind of knowledge that is inspired, and in fact it is the highest form of knowledge. According to the *Phaedo*, the seeker of wisdom wants to be released from pleasure, pain, fear, and desire, and achieves this by "contemplating the true and divine and unconjecturable, and drawing inspiration from it" (84a). The lover of wisdom is impelled by a divine power. Plato develops this in the *Phaedrus*, where philosophy is a kind of good madness (249d–e). While others have forgotten, philosophers remember the vision of truth that every soul once had, and are impelled toward it as if out of their wits.

An important consequence of the idea that the mind is a spiritual automaton is that it made room within immaterialist theories of mind for a key feature of materialist theories. We tend to look toward Hobbes for the roots of materialism because he is explicitly committed to the view that mental states and processes are physical. However, it is equally important that the idea that the mind is an automatic mechanism with respect to which we, as conscious selves with overt beliefs and desires, can be wholly passive is part of 17th-century immaterialism. As we see below, for both Spinoza and Leibniz, the mind is a spiritual automaton that is governed involuntarily by the laws of the intellect in much the same way that a physical machine is governed by the laws of motion.

Belief and Volition

Although both Leibniz and Spinoza emphasize automatic features of the mind, they disagree on the role human volition plays in the conduct of the understanding. While for Spinoza and 17th-century enthusiasm the denial of the will was the key to enlightenment, Leibniz found a place for volition and voluntary control over our minds. Leibniz offers a resolution to the 17th-century opposition between cognition as involuntary divine or intellectual inspiration

5

and cognition as a voluntary achievement by suggesting a natural and acquired surrogate for inspiration. Leibniz develops Hobbes's notion of reason as the manipulation of public symbols, turning it into a remedy for irresolution. By manipulating symbols – a public and voluntary exercise of reason – we can increase the power of our own minds, guide our own meditations, settle our own doubts, and adjudicate conflicts between other people. The effort Leibniz expended on developing calculi that would serve both the art of discovery and the art of judgment or justification was in part motivated by his desire to play his part in resolving the conflicts and irresolution on religious and other matters that dominated 17th-century Europe.

Thus the will can play an indirect role in the acquisition of conviction for Leibniz. Calculation is a voluntary action, and thus the inspiration achieved through calculation is not itself voluntary, but an indirect product of voluntary activity. So it is a kind of inspiration or infusion, but a natural, not supernatural, infusion of knowledge. Moreover, we achieve conviction not simply through internal mental activity, but with the aid of bodily activity, be it computing an equation on paper or the physical search for evidence. Thus we "can work on our own minds," as Kant puts it, not simply by thinking alone, but by thinking in public, using our bodies and their environments.

The question about the role of volition in belief fixation is not just of historical interest (Losonsky 2000). Divergent philosophers such as H. H. Price (1954), C. I. Lewis (1955), William James (1956), Roderick Chisholm (1968), and, more recently, Bas van Fraassen (1984) have given a central role to volition in belief formation.[4] What ties these positions is the view that to believe a proposition, which involves assigning to it some chance of its being true, is a mental action that directly involves an act of will on the part of the believer. What this means is that we can believe a proposition because we have some inducements to believe it, that is, we believe it because we have some practical reasons, such as that belief satisfies a certain desire. Moreover, since belief fixation turns out to be a voluntary action, there is an ethics of belief that gives us the norms for proper belief fixation.

Although much of our language of belief treats beliefs as if they are actions, many, if not most, philosophers today reject the view that

---

4. Also see Nagel (1969) and Naylor (1985).

beliefs are actions. Instead, they hold that belief and belief acquisition are involuntary events or states of mind (Hampshire 1959; Williams 1973; Curley 1975; Bennett 1990; Cohen 1992).[5] In fact, it is the involuntary nature of thought that supposedly makes thinking exhibit lawlike regularities that can be discovered by a science of the mind (Fodor 1987: 100), and it seems that voluntary behavior is to be understood in terms of these involuntary internal states of the mind (Nagel 1969).

Nevertheless, even philosophers who deny that belief is an action will grant, with Leibniz, that volition at least plays an indirect role in belief formation. For instance, Edwin Curley (1975) distinguishes between belief, which is a state one finds oneself in, much like a headache, and inquiry, which is an action. He writes that "though belief is not a voluntary action, we must allow that it is often connected with activities of reflection and inquiry which are or can be voluntary," and adds that the fact that we can have an "indirect influence of the will on belief" and "produce belief in ourselves by our actions, or preserve it by our inactions" is sufficient to justify the moral appraisal of belief (183–4).[6] Although we cannot control our belief directly, we can use voluntary activity to indirectly influence our beliefs.

Thinking in Public

But how can our actions influence our beliefs? What is significant about Leibniz is not simply the recognition that volition can control beliefs indirectly, but that Leibniz develops this view by finding a place for thinking in public. Thus Leibniz sets the stage for Kant's notion of the "public use of reason" and the role it plays in enlightenment, particularly in the overcoming of irresolution and indecision. The starkest case of this, and the case to which Leibniz devoted much of his thinking, is calculation, where we externalize our thinking in order to improve our understanding. It is as if in the 17th century the

---

5. Also Pojman (1985) and Montmarquet (1986).
6. Also see Pojman (1985) and Bennett (1990). Curley's essay is on Descartes and Spinoza, and he sides with Spinoza's views on involuntary belief, but emends this position with the idea that beliefs can be under the indirect control of voluntary activity. He does not notice that this emendation is precisely the one Leibniz offers and develops.

automatic and voluntary functions of the mind are being sorted out, and that as internal mental activity is seen more and more to be automatic and passive with respect to human volition, voluntary mental activity is located in our external and bodily interactions with our environments.

The idea that thinking can take place in public in our actions and in turn have an effect on our internal mental states is also one that has a place in contemporary thinking about the human cognition. Recently, many philosophers and cognitive scientists have come to defend and develop the view that we develop and change our cognitive capacities through the use of environmental structures (Clark 1989: 63–6 and 132–5). For example, David Rumelhart et al. (1986) have argued that our capacity to perform complex calculations and other forms of serial reasoning in the head is a result of our capacity to model and change our environment. We are able to create and manipulate public symbolic structures, and by modeling these structures and manipulations internally we augment our capacity for serial reasoning.

Annette Karmiloff-Smith has concluded from her work in child development that innate and domain-specific predispositions are developed by "a dynamic process of interaction between mind and environment" (1992: 9). During development "the environment acts as much more than a trigger . . . it actually influences the subsequent structure of the brain via rich epigenetic interaction between the mind and the physical/sociocultural environment" (1992: 15). On the basis of infant development, Julie Rutkowska (1993) has argued that thinking must be understood not only in terms of internal processing, but also in terms of interaction with the environment, and that a proper modeling of certain kinds of cognitive capacities must include the environment in the model.

This turn in our understanding of the mind is a confluence of two currents in 20th-century thinking about the mind. The first half of this century was dominated by views that, roughly speaking, explained the mind and its properties in terms of human action, including interaction with the environment. Pragmatism, beginning with Charles Sanders Peirce's characterization of a belief as a habit of action (1955: 29), has always been associated with the view that mind must be characterized in terms of human practices (Dewey 1931). Other major trends in philosophy and psychology that believe that human thinking is embedded in our behavior and its environment are behaviorism (Watson 1930; Ryle 1949), Piagetian constructivism (Piaget 1952; Beilin 1989), the philosophy of the later Wittgenstein (1953), Heideggerian philosophy (Dreyfus and Dreyfus 1986), and the thinking of ecologists (Gibson 1979). According to this trend, to use Gilbert Ryle's well-known distinction, *knowing how* to perform some activity is the more basic notion in terms of which we must explain and understand *knowing that* something is the case, that is, propositional or theoretical knowledge (Ryle 1949: 27–32).

Although this view had the edge during the first half of the 20th century, the latter half of the century saw a swing to a competing mentalist or cognitivist conception that reversed the depencence and made *knowing that* fundamental. Cognitivism, which was primarily a response to the hegemony of behaviorism, came to understand thinking as a process internal to us – usually somehow part of the brain – and action as an effect of this internal and mostly subconscious process consciousness, as is the case for the mental states that guide our eye movements when we scan something (Haugeland 1978: 243). On this view, action, to again borrow a phrase from Gilbert Ryle, is a "step-child" of thinking (1949: 26), and actions are like conclusions of internal cognitive processes (Cummins 1991: 94). The major proponents of 20th-century cognitivism are classical computationalists, according to which these internal mental states are like the formal information-processing states of a digital computer (Haugeland 1985).

The cognitivist reaction to behaviorism often placed 17th-century rationalism on its banner, particularly in the name of Descartes (Chomsky 1966). Although this is not wholly false, it is misleading because in important respects 17th-century rationalism is much closer to a synthesis of cognitivism and behaviorism than either of these two approaches. From Descartes to Leibniz we can see the development of the idea that thinking, at least sometimes, for instance when we calculate, unifies both internal mental states and external bodily behavior (Dascal 1978, 1987; Sutton 1998). As I try to argue, this idea is part of a larger network of ideas that finally come together in Kant's conception of public and voluntary reason as the source of enlightenment. When manipulating a symbol system, including our own language, we are not only thinking in public, but also engaging in voluntary activity that contributes to the making of our minds. If the symbol system we use is a good one, then we are also improving our understanding and overcoming the debilitating influence of irresolution.

Enlightenment, Politics, and Progress

For Kant, the mind's enlightenment had a political dimension. If we are to contribute to enlightenment, we must ensure a social and political context in which reason can be exercised in public. We need to build a community of cosmopolitan citizens in which the public exercise of reason is free in all matters. We need to be able to "speak in our own person," but speak freely and in public in a community of people who are equally committed to the free and public exercise of reason.

The defense of freedom of speech is not new to Kant. Spinoza already defended it in his *Theologico-Political Treatise*, and his defense is not based in law or morality, but in his metaphysics and psychology. Inner conviction cannot be controlled, and inner conviction and speech are bound tightly together. Unfortunately, Spinoza shows little concern for those weakened by irresolution and offers no remedies that human beings can apply to strengthen the mind. Freedom of speech, in effect, is for those with convictions, but Spinoza fails to see that freedom of speech is also important because it is a means for gaining conviction and overcoming irresolution.

Leibniz recognizes the role language and, more generally, symbol systems can have in strengthening our capacities to reason, and accordingly he begins to tie the idea of enlightenment to publicity. Leibniz believes that you maintain your own enlightenment best in the company of other people and in the quest for the common good, which includes contributing to the enlightenment of other people as well as freeing them "from annoying inconveniences, in so far as this is feasible" (PW: 107). Princes and ministers should make extraordinary efforts toward this end, and Leibniz himself saw his quest to improve the art of reasoning with a public symbol system – the universal characteristic – part of his contribution to the improvement of the human lot.

Nevertheless, Leibniz does not recognize the significance of the political freedom of speech. Thus Kant appears to be the first major philosopher who explicitly brings together political freedom of speech endorsed by Spinoza and the notion present explicitly in Leibniz's philosophy that the public use of reason exemplified in our use of language and other symbol systems is needed for enlightenment. Freedom to exercise reason in public, that is, in speech and writing, is important not only for those who have convictions and are enlightened, but for the vast majority whose reason and understanding remain in immaturity to the authority of others.

In this light, 17th-century philosophy was the intellectual ground that nourished the various elements needed to begin the cultivation, both politically and philosophically, of the proposition that publicity, particularly the free public exercise of reason, is a means for improving the human condition. Of course, the idea that progress and freedom depend on each other blossoms in 18th- and 19th-century liberal and radical intellectual thought, but this could not have happened if 17th-century philosophers in their search for ways to improve the human understanding had not come to recognize the dependence of individual enlightenment on the public exercise of reason. How this recognition came about is the story of the following chapters.

2

Descartes: Willful Thinking

The Will to Know and Doubt

Descartes aimed to find a method that would nullify all his ideas and judgments that were a source of confusion and uncertainty and lead his mind to clarity and certainty. One source of confusion, Descartes believed, is the reliance on forces outside of his own understanding, such as the authority of other people, and so a key to improving his mind was to rely solely on his own understanding and its operations. The idea that the mind needs to be improved and that its improvement requires the mind's reliance on its own devices is a guiding idea of modern philosophy from Descartes to Kant, who captures it with the motto from Horace "*Sapere aude!*" and his paraphrase "Have courage to use your *own* understanding [Kant's emphasis]."[1]

It is very common to give Descartes's project a purely intellectualist interpretation.[2] His philosophy is commonly thought to be a philosophy of pure intellect alienated from all passion and action, but this is not quite right. The *Meditations* themselves are not a product of pure intellect, but of an act of will. In a letter from 1648 Descartes classifies together "meditations and acts of will" (AT II: 36/CSMK III: 97), and in the opening paragraph of his First Meditation he explicitly affirms the volitional nature of his project:

I realized that it was necessary, once in the course of my life, to demolish everything completely and start again right from the foundation *if I wanted*

---

1. On these grounds it has been argued that the Age of Enlightenment stretches back to Descartes (Schouls 1989 and Hinchman 1996: 490–2).
2. This intellectualistic reading of Descartes is common to sympathetic (Guéroult 1984) and unsympathetic (Lloyd 1984) readers of Descartes.

to [cupiam] establish anything at all in the sciences that was stable and likely to last" (AT VII: 17/CSM II: 12, my emphasis).

It is this desire for something stable and lasting in the sciences that directs Descartes to do his *Meditations*, rather than, as Rorty puts it, keep "running through the proofs for the existence of God over and over, over and over and over" (Rorty 1992: 386).

The underlying desire and decision of the *Meditations* are described in more detail in the *Discourse on Method*, where Descartes notices that we "*direct our thoughts* along different paths and do not attend to the same things" (AT VI: 2/CSM I: 111, my emphasis). Consequently "it is not enough to have a good mind; the main thing is *to apply it* well" (ibid., my emphasis). Descartes resolved "to seek no knowledge other than that which could be found in myself or else in the great book of the world" (AT VI: 9/CSM I: 115) and he was motivated by his "most earnest desire to learn to distinguish the true from the false in order to see clearly into my own actions and proceed with confidence in this life" (AT VI: 10). This desire is affirmed by Descartes to the end of his life. In his last letter to Elizabeth of Bohemia he writes that the search for truth "is where my chief good in this life lies" (AT V: 430/CSM III: 383).

To find knowledge, Descartes "spent . . . time in planning the work I was undertaking and in seeking the true method of attaining . . . knowledge" (AT VI: 17/CSM I: 119). The method, as described in the *Discourse*, involves "a strong and unswerving resolution . . . to direct my thoughts in an orderly manner" (AT VI: 18/CSM I: 120). Knowledge must be developed systematically, and that requires willful mental activity. Descartes compares customary knowledge with medieval cities with their crooked streets and diverse architecture or societies based on customary laws. Such organizations are the results of chance and they are not as perfect as cities developed by "the will of men using reason" or "some wise law-giver" (AT VI: 12/CSM I: 116–17). More perfect knowledge will also be the product of will and reason.

Descartes's decision to pursue perfect knowledge is the culmination of his deliberation about what to do. Descartes writes in the *Discourse* that after several years studying "the book of the world" he "*resolved* one day to undertake studies within myself . . . and to use all my powers of my mind in choosing the paths I should follow" (AT VI:

10/CSM I: 116, my emphasis). In November 1619, while "shut up alone in a stove-heated room" near Ulm in Bavaria, he had a vision of human knowledge organized along geometric lines, and he decided to show this. He then had his famous three dreams, the last of which was about reading Ausonius's Seventh Ode, which begins with the question, "What road in life shall I follow?" Descartes took this dream to be a divine confirmation of his decision to pursue what he calls "first philosophy" in his *Meditations* (AT X: 216, CSM I: 4; AT10: 180ff).[3]

The role of resolve in the acquisition of knowledge is highlighted in Descartes's Dedication of the *Principles of Philosophy* to Elizabeth of Bohemia. Wisdom depends on both "the perception of the intellect and the disposition of the will" (AT VIIIA: 3/CSM I: 191). One needs "the firm and powerful resolve always to use one's reasoning powers correctly, as far as one can, and to carry out whatever one knows to be best" (AT VIIIA: 2/CSM I: 191). People come with different intellectual capabilities, and those with weaker intellects should simply try to pursue knowledge of what is right. Yet some will have "the sharpest intelligence combined with the utmost zeal for acquiring knowledge of the truth" (AT VIIIA: 3/CSM I: 191). Descartes goes on to praise both Elizabeth's zeal for truth and sharp intelligence, but it is clear in this dedication that Descartes also believes that he has this zeal.

The will to know sustains Descartes's doubt in the First Meditation about all his customary beliefs, such as that there is an earth, sky, his own body, and the like. "I must withhold assent from these former beliefs . . . if I want to discover any certainty," he writes (AT VII: 22/CSM II: 15). Withholding assent in this case is not easy. He must "make an effort" to withhold assent, and the reason for this is that these customary beliefs keep coming back "despite my wishes." He has a "habit" of assenting to propositions that are reasonable but not certain. To overcome this habit Descartes devises a plan:

I think it will be a good plan to *turn my will* in completely the opposite direction and deceive myself, by pretending for a time that these former opinions are utterly false and imaginary. (AT VII: 22/CSM II: 15, my emphasis)

He does this by using the famous and fantastic hypothesis that there is a malicious demon that deceives Descartes into having all these cus-

---

3. See the account of these events by Rodis-Lewis (1992: 30–3).

tomary beliefs. This hypothesis helps him to "stubbornly and firmly persist in this meditation" and do what is in his power, namely, to withhold assent from these customary beliefs and so "resolutely guard against assenting to any falsehoods." "This is an arduous undertaking," Descartes writes, and he repeats that he must "toil not in the light, but amid the inextricable darkness of the problems I have now raised" (AT VII: 23/CSM II: 15).

Descartes's doubt, then, is an act of will. It is not thrust upon him by pure reason. As Descartes writes in the Synopsis that precedes the *Meditations*, his "mind uses its own freedom and supposes the non-existence of all things about whose existence it can have the slightest doubt" (AT VII: 12/CSM II: 9).[4]

Willful Judgments

For Descartes, doubt, like all other kinds of judgments, is a mental action. Judgments are actions of the soul, not passions (AT IV: 312/CSMK III: 271). They consist of two capacities – the intellect and volition – and, as is well known, in the Fourth Meditation Descartes argues that epistemic error, namely, affirming something that is false or denying something that is true, is due to the will of the judge, not God (AT VII: 56). The willful nature of judgments is stated clearly in the *Principles*:

Making a judgement requires not only the intellect but also the will. In order to make a judgement, the intellect is of course required since, in the case of something which we do not in any way perceive, there is no judgement we can make. But the will is also required so that, once something is perceived in some manner our assent may then be given. (AT VIIIA: 18/ CSM I: 204)

Sometimes Descartes characterizes a judgment simply as an operation of the will (AT V: 159/8B: 363).

The basic idea is that the intellect provides the perception of ideas, specifically, propositions, namely, what is expressed with that-clauses:

---

4. However, this does not mean that for Descartes the will is primary and reason secondary, as is argued by Schouls (1989: 31–62). Descartes's will is guided by a perception of what he desires, namely, a true, stable, certain, and systematic knowledge, and this perception, like all perceptions, is provided by his intellect.

that there is a sky, that $2 + 3 = 5$, or *that I exist.*[5] In and of themselves these propositions are neither true nor false, and thus error cannot be attributed to them (AT VII: 37/CSM II: 26). Error is possible when propositions are judged, for example, they are affirmed, denied, or doubted. Doubt, affirmation, or denial are mental attitudes, along with attitudes such as fear or hope, and for Descartes, the attitudes of doubt, affirmation, or denial are operations of the will just as much as are desire or aversion (AT VIIIA: 17/CSM I: 204).[6]

Commentators in the recent past have found Descartes's view that cognitive judgments involve conative factors implausible.[7] For instance, Descartes claims that he turned his will and decided to believe that there is a powerful deceiver in order to strengthen his doubt and to help him gain the certain knowledge he was after. On Descartes's theory of judgment this is possible, but this – believing something to be true simply by deciding to believe it – is exactly what strikes commentators as psychologically impossible. Their argument is that simple introspection shows that we cannot just decide to believe something and then really believe it; what we believe is not really up to us (Curley 1975: 176–8; Wilson 1978: 145).[8]

What these writers ignore is the inner life of those in whom self-doubt plays an important and sometimes dysfunctional role. Unlike Descartes, they do not take seriously enough the cognitive lives of those who suffer from doubt and anxiety about their own capacities to fix their beliefs (even if it is to fix on withholding judgment on some topic). People endowed with resolute minds will ordinarily find themselves with their beliefs already fixed; usually they do not need to decide what to believe and how strongly to believe it. But simple introspection by those who suffer from and try to overcome cognitive

---

5. Descartes uses "idea" to cover many things, but it does cover propositions because ideas are, among other things, what we affirm or deny in a judgment (AT VII: 56/CSM II: 39). On the variety of Descartes's usage, see Wilson (1978: 141 and 156–7). On Descartes's commitment to propositions as the objects of his psychological attitudes, see Markie (1986: 73–7).
6. For a full account, see Rosenthal (1986: 405–34).
7. See Kenny (1972: 1–31), Curley (1975: 159–89), and Wilson (1978: 144).
8. It is important to distinguish voluntarily raising the subjective probability of a proposition from voluntarily accepting a proposition (Bennett 1990: 90). For Descartes both accepting propositions and the setting of subjective probabilities involve the will.

self-doubt reveals a more willful cognitive life in which they spend some time trying to decide what they should believe.

To what degree Descartes himself suffered from self-doubt or only pretended to be in doubt about his cognitive capacities is an open question, but clearly he was keenly aware of the phenomenon of self-doubt.[9] After all, the *Meditations* are an attempt to overcome cognitive self-doubt. But in *The Passions of the Soul* Descartes is concerned about treating more pathological forms of self-doubt than the self-induced doubt of the First Meditation.

There he writes that the passions of "esteem and contempt," which are species of wonder, Descartes's first passion (AT XI: 373–4/CSM I: 350), are "chiefly noteworthy when we refer them to ourselves" (AT XI: 444–5/CSM I: 383–4).[10] Self-esteem involves recognizing that the only things for which I am responsible are my own volitions and firmly resolving "never to lack the will to undertake and carry out whatever" I judge to be the best (AT XI: 445–6/CSM I: 384). Self-contempt involves the anxiety of irresolution (AT XI: 459/CSM I: 390).[11] This is not uncertainty due only to lack of information, but this is a dysfunction where the uncertainty is brought about by "our anxiety of choosing wrongly." He observes:

This anxiety is so common and so strong in some people that although they have no need to make a choice and they see only one thing to be taken or left, the anxiety often leads them back and makes them pause to search in vain for something else. In this case an excess of irresolution results from too great a desire to do well and from a weakness of the intellect, which contains only a lot of confused notions, and none that are clear and distinct. (AT XI: 460/CSM I: 390–1)

Descartes's remedy against such excess is this:

9. In a letter to Elizabeth of Bohemia, Descartes makes the following interesting observation: "When everything goes according to our wishes, we forget to think of ourselves" (AT IV: 283/CSMK III: 263).
10. Descartes vividly describes how the causes of self-esteem and self-contempt are sometimes "so manifest that it changes even the appearance, gesture, gait and, generally, all the actions of those who conceive an unusually better or worse opinion of themselves" (AT XI: 445/CSM I: 384).
11. Although Descartes was always concerned with irresolution and the vice of indecision (see AT II: 34–6/CSMK III: 97), in *Passions* irresolution can infect our judgments as well as our behavior.

Become accustomed to form certain and determinate judgments regarding everything that comes before us, and to believe that we always do our duty when we do what we judge to be the best, even though our judgments may perhaps be a very bad one [sic]. (AT XI: 460/CSM I: 391)

In other words, make a judgment and then stick with it! Get into the habit of committing yourself to your judgments when obsessive behavior undermines your capacity to make judgments.

Cases of cognitive irresolution that fit the dysfunctional pattern Descartes describes are ones in which noncognitive factors undermine cognitive processes. Excessive fear of making mistakes can keep one from settling on a belief in certain circumstances even when there are no competing hypotheses and all the evidence – which is good even if not clear and distinct – supports a proposition. Instead, irresolute persons search for competing hypotheses, no matter how outlandish, and they waffle between them. Their good cognitive instincts are destroyed by excessive second-guessing induced by fear of being wrong, and thus they forgo the benefits of making quick and efficient cognitive commitments. People with the same information but uninhibited cognitive faculties make judgments in this situation, and move down the road of inquiry, while the irresolute remain stalled. Of course, not all situations are like that, and we should withhold judgment when we have good reasons for irresolution. But the dysfunctional situation is one in which compulsive anxiety or some other noncognitive factor undermines cognitive commitments, including our assignment of subjective probabilities.

Descartes's remedy is to treat the noncognitive anxiety that undermines cognition by noncognitive means: conation. Use your willpower to overcome the fear of being wrong and commit yourself to believing something. For instance, raise your subjective probability assignments in order to counteract the deleterious effect on your cognitive faculties by your dysfunctional anxieties. Or, stop asking so many questions and start drawing some conclusions. Even in Descartes's day, this was old-fashioned advice for bad habits – use your willpower to change yourself.

Of course, for Descartes the situation is reversed. Instead of overcoming irresolution with an act of will, in the *Meditations* he tries to overcome dogmatism, or excessive resolution, with an act of will, namely, his self-induced doubt. But it is still an intentional cognitive act – a decision to doubt whatever can be doubted – and the reason he does this is that he wants to find out if anything can escape the strongest doubt he is capable of mustering.

The Willful *Cogito*

The first thing that escapes Descartes's doubt is knowledge of his own existence. This is Descartes's *cogito*, usually identified with the phrase "*I think, therefore I am.*" I focus on the *cogito* as it actually appears in the Second Meditation:

I have persuaded myself [*mihi persuasi*] that there is absolutely nothing in the world, no sky, no earth, no minds, no bodies. Does it now follow that I too do not exist? No: if I persuaded myself of something then I certainly existed. But there is a deceiver of supreme power and cunning who is deliberately and constantly deceiving me.... [L]et him deceive me as much as he can, he will never bring it about that I am nothing so long as I shall think that I am something. So after considering everything very thoroughly, I must finally conclude that this proposition [*pronuntiatum*], *I am, I exist*, is necessarily true whenever it is put forward or mentally conceived by me [*quoties a me profertur, vel mente concipitur*]. (AT VII: 25/CSM II: 16–7)

The so-called *cogito* in this passage is Descartes's conclusion that "this proposition, *I am, I exist*, is necessarily true whenever it is put forward or mentally conceived by me" (Wilson 1978: 52).

The first thing to notice is that the *cogito* is a judgment. It is not simply the proposition that *this proposition, I am, I exist, is necessarily true whenever it is put forward or mentally conceived by me*. The *cogito* is a propositional attitude, namely, an affirmation of this proposition. Descartes writes, "*I must . . . conclude* that . . . I am, I exist, is necessarily true whenever it is put forward or mentally conceived by me" (AT VII: 25, my emphasis). Later on in the Third Meditation Descartes writes that "in this first item of knowledge there is simply a clear and distinct perception *of what I am asserting*" (AT VII: 35, my emphasis). In the Fourth Meditation Descartes summarizes what has happened in the first two *Meditations* as follows:

During the past few days I have been asking whether anything in the world exists, and I have realized that from this very fact of my raising this question it follows quite evidently that I exist. I could not but judge (*judicare*) that something which I understood so clearly was true. (AT VII: 58/CSM II: 41)

Descartes did not simply perceive a proposition in the *cogito*; he also had to judge that it was true.[12] In the *Discourse*, Descartes writes about the decision involved in the affirmation of the *cogito*: "I decided that I could *accept* ['I am thinking, therefore I exist'] without scruples as the first principle of the philosophy I was seeking" (AT VI: 32, my emphasis).

So the *cogito* is a judgment or affirmation, and as such, it is like any other judgment for Descartes, namely, an act of will. It is for this reason that Descartes refers to the *cogito* as a "cognition [*cognitio*]" (AT VIIIA: 7/CSM I: 195) or an "inference [*ratiocinium*]" (AT X: 523/CSM II: 417 and AT V: 147/CSM III: 333). He does not think of it as a general proposition, but as a "particular instance" of thinking (AT V: 147/CSM III: 333).[13]

Let us now turn to the proposition affirmed by the *cogito*. It is a complex proposition consisting of two simpler propositions: *that I exist* and *that I put forward or mentally conceive it*. For our purposes, we can simplify the second proposition to *that I think* or, more appropriately, *that I am thinking*.[14] Moreover, there is some kind of dependence relation between these two propositions in the *cogito*: the proposition *that I exist* in some sense follows from or is supported by the proposition *that I am thinking*.[15] Descartes knows of himself that he exists in virtue of his knowing of himself that he is thinking. I will call the proposition *that I am thinking* the "thought proposition" and the proposition *that I exist* the "existence proposition."

---

12. The fact that Descartes *had* to judge in this way does not make it any less of an action. My action motivated by a desire that is too strong to resist is still an action. On the parallels between judgment and desire, see Rosenthal (1986: 411–16).

13. Sometimes Descartes refers to the *cogito* as a proposition (AT VI: 32/CSM I: 127 or AT II: 38/CSM III: 98). This is because the *cogito* also has a propositional content and sometimes Descartes is discussing the proposition rather than his affirmation of the proposition. This comes out quite clearly in his reply to Gassendi's *Counter-Objections*, where he distinguishes between the proposition and our attention, belief, and judgments about it (AT VII: 271/CSM II: 271).

14. Cottingham (1986: 36) correctly observes that the continuous present tense "I am thinking" rather than the simple present "I think" is the correct translation of both the Latin "*cogito*" and the French "*je pense*." This captures the fact that Descartes's knowledge of his existence is based on the fact that he at the time he is engaged in the *cogito* is engaged in thinking. I discuss how it is based on his thinking in sections below.

15. I am staying neutral on whether the *cogito* is an inference, intuition, combination thereof, or still something else. See Markie (1992).

What sorts of thoughts play a role in the thought proposition of the *cogito*? Descartes divides thoughts into two classes: operations of the intellect and operations of the will. Operations of the intellect are perceptions, and this includes "sensory perception, imagination and pure understanding," while "desire, aversion, assertion, denial and doubt are various modes of willing" (AT VIIIA: 17/CSM I: 204) or "inclinations of the will" (AT III: 665/CSMK III: 218). In *Passions of the Soul*, Descartes characterizes all the various perceptions of the mind as passions and distinguishes them from actions of the soul, which are volitions (AT XI: 342, 349, and 359/CSM I: 335, 339, and 343). In a letter from 1641 he writes that "understanding is the passivity of the mind and willing is its activity" (AT III: 372/CSMK III: 182), and he repeats this later in another letter where he writes of the mind that "only its volitions are activities [*actio*]" (AT IV: 113/CSM III: 232).[16]

There are several reasons for thinking that the thought proposition of the *cogito* has to be about mental action and not a passion. The main reason for this is that the structure of the propositions in Descartes's *cogito* requires this, and I try to show this in the sections below. Another reason is that Descartes only uses attitudes such as doubt, denial, or affirmation when he actually states the *cogito*. For example, he typically argues that it is doubt itself that grounds his confidence in the proposition that he exists. In the passage from the

16. Unfortunately, sometimes, although very rarely, Descartes also describes any operation of the mind, be it a perception or a volition, as an act of the soul (AT VII: 176 and 256/CSM II: 124 and 172). But in these passages Descartes tends to use the term "*actus*," which is distinct from "*actio*" (see Chappell 1986: 196n17). An apparent exception to this is the following passage in the Second Meditation: "The next thought was that I was nourished, that I moved about, that I sensed [*sentire*], and that I thought [*cogitare*]; and these actions [*actiones*] I attributed to the soul" (AT VII: 26/CSM 17). If "*sentire*" refers to the having of sense perceptions, then he is calling passive perceptions "actions [*actiones*]." But Descartes distinguishes between perceptions that are formed by the will and thus are actions of the soul from perceptions that are not formed by the will (AT XI: 345/CSM I: 336). He describes remembering something, imagining something, and fixing one's visual attention on an object as volitions (AT XI: 360-1/CSM I: 343-4). It is not implausible to suppose that "*sentire*" in this passage refers to the activity of engaging in sense perception, as when one fixes one's attention on an object, not just passively receiving ideas. Thus Cottingham's translation of the phrase "*me . . . sentire*" as "I engaged in sense perception" (CSM II: 17) seems correct. Moreover, these passages are uncommon; when he is explicitly characterizing action it always involves volition.

Fourth Meditation quoted above Descartes writes that "from this very fact of *my raising this question*" it follows quite evidently that I exist" (AT VII: 58/CSM II: 41). In the Synopsis he writes that the "mind uses its own freedom and supposes the non-existence of all things" and he adds that "in so doing the mind notices that it is impossible that it should not exist during this time" (AT VII: 2/CSM II: 9).[17] He never uses the form "I perceive, therefore I exist" or "I imagine, therefore I exist."

A third reason to believe that Descartes thinks that the thought proposition must be about a mental action is that there is some textual evidence that he thinks this. When Gassendi argues that the *cogito* is an inference that is valid "from any one of your other actions [*actione*]" besides thinking, for example, walking (AT VII: 259/CSM II: 180), Descartes responds by writing, "I am not wholly certain of any of my actions [*actionis*], with the sole exception of thought [*cogitationis*]" (AT VII: 352/CSM II: 244). Thus Descartes seems to narrow the scope of thoughts relevant to the *cogito* to the thoughts that are actions or operations of the will.

The example Descartes discusses in this reply might suggest that he is referring to a passion. He writes that "the consciousness of walking [*ambulandi conscientia*]," not the walking itself, supports the inference that he exists (AT VII: 352/CSM II: 244). This could be taken to refer to the perception or awareness of walking, but it is significant that Descartes does not use the term "*perceptio*" here, which is the term he usually uses when referring to the operations of the intellect which are passive (AT VIIIA: 17–18/CSM I: 203–4). Moreover, he describes his consciousness as "I seem to myself to be walking [*mihi videor ambulare*]" and "I think I am walking [*putem me ambulare*]." The use of the Latin verbs *video* and *puto* suggests that Descartes is not thinking just about the perception of my walking, but the judgment *that I seem to be walking*.[18] *Video* indicates that this is an act of seeing on purpose, as when I intentionally look at something, while *puto* is a verb indicating the mental affirmation or acceptance of a proposition.

---

17. So pace Guéroult (1984: 42), in the *Meditations* Descartes does use the act of doubting to argue for his existence.
18. These are, in Kant's terminology, judgments of perception, which are to be distinguished from judgments of experience (Kant Ak IV: 298).

I suggest, then, that in all of the following phrases in the *cogito* passage of the Second Meditation Descartes is referring to propositional attitudes: "if I persuaded myself of something," "so long as I shall think that I am something [*esse cogitabo*]," "whenever it [the proposition that I am, I exist] is put forward or mentally conceived by me [*quoties a me profertur, vel mente concipitur*]" (AT VII: 25). To be persuaded of something is clearly a judgment, and hence, on Descartes's view, a mental action. If I think that I am something, say, something that walks, then I have a propositional attitude: either I affirm that I am walking or I affirm that it seems to me that I am walking. Putting forward some proposition is also an action. It involves directing the mind to a proposition and considering or entertaining it. In the *Passions* Descartes distinguishes between purely mental actions (volitions of the soul "which terminate in the soul itself" from bodily actions ("which terminate in our body, as when our merely willing to walk has the consequence that our legs move and we walk"), and "generally speaking," a mental action is "to apply our mind to some object which is not material" (AT XI: 343/CSM I: 225). Putting forward a proposition for consideration is a good example of the mental action of applying one's mind to a proposition.

I will, therefore I am

In other words, I am suggesting that Descartes could have written "I will, therefore I am" as well as "I think, therefore I am."[19] This is in fact suggested by Descartes's introduction of the will in *Principles of Philosophy*. Even before he gets to the *cogito* in Principle 7, Descartes writes that "we have a free will, enabling us to withhold our assent in doubtful matters" (AT VIIIA: 6). He argues, echoing the *cogito* reasoning in the *Meditation*, that no matter how "powerful and however deceitful" our creator may be, "we nonetheless experience [*experimur*] within us the kind of freedom which enables us always to refrain from believing things." This makes his will into one of the first things he knows, as he admits in Principle 39: "That there is freedom in our will, and that we have power in many cases to give or withhold our assent at will, is so evident that it must be counted among the first and most common notions that are innate in us" (AT VIIIA: 19/CSM I: 205–6).

19. Pace Gueroult (1984: 42).

Descartes's reference to liberty here should not obscure the important point that what is at issue is a certain mental state or event, namely, volition. This can be seen by looking more closely at Descartes's characterization of the will. In the Fourth Meditation, where Descartes uses "will," "freedom of the will," "choice," and "freedom of choice" synonymously (AT VII: 56–7), he writes:

> The will simply consists in our ability to do or not to do something (that is, to affirm or deny, to pursue or to avoid); or rather, it consists simply in the fact that when something is put forward for our consideration by the intellect, we are moved to affirm or deny it, or pursue or avoid it, in such a way that we feel we are not determined by an external force. (AT VII: 57)

Descartes is really characterizing two distinct properties, namely, freedom of the will and voluntary action. Freedom involves having alternative actions available, for example, to either affirm or deny a perception. The other property is that of having an effective and occurrent want or desire.[20] For example, the *cogito* is a voluntary action. The clear and distinct perception of the proposition affirmed by the *cogito* is accompanied by a "great inclination in the will" to affirm it, and this moved Descartes to affirm it (AT VII: 58–9/CSM II: 41). He is doing what he consciously wants to do, and hence his action is voluntary.

A voluntary action need not be free. Locke illustrates this with a man who happens to be in a room that (unbeknownst to him) he cannot leave but that also happens to contain his good friend with whom he wants to converse (II.21.10). So he stays in the room voluntarily, doing what he wants to do without any impediment, but his action is not free because there is no choice but to stay in the room. Although in the *Meditations* Descartes includes freedom and voluntary action under the same heading, he distinguishes them in a letter written in 1645. He distinguishes between free actions that have been performed and free actions that have not been performed (AT IV: 173/CSM 245). Before they are performed, we have alternative courses of action and either we can be indifferent to the alternatives (which is the lowest grade of freedom) or we are not indifferent "morally speaking" because "a very evident reason moves us in one direction." Nevertheless, "absolutely speaking" we still have a choice

---

20. The notion of an *effective desire* is borrowed from Frankfurt (1971). On occurrent wants, see Goldman (1970: 86–8).

because "it is always open to us to hold back from pursuing a clearly known good, or from admitting a clearly perceived truth, provided we consider it a good thing to demonstrate the freedom of our will by doing so" (ibid.). For example, even when I perceive clearly and distinctly that I exist whenever I think, I can refrain from affirming this.

Once an action is under way or completed, we do not have a choice anymore and we cannot be indifferent because we are acting on or have acted on some effective reason or desire. Then freedom consists simply in "ease of operation; and at that point freedom, spontaneity and voluntariness are the same thing" (AT IV: 174–5). Descartes points out that this is what he had in mind when in the *Meditations* he wrote that we can be free even when we do not have a choice and are compelled as long as we are compelled by our own reasons or "inmost thoughts" (AT VII: 58/CSM II: 40). In fact, even if these inmost thoughts are divinely produced they are free in the sense of being voluntary.

For Descartes, a voluntary mental action is something "we are aware of as happening within us" (AT VIIIA: 6–7) and it is "as self-evident and as transparently clear as anything can be" (AT VIIIA: 20). This suggests that when Descartes identifies voluntariness with freedom, he is not using "freedom" in the sense that requires the existence of alternative courses of action. Whether or not there are real alternatives is an objective fact that cannot be known by reflection or introspection. A voluntary mental action is a kind of mental event that can be known by introspection.

The failure to distinguish freedom and volition underlies the following objection to the voluntarist reading of the *cogito*:

One can doubt that I am willing and affirm that my will, my effort, is but an illusion, state that it only *seems* that I will, in the same way that it *seems* that I sense or imagine; but in any case one cannot doubt that I think that I will. (Guéroult 1984: 44)

It is true that I can doubt that I have a choice of actions, that I could have done otherwise, or that my will is free. I may also have doubts about the unconscious determinants of my actions, including mental actions. For example, if I want to think about the proposition that I am drinking a cup of tea and I think about it, then perhaps my wish and my thinking about it are caused by to me unknown factors, and my thought about this proposition is not brought about by my wish to think it. But none of this affects the claim that I have the volition, whether or not it is free. For Descartes, if it seems to me that I want something, then I want it, just as if it seems to me that I am thinking, then I am thinking.

Propositional Attitudes and Self-Doubt

Nevertheless, there is still room for doubting the *cogito*. If a volition that grounds the *cogito* is an object of thought – something I think about – and all objects of thought are represented only by my thoughts, then my volitions can indeed be illusions. Perhaps nothing corresponds to or satisfies my thoughts of volitions. This doubt, however, does not discriminate between volitions and other kinds of thoughts. As we see in this section, this doubt infects all thoughts about oneself.

What Descartes has to say about thoughts very easily fits a model according to which thoughts have the structure of propositional attitudes. This is the model I have been using in discussing Descartes's *cogito*. There are psychological attitudes, such as doubt, hope, and belief, and propositions are the meanings or contents of these attitudes. We can think of the attitudes as being directed toward a proposition, but it is important not to confuse this with thinking that the attitude is about a proposition. Hoping that there is a world has as its content the proposition *that there is a world*, and this is distinct from hoping something about the proposition that there is a world, for instance, hoping that there is a proposition that there is a world. In the latter case the content of the attitude is the second-order proposition *that there is a proposition that there is a world*.

What about the structure of a proposition? A standard view that can be associated with Frege (1967) goes like this. Propositions are built out of concepts, and thus we can say that they are structures of concepts. The proposition *that a cat is on the mat* is a structure that consists of the concept CAT, the concept MAT, as well as the relational concept of BEING ON SOMETHING. Concepts bear semantic relations to objects: they either apply or do not apply to objects. The concept CAT applies to cats but not to dogs, while the concept UNICORN applies to nothing. Propositions themselves also have semantic properties – for example, that they are true or false – and the semantic properties of propositions are determined by the semantic properties of the propositions' concepts.

On this view, the *cogito* is a propositional attitude involving a belief or affirmation and the propositions that I exist and that I think, which are structures of concepts. Unfortunately, this reading of the *cogito* condemns Descartes's project to immediate failure (Henry 1993; Marion 1993). The reason for this is a distinction that is essential to this Fregean understanding of the structure of propositions: propositions are made of concepts, but Fregean concepts are distinct from the objects that satisfy them (Frege 1892). The concept of a horse is not a horse. By the same token, the concept I have of myself is not identical to me. I satisfy this concept, but I am not identical with this concept. Consequently, what I affirm in the *cogito* is a proposition that bears a semantic relation to me. I affirm the proposition that I exist, and this is an affirmation of my own existence in virtue of a semantic relation this proposition bears to me.[21]

The distinction between concept and object, in the dramatic words of Jean-Luc Marion,

rends with an impassible *caesura* ... the represented from what represents; the being which carries out the *cogito* remains separated from the being which it knows as its *cogitatum*, whatever it may be. Therefore, the *ego*, far from being reconciled to itself by reconciling itself to a certain existence – which Descartes certainly meant to establish – must admit that it ... remains alienated by itself from itself. (1993: 56)

Although Marion's worry is informed by a phenomenological understanding of the *cogito*, an understanding rooted in Edmund Husserl, not Frege, Marion's concern applies with equal force to the Fregean reading of the *cogito*.[22]

The aim of the *cogito* (if I am the one following the meditative path Descartes laid out in the Second Meditation) is to know myself and

---

21. This Fregean reading of the *cogito* is endorsed by Markie (1986: 88–9 and 1992: 147).
22. This should not be surprising because the Fregean account of propositional attitudes and Husserl's theory of intentionality are very close kin (Foellesdal 1982). For Husserl, a judgment is a mental act directed toward an intentional object: the *noema*. This *noema* is what a judgment affirms or denies, and it is said to be its intentional content. The *noema* also determines what are the objects, if any, of the judgment. In the case of the *cogito*, I am the object of the judgment – its *cogitatum* – and this object is determined by the intentional content of the *cogito*.

my mental states with certainty. But on the Fregean reading of the *cogito* what I affirm is a proposition, and this proposition is about me in virtue of semantic relations its concepts bear to me. It is about me because it contains a concept of me and it is about my thinking because it contains a concept of my thinking. The dependence on concepts and the semantic relations they bear to their objects is the source of Marion's doubt. If I am following Descartes's path in the *Meditations*, I am supposed to gain knowledge of my own existence, and the *cogito* is an item of knowledge only if doubt does not infect the semantic relation that obtains between the proposition affirmed in the *cogito* and myself. For the *cogito* to be successful, I cannot doubt that the concepts that make up the proposition affirmed in the *cogito* are satisfied. But this relation is not immune to Cartesian doubt, as is vividly described by Marion:

> If doubt disqualifies the relation between every idea (every representation) and its *ideatum* (what is represented), and if the existence of the *ego* or even its performance of thinking constitutes an *ideatum*, then how are we to certify that the representation of that *ideatum* and it alone constitutes an exception to the disqualification of even the most present of things that are evident? In short, if the *cogito, ergo sum* heightens representation, then it too, like all representations, must be vanquished by the blow of doubt. For why should it be certain that I think, if I also represent these things to myself? (1993: 56–7)[23]

Perhaps the deceiver makes me judge that I doubt, understand, think, and so on, but also makes it the case that these judgments are false (Wilson 1978: 59). It is worth repeating that this problem infects all aspects of the *cogito* including the judgment that I think, as long as what I affirm is a proposition that bears semantic relations to my thinking. We can label this doubt "conceptual self-doubt" in order to capture the fact that I am doubting the *concepts* I use to make first-person judgments about myself.

We can rely on Descartes's deceiver to generate conceptual self-doubt, but there are much more troublesome sources of doubt in contemporary philosophy of mind and language. If all semantic relations are natural relations known a posteriori, not a priori, then we have Cartesian reasons to suspend judgments about all semantic

---

23. Zemach (1985: 192) raises a similar objection.

relations, including the ones relevant to the *cogito*.[24] Moreover, if our ordinary, common-sense psychological judgments about believing, desiring, thinking, willing, and so on are all either false or too ambiguous to get a truth value and thus warrant elimination from a true account of human nature,[25] then the *cogito* is also either false or too ambiguous to get a truth value. Of course, there seems to be a phenomenology because we judge that we think, desire, and so forth, but it does not follow that there really is a phenomenology (Dennett 1991: 365–7). In sum, perhaps the science of mind undermines our trust in the concepts we use to think about ourselves, including the concepts used in the *cogito*.

Immediate Self-Awareness

One conclusion that could be drawn from this is that Descartes's *cogito* reasoning is just faulty. However, I think Descartes would have recognized and confronted the dangers the deceiver poses for the *cogito* understood as an attitude involving concepts distinct from their objects.[26] A more charitable conclusion is that the *cogito* is not a propositional attitude, but a case of direct self-awareness that is unmediated by concepts. The thinking self is immanent in the perception that constitutes the *cogito*.

There is textual evidence that Descartes believed he had immediate self-awareness of the *cogito*. In the Synopsis to the *Meditations* he writes that the "mind notices [*animadvertit*] that it is impossible that it should not itself exist during this time [while it doubts]" (AT VII: 12/CSM II: 9).[27] He ends the Second Meditation by reminding himself, "I know plainly that I can achieve an easier and more *evident perception of my own mind* than of anything else [*aut evidentius mea mente posse a me percipi*]" (AT VII: 34/CSM II: 22–3, my emphasis). In the Third Meditation he

---

24. For example, all causal theories of content undermine Descartes's *cogito* and all varieties of what Millikan (1984: 325–33) calls "meaning rationalism."
25. For a comprehensive collection of the influential essays on the validity of ordinary psychological concepts, see Christensen and Turner (1993).
26. Pace Wilson (1978: 59).
27. The whole quote reads as follows: "*Mens quae, propria libertae utens, supponit ea omnia non existere de quorum existentia vel minimum potest dubitare, animadvertit fieri non posse quin ipsa interim existat.*"

writes, "I will . . . scrutinize myself more deeply [*penitius inspiciendo*]; and in this way I will attempt to achieve, little by little, a more intimate [*familiarem*] knowledge of myself" (AT VII: 34/CSM II: 24). He wants to "cast around [*circumspiciam*] . . . to see whether there may be other things within me which I have not yet noticed" (AT VII: 35/CSM II: 24). Descartes's language in these passages accords with his general view that we are "immediately aware [*conscii*]" of all our thoughts, and he adds, "I say 'immediately' so as to exclude the consequences of thoughts" (AT VII: 160/CSM II: 113), and by "consequences" he means relations thoughts have to other things, such as behavior that is caused by thoughts. It seems that this excludes all relations, including semantic ones. We are immediately aware of our thoughts, not what relations our thoughts bear to other things.

Additional support for the claim that the *cogito* involves immediate self-awareness is found in a letter Descartes wrote in 1648, where he compares the *cogito* to intuiting God (AT V: 136–9/CSM III: 330–2). Intuitive knowledge of God is a product of "direct illumination," and such knowledge allows us to "know God by himself," that is, "by an immediate light cast by the Godhead on our mind," and this we do not now have. Our knowledge is discursive and deduced from propositions and principles. The only example we now have of such intuitive knowledge is the *cogito*. Descartes writes that "the truth of the proposition 'I am thinking, therefore I exist' . . . is not the work of . . . reasoning, [but] it is something that your mind sees, feels and handles" (AT V: 138/CSM III: 331). In fact, the intuitive self-knowledge we have in the *cogito* is evidence for Descartes that we have a capacity for intuitive knowledge, particularly, the capacity to have intuitive knowledge of God "in the beatific vision" that he expects to have after death.[28]

However, if we interpret the *cogito* as a case of immediate self-awareness and reject the idea that the *cogito* is an attitude directed to a structure of concepts, where the concepts are distinct from their objects, then the Fregean model of propositions does not apply to Descartes's *cogito* anymore. One way to handle this difficulty is to reject the propositional model for the *cogito* altogether.[29] Unfortu-

---

28. Also see the last paragraph to Descartes's Second Meditation (AT VII: 52/CSM II: 36).
29. This alternative is affirmed by Henry (1993) and Marion (1993).

nately, this leaves us with the problem of how to handle other judgments. Is the *cogito* in a class of its own while other judgments are propositional attitudes? This is not very satisfactory because Descartes always discusses judgments in a unified way. He writes about only one faculty of judgment (AT VII: 53/CSM II: 37); a judgment always requires the operation of the intellect, namely, perceptions (AT VIIIA: 17); and the immediate objects of perception are always ideas (AT VII: 160 and 181/CSM II: 113 and 127).

Still another problem for rejecting the propositional attitude model for the *cogito* is that Descartes describes the *cogito* as involving a proposition. In the Second Meditation he writes that "this proposition [*pronunciatum*], *I am, I exist* is . . . true whenever it is put forward by me or conceived by my mind" (AT VII: 25). In the Third Meditation Descartes reports that "in this first item of knowledge there is simply a clear and distinct perception of what I am asserting" (AT VII: 35). In the Fourth Meditation he writes about the *cogito* that ". . . he could not but judge that something which he understood so clearly and distinctly is true" (AT VII: 58). Moreover, the philosophy he is seeking is one in which the first principles can serve as premises in sound deductive arguments. After all, "*cogito, ergo sum*" is for Descartes a "truth . . . that I decided I could accept . . . without scruples as the first principle of the philosophy I was seeking" (AT VI: 32). It is difficult to see how self-awareness, in itself, can serve as a premise in an argument. If the *cogito* is to play this role, it needs to be a proposition or something with propositional content, such as a judgment or statement.

So it seems that for Descartes the *cogito* must be both a case of immediate self-awareness *and* a propositional attitude. This means that we cannot interpret the *cogito* in a Fregean manner as an attitude toward a structure of concepts. If the *cogito* is a case of immediate self-awareness, it cannot be a propositional attitude that is about myself in virtue of concepts that apply to me because, as we saw, this opens the *cogito* to conceptual self-doubt.

Fortunately, Frege's account of propositional attitudes is not the only available account. Bertrand Russell's alternative account of the nature of propositions avoids this problem. In a famous exchange, Russell responds to Frege's claim in a letter that "Mont Blanc with its snowfields is not itself a component part of the thought that Mont Blanc is more than 4,000 meters high" as follows: "I believe that in spite of all its snowfields Mont Blanc itself is a component part of what is actually asserted in the proposition 'Mont Blanc is more than 4,000 meters high.' "[30] What is asserted is a complex entity Russell calls an "objective proposition" and this is what includes Mont Blanc itself. Russell believes that the object is a component of what is asserted when we use proper names or indexicals such as "that" or "I." The meaning of these terms just is their denotation.[31]

I suggest that this is precisely the view Descartes had in mind for the proposition of the *cogito*.[32] When Descartes is affirming that he thinks, he is affirming a proposition, but it is an objective proposition. This proposition in some sense actually involves him, and not a concept that stands in a semantic relation to himself. We can think of this proposition as consisting of or being a state of affairs, event, or happening that involves me, namely, the occurrence of my thinking. Thus, the *cogito*, in my own case, is a propositional attitude whose content consists of my thinking *and* it is also a case of self-awareness because it is an attitude directed toward me as opposed to a concept of me. Objective propositions overcome the *caesura* between content and object that threatens Descartes's project, while preserving his commitment to propositional attitudes.

Ideas and Self-Awareness

What exactly is the immediate object of awareness when Descartes is aware of himself? An important constraint on how we answer this question is Descartes's explicitly stated view that an idea is "whatever is immediately perceived by the mind" (AT VII: 160 and 181/CSM II: 113 and 127). What is needed is an idea, perception of which is a case of direct acquaintance of himself.[33] This idea will be a component of the proposition he affirms in the *cogito*, but it will not be like a concept of Descartes, namely, something that bears a semantic relation to Descartes. How can this be?

---

30. This exchange is reprinted in Salmon and Soames (1988: 56–7). The original letters are in Frege (1980: 153 and 169).
31. This theme is developed by David Kaplan (1989).
32. This is already suggested by Zemach (1985: 195–6).
33. Markie (1992: 163) rejects the view that Descartes is committed to direct, non-conceptual self-awareness on the grounds that on Descartes's view you think about yourself by grasping ideas. He assumes without argument that you cannot both be directly acquainted with yourself and thinking about yourself by grasping ideas.

It is easy to assume that for Descartes all ideas are like concepts in that they have semantic properties (Wilson 1978: 102). For example, in the Third Meditation he writes that "there can be no ideas which are not as it were of things." The French translation of this passage, which Descartes approved, is even stronger: "since ideas, being like images, must in each case appear to us to represent something" (CSM II: 30). However, Descartes distinguishes between ideas in a "strict and narrow sense" and ideas in an "extended" sense (AT V: 153/CSM III: 338).

Ideas in the narrow sense always have semantic properties: they resemble, conform to, refer to, or represent something (AT VII: 37–40/CSM II: 25–8). Such ideas "represent [*repraesentant*] God, corporeal and inanimate things, angels, animals and finally other men like myself" (AT VII: 42/CSM II: 29). An idea in the broader sense is any mode of thought that is accessible to immediate awareness (AT VII: 160/CSM II: 113). This includes not only ideas that represent, but ideas that, in and of themselves, do not have semantic properties, such as sensations, emotions, and the psychological attitudes such as "when I will, or am afraid, or affirm, or deny" (AT VII: 37/CSM II: 26).[34]

Ideas in the narrow sense are also modes of thought: they have ontological status and their own intrinsic natures in addition to their semantic properties. Descartes highlights these two aspects of ideas in the Preface to the *Meditations*: "'Idea' can be taken materially, as an operation of the intellect. . . . Alternatively, it can be taken objectively, as the thing represented by the operation" (AT VII: 8/CSM II: 7).[35] This important distinction between ideas as operations or modes of the intellect and ideas as representations is made in the Third Meditation in terms of his distinction between formal and objective reality. An idea's formal reality consists in the fact that it is a mode of thought or a way of thinking (AT VII: 41/CSM II: 28). But it also contains objective reality, namely, what it represents. Just as a book has both semantic properties (e.g., that it is about two people) and

---

34. Although attitudes have propositional content, the attitudes are distinct from this content because, as Descartes puts it succinctly in response to Hobbes, seeing and being afraid of a lion is distinct from seeing a lion fearlessly (AT VII: 182/CSM II: 128).

35. Chappell (1986: 177) notes the importance of this distinction to a proper understanding of Descartes.

nonsemantic properties (e.g., that it is a paperback), an idea in the narrow sense has nonsemantic as well as semantic properties.

In ordinary cases, the features of an idea that play a role in determining propositional content are its semantic properties. It is an idea taken objectively, in Descartes's sense of this term, that plays a role in propositions. For example, if the proposition that I affirm in my belief that the sun exists contains an idea of the sun, then the role of this idea is to pick out what it is, if anything, that my belief is about. However, there is another way that an idea can contribute to the proposition. It can contribute in the way Mont Blanc contributes to Russell's objective proposition, as we saw above. An idea can contribute to the proposition by being itself a component of the proposition. Consequently, if a propositional attitude is directed at a proposition that incorporates an idea in this way, then the idea itself is an object of the attitude.

What allows an idea to be a component of a proposition is that it is something with formal reality. It is an event or state that occurs for some finite duration (Chappell 1986: 181). In this respect, ideas that do not have semantic properties can play a role in propositions and determine the content of propositional attitudes. In fact, as far as the *cogito* is concerned, the semantic properties of ideas are irrelevant. It is the having of thoughts, not what one thinks, that matters to the *cogito*. Thus the *cogito* is directed at an idea *and* it is directed at myself at the same time because it is directed at the idea's material aspects or formal reality. That is, it is directed at the idea as a certain mental state I am in.

This is borne out by the way Descartes describes the *cogito*. In the *Meditations* it is the persuading oneself of something, the putting forward or conceiving of a proposition that underwrites the *cogito*.[36] As long as I think anything at all I exist (AT VII: 25/CSM II: 17). The knowledge he has of his existence depends on this state of affairs: "I am, I exist, that is certain. But for how long? For as long as I am thinking." The certainty of my existence depends on a certain happening: my thinking. This is why Descartes can also write about thought as if it were a discovery: "At last I have discovered [*invenio*] it – thought; this alone is inseparable [*divelli*] from me." (AT VII: 27/CSM II: 18). In the *Discourse* Descartes writes, "I noticed that while I was trying thus

---

36. See the discussion of *cogito* above.

to think ... it was necessary that I ... was something" (AT VI: 32/CSM I: 127). He knows himself insofar as he is trying to think something.

In the *Principles* he writes that "we cannot for all that suppose that we, who are having such thoughts, are nothing." Restated for the first person, this says that I, who am having certain thoughts, cannot suppose that I am nothing. What is contradictory is to suppose that I do not exist "at the very same time when [I am] thinking" (AT VIIIA: 7/CSM I: 195). He adds: "For it may perhaps be the case that I judge that I am touching the earth even though the earth does not exist at all; but it cannot be that, when I make this judgment, my mind which is making the judgment does not exist" (AT VIIIA: 9/CSM I: 196). Again, it is the event of making a judgment that is involved in the *cogito*, not what it represents. Descartes makes this explicit when he characterizes thought as "everything which we are aware of as *happening* within us (AT VIIIA: 7/CSM I: 195). This reference to thoughts as happenings comes after he introduces the *cogito*, and it explains what he means by thinking in the *cogito*.

However, the most compelling evidence for the claim that Descartes's *cogito* is a case of immediate awareness of one's own thoughts comes from his discussion of volition in the *Passions of the Soul*.[37] For Descartes, all perceptions are passions because the mind is passive with respect to them (AT XI: 328 and 342/CSM I: 328 and 335). Yet some perceptions are caused by the mind, and those are the perceptions of our volitions. He writes:

[Perceptions] having the soul as their cause are the perceptions of our volitions and of all the imaginings or other thoughts which depend on them. For
it is certain that we cannot will anything without thereby perceiving that we
are willing it. And although willing something is an action with respect to our
soul, the perception of such willing may be said to be a passion in the soul.
But because this perception is really one and the same thing as the volition,
and names are always determined by whatever is most noble, we do not nor-
mally call it a "passion," but solely an "action." (AT XI: 343/CSM I: 335-6)

The perception of volition, that is, the having of an idea of volition, is identical to the volition itself. The ideas that I have of my volitions, at least while I am willing, do not stand in any semantic relation to my volition but simply *are* the volition. Consequently, propositions

37. This was noticed by Marion (1993: 64).

about my volition that consist of these ideas will be composed of the volition itself, and an affirmation of such a proposition will be both a propositional attitude and a case of self-awareness.

Moreover, that mental actions, rather than passions, are what underwrite Descartes's *cogito* is shown immediately in the next paragraph. There Descartes states that when "our soul . . . applies itself to consider something that is purely intelligible . . . , for example, in considering its own nature, the perceptions it has of these things depend chiefly on the volition which makes it aware of them." So, the perceptions that are involved in the knowledge of our intelligible selves, namely, the self-knowledge Descartes achieves in the Second Meditation, are regarded "as actions rather than passions" (AT XI: 344/CSM I: 336).[38] Perceptions of our will are distinct from all the other passions because all other passions – imaginings, external sensations such as vision, internal bodily sensations such as pain, or emotions and desires such as joy or love – "are not actions of the soul or volitions" (AT XI: 349/CSM I: 339).

Voluntary mental activity, then, is needed for the *cogito*, and Descartes is surely right about that. Just as we when we were children acquired a sense of our own bodies through our physical activity – for example, by trying to lift our heads, reach for objects, or scoot around the floor – we come to know our minds through our mental activity, for example, by trying to form and fix our beliefs. I know I exist only as long as I am actively engaged in thinking, and this activity is what the *cogito* is about. It is about the kind of thinking Descartes has in mind when he writes that "we are responsible only for our thoughts" (AT IV: 307/CSMK III: 269).

Understood in this way, it is easy to see why Descartes did not worry about what appears to be a fundamental objection to his *cogito*. A mystery figure called "Hyperaspistes" first raised this objection in 1641 as follows: "You do not know whether it is you yourself who think or whether the world-soul in you does the thinking, as the Platonists believe" (AT III: 403/CSM III: 192). In other words, Descartes is not entitled to use the first-person pronoun "I" in the *cogito*. At most he

---

38. Also see his letter to Elizabeth of Bohemia dated October 6, 1645 (AT IV: 310–1/CSMK III: 270). The dependence of the ideas of the *cogito* on the mental action of thinking may be the source of the notion of causality Descartes uses in the Third Meditation to prove God's existence (see Baier 1986).

is entitled to claim that there are now thoughts or that thinking is now occurring, but these claims cannot support the judgment that he exists.[39]

Descartes does not reply to this argument specifically, but he treats it together with the objection that he is not entitled to believe that he knows what thinking or existence is. To all this Descartes writes:

I utterly deny that we do not know . . . what thought is, or that I need to teach people this. It is so self-evident that there is nothing which could serve to make it any clearer. (AT III: 426/CSM III: 192)

The self-evidence of thought is echoed later in the *Principles* (AT VIIIA: 8/CSM I: 196). In the *Meditations*, Descartes makes a similar appeal to self-evidence:

The fact that it is I who am doubting and understanding and willing is so evident that I see no way of making it any clearer. (AT VII: 29/CSM II: 19)

Here Descartes's main concern is the identity of the subject across these different mental states: whether or not it is "same 'I'" who doubts, understands, affirms, desires, and so on. But in the same breath he also asks the questions, "Which of these activities is distinct from my thinking? Which of them can be said to be separate from myself?" and his answer is the same appeal to self-evidence. For Descartes it is as self-evident that when thinking, it is he who is think-ing, when doubting, it is he who is doubting, when understanding, it is he who is understanding, and so on, as it is self-evident that it is always he – the "same 'I'" – who is thinking, doubting, under-standing, and so on.

I suggest that the reason this seemed so self-evident to Descartes and that Hyperaspistes's objection seemed unproblematic was that Descartes did not separate agency from thinking. If the thinking of the *cogito* is a passive and involuntary activity, then Hyperaspistes's objection has some intuitive plausibility. After all, at times it might seem that the passive, involuntary thoughts one has are not one's own thoughts.[40] Granting this, it is nevertheless difficult to generate such a concern for our deliberate and voluntary thoughts, and it is volun-tary thinking that plays a role in Descartes's *cogito*. The thinking that

---

39. See Russell (1945: 576) and Kenny (1968: 93).
40. For example, Mozart supposedly claimed that at times it seemed to him that when he was composing it was not he who was composing, but someone else.

grounds Descartes's self-knowledge is not passive perception of the intellect, but his own deliberate and willful thinking: his trying to doubt, his trying to find certainty, his ordering of his beliefs according to degrees of simplicity and certainty, and so on. These are examples of first-person mental agency, and there is no better way to refer to these mental states or occurrences than by using phrases such as "I am thinking" or "I am doubting."[41]

Will and Environment

Not only do the mental states of first-person mental agency ground Descartes's knowledge of his own existence, but his conscious volition also embeds Descartes in an environment. Strictly speaking, Descartes's conception of mind is not individualistic, that is, it is not true that for Descartes "the nature and individuation of an individual's mental kinds are 'in' principle independent of the nature and individuation of all aspects of the individual's environment" (Burge 1986: 117). The very nature of Descartes's idea of God requires that there is "something distinct from [himself], namely God" (AT VIIIA: 12/CSM I: 199). The feature of this idea that ties it to the world is that it represents a supremely powerful creator who has everything it wants (AT VII: 45/CSM II: 31), and Descartes comes to understand that he has such an idea from the fact he has a will. He writes that "it is above all in virtue of the will that I understand myself to bear in some way the image or likeness of God" (AT VII: 57/CSM II: 40). The will is the source of Descartes's perfection (AT VIIIA: 18/CSM I: 205). There is nothing in him that is as perfect as his will, including his intellect, because it "is not restricted in any way" (AT VII: 56–7/CSM III: 39–40). It is, in a sense, infinite because there is no object, including objects of God's will, that cannot be an object of his will (AT VIIIA: 18/CSM I: 204). So Descartes's will leads him to an idea of God, which in turn is tied to his divine environment.

It is not clear precisely how Descartes's volition leads him to his idea of God, but a way of understanding this is that Descartes's will itself is a constituent of his idea or image of God, and it is the per-

---

41. These are, to borrow a phrase from Elizabeth Anscombe (1975), unmediated agent conceptions of actions, happenings, or states.

fection of volition that Descartes cannot explain in terms of himself only. The powerful and unlimited nature of his volition needs a cause that is greater than he is, and this, in Descartes's view, turns out to be God. Descartes's argument for God's existence is not specific about the perfections that are used to generate the conclusion, and it is intended to apply to all perfections. He writes:

All these attributes [of God] are such that, the more carefully I concentrate on them, the less possible it seems that they could have originated from me alone. So from what has been said it must be concluded that God necessarily exists. (AT VII: 45/CSM II: 31)

However, the reason he cannot be the source of this idea is that although his volition is unlimited, he nevertheless does not have everything he wants. Descartes's proof for the existence of God rests on the assumption that Descartes is imperfect and he knows he is imperfect because he has frustrated wants. For example, he does not have the knowledge he wants about many things (AT VII: 48/CSM II: 33). So although his wants are unlimited (and perfect in this sense), their satisfaction is not. But if he were the author of his existence, all his wants would be satisfied – including his will to know – and, in his words, "I should myself be God" (AT VII: 48/CSM II: 33). The will he has can be directed at any object whatsoever because it is simply the capacity "to affirm or deny, pursue or avoid," but it is not always "firm and efficacious" in its affirmations and pursuits (AT VII: 57/CSM II: 40). This defect needs to be explained by the existence of something distinct from Descartes.

Descartes's awareness of his own agency, particularly its limits, leads him not only to God, but to a material environment as well. In the Sixth Meditation Descartes proves the existence of material objects on the basis of the fact that he has ideas that are not in his conscious control. These are "ideas of sensible objects," such as his own body and other corporeal objects (AT VII: 79/CSM I: 55). Descartes writes: "The ideas in question are produced without my cooperation and often even against my will. So the only alternative is that it is another substance distinct from me" (AT VII: 79/CSM I: 55). Descartes goes on to identify this substance with corporeal things, because if anything noncorporeal causes these ideas, God is a deceiver, which is not the case. So it is the fact that I have a "passive faculty of sensory perception" (AT VII: 79/CSM II: 55) that is not only beyond my voluntary control, but that sometimes even frustrates my wants, that shows there are material bodies distinct from my mind.

In short, for Descartes it is on account of the fact that we have a will that we come to know that there are other things besides us. This is a far cry from the Kantian proposition that enlightenment requires public activity, and yet here in Descartes we can see the rough outlines of this notion. Proper rational Cartesian knowledge depends on voluntary mental activity, and it is this very activity that leads us to know that we are embedded in a divine and material environment.

Not only does volition ground our knowledge of what is external to us, but we use volition to distinguish rational from nonrational bodily activity. Rational bodily action requires volition. What distinguishes human beings from automatons and "beasts," according to Descartes, is that while animals and automatons are always moved by "dispositions of their organs" (AT VI: 57 and 59/CSM I: 140 and 141), human beings have the "power of movement" that belongs to the rational soul, and volition is this power. Although the external movements of animals, automatons, and human beings may resemble each other, there is no resemblance "between the corresponding interior actions" (AT II: 41/CSMK III: 100). What is missing in animals and automatons and what we have is "the command of [a] soul" (AT II: 37/CSMK III: 98).

Of course, Descartes believes that reason and its volitions are internal to the mind and are not found in public. What is public are reason's external consequences, for example, the body's movements. Nevertheless, even in Descartes we can find the idea that reason is not only "in the head," but spread throughout the body.[42] At one point Descartes writes,

I also think that some of the impressions which serve the memory can be in various other parts of the body: for instance the skill of a lute player is not only in his head, but also partly in the muscles of his hands, and so on. (AT III: 20/CSMK III: 144).

---

42. Sutton (1998: 60–6) has an extended discussion of how memory is distributed for Descartes and not localized in one place. Unfortunately, Sutton's excellent study came to my attention after my manuscript was written.

Descartes does not develop this remark, but the idea that the mind involves the whole body is developed in great detail by Hobbes and will have a firm place in subsequent 17th-century philosophy of mind. Although for Descartes the body does not have much of a role in the improvement of the understanding, he does see voluntary activity as a remedy for the mind's defects, particularly irresolution, and it is a deeper understanding of volition that will bring the body into focus for 17th-century philosophy.

3

Hobbes: Passionate Thinking

Computationalism

It is a curious fact that Hobbes has been claimed by all three major
20th-century materialist theories of mind. During the heyday of
behaviorism it was common to read Hobbes as a protobehaviorist
(Peters and Tajfel 1957). As behaviorism lost favor, it was not uncommon to interpret Hobbes as a "conspicuous defender of a central-state
theory," namely, the view that mental states are identical to states
of the brain or nervous system (Armstrong 1968: 110). Now that
central-state theories have been succeeded by computational theories
of mind, Hobbes is being called the "grandfather of AI [artificial
intelligence]" and it is widely accepted that in Thomas Hobbes's
philosophy of mind we find a rudimentary formulation of a computational theory of mind.[1]

Perhaps all these interpretations are partially right. Hobbes was
interested in internal physical states as well as their semantic properties, and he was also concerned with external embodied states. What
these partial interpretations miss was that Hobbes saw thinking as a
unity of internal and external states. We can see this best by looking
at the most recent appropriation of Hobbes's philosophy of mind by
the computationalists.

According to computationalism, thinking is a computation or
manipulation of mental representations that have language-like

---

1. Haugeland (1985: 23–8). Also see Kneale and Kneale (1962: 312); Styazhkin
   (1969: 60); P. Remnant's and J. Bennett's notes in NE; Cummins (1989: 6); and
   Bechtel and Abrahamsen (1991: 10). An endorsement is also suggested by Tuck
   (1989a: 46–7).

properties. These mental representations are language-like in that they have semantic features, for example, they have properties such as denoting or representing something or contributing to the meaning of other symbols in their context, and they bear semantic relations to other representations, such as entailment. Moreover, just as symbols of a public language have nonsemantic properties, mental representations have nonsemantic properties, roughly speaking, the physical and formal properties of the representations themselves and the causal or formal relations between mental representations.[2]

Another feature of computational theories is that they give cognitivist accounts of human action, and cognitivism explains action in terms of internal thinking.[3] An instance of behavior (e.g., lifting one's arm above one's head) is an action (say, volunteering for a task) because that behavior is a consequence of certain internal mental states (such as desiring to volunteer and believing that raising one's hand on this occasion will communicate this desire). For the computationalist, human action rests on internal computations over mental representations, and these operations can be characterized without relying on some prior notion of intelligent behavior. This point can also be made in terms of Gilbert Ryle's well-known distinction between *knowing how* to perform some activity and *knowing that* something is the case (Ryle 1949: 27–32). On the computational view, *knowing how* rests on *knowing that*, for example, a certain type of behavior is intelligent because it is a product of, say, internally represented production rules, that is, rules of the form "IF <condition> obtains, DO <action>." *Knowing that*, however, can be explained without appealing to a previously understood notion of *knowing how*. In short, for the computationalist, propositional knowledge and

2. It is important to distinguish between two senses of formal that are easily confused: (1) the syntactic properties of a system, and (2) the physical properties such as the shape of a symbol or the pattern of on and off states of a digital computer. See Devitt (1990: 371–98). I am covering both senses here in part because they are not distinguished in 17th-century discussions of mind.
3. In recent discussions, the terms "cognitivism" and "classical computationalism" are often synonymous, e.g., Lycan (1990: 8). However, I think it is useful to use "cognitivism" synonymously with "mentalism" as it was used in connection with Chomsky's language theory, e.g., Lyons (1981: 231 and 241–8). A cognitivist, in this weaker sense, is committed to the existence of internal mental or psychological states. Thus a cognitivist need not be a classical computationalist, although all classical computationalists are cognitivists.

internal mental processes, not human activity, play the primary role in psychological explanations.

A third feature of computationalism is that the mind is medium-independent (Haugeland 1985: 63). The mind is a system that does not depend on any specific features of the material that embodies the system. Just as chess can be played with a standard board and wooden figures or just on paper with algebraic notation, the mind can be a biological system or an artificial system. All that matters is that the states of the system can be characterized in terms of or mapped onto computable cognitive functions such as doing arithmetic, speaking language, or going to a restaurant (Cummins 1989: 87–113).[4]

I try to show that Hobbes does not endorse, even in a rudimentary fashion, these central ideas of computationalism. For Hobbes, not all thinking is computation, not all mental representations are language-like symbols, and thinking is not medium-independent. Moreover, Hobbes grounds thinking in intelligent behavior, and intelligent behavior is, to borrow Ryle's phrase, "not a step-child of theory" (Ryle 1949: 26). On the other hand, Hobbes is not a protobehaviorist, either. Hobbes offers an account of mind in which neither *knowing how* nor *knowing that* is more basic than the other, and both are equally necessary for cognition. The locus of Hobbes's synthesis of action and internal information processing is his concept of "passionate thought," thought that is willful, embodied, and embedded in a natural environment.

"The Grandfather of Artificial Intelligence"

The central piece of evidence for calling Hobbes "the grandfather of AI" is his claim that all reasoning, or ratiocination, is calculation. In the *Leviathan*, Hobbes writes:

---

4. New connectionists and classical computationalists have this commitment in common. Connectionists drop the demand that the mind has to be computing over language-like symbols. Instead, the objects of computation are neuron-like (rather than language-like) units that can have various activation values and pass them to other units to which they are connected. Nevertheless, the mind is characterized in terms of a function on vectors of activation values (Churchland and Sejnowski 1992: 61–2). On the differences between connectionism and classical computationalism, see Clark (1989) and Bechtel and Abrahamsen (1991: 1–20).

When a man *Reasoneth*, hee does nothing else but conceive a summe totall, from *Addition* of parcels; or conceive a Remainder, from *Subtraction* of one summe from another: which (if it be done with Words) is conceiving of the consequence of the names of all the parts, to the name of the whole; or the names of the whole and one part, to the name of the other part. . . . These operations are not incident to Numbers onely, but to all manner of things that can be added together, and taken one out of another. . . . In summe, in what matter soever there is place for *addition* and *subtraction*, there is also a place for *Reason*; and where these have no place, there *Reason* has nothing at all to do. (L 1.5/110–11)

To reason, then, is to compute, and one can compute over anything that can be added or subtracted.

This claim is repeated in the opening chapter of the first part of *De Corpore*, called "Computation or Logic":

By RATIOCINATION, I mean computation. Now to compute, is either to collect the sum of many things that are added together, or to know what remains when one thing is taken out of another. *Ratiocination*, therefore, is the same with *addition* and *subtraction*; . . . So that all ratiocination is comprehended in these two operations of the mind, addition and subtraction. (DC 1.1.2)

Hobbes then goes on to give an example of how we "add and subtract in our silent thoughts, without the use of words" (DC 1.1.3).

In these passages Hobbes appears to anticipate essential elements of computationalism. John Haugeland writes that in these passages Hobbes is suggesting that

thinking is "mental discourse"; that is, thinking consists of *symbolic operations*, just like talking out loud or calculating with pen and paper – except, of course, that it is conducted internally. Hence thoughts are not themselves expressed in spoken or written symbols but rather in special brain tokens, which Hobbes called "phantasms" or thought "parcels." (1985: 23)

In other words, the elements of thinking are language-like symbols, and to think is to compute over these language-like symbols.[5] This

---

5. These language-like symbols are the *direct* objects of computation: they are the objects that are manipulated by the computation; that is, the computation is causally sensitive to and it alters the formal and physical properties of these symbols. I distinguish direct objects from *indirect* objects of computation. Indirect objects of a computation are not causally altered by the computation, but they nevertheless can be appropriately mapped onto the direct objects of this computation. For example, when working out an equation on a piece of paper, the direct objects of the

reading was anticipated by Leibniz, who writes that for Hobbes, all our mental operations, not just reasoning, are computational:

Th. Hobbes, a profound investigator of the principles of all things, rightly maintained that everything our mind does is a computation, by which is meant either the addition of a sum or the subtraction of a difference. (GP IV: 63; my translation)

The computationalist reading of Hobbes is corroborated by the fact that Hobbes seems to believe that human actions are the products of internal mental operations. Hobbes distinguishes vital motion, which is unthinking reflexive motion, from voluntary motion as follows:

Voluntary motion; as to *go*, to *speak*, to *move* any of our limbes, in such a manner as is first fancied in our minds. . . . And because *going, speaking*, and the like Voluntary motions, depend alwayes upon a precedent thought of *whither, which way*, and *what*; it is evident, that the Imagination is the first internall beginning of all Voluntary Motion. (L 1.6/118)

In other words, what distinguishes mere behavior from action is that the action is behavior caused by internal mental processing. Consequently, Hobbes cannot identify human thinking with the manipulation of external symbols (e.g., when we speak to communicate with others or make marks to aid our own memory) (Kneale and Kneale 1962: 312). The manipulation of external symbols is intentional behavior (DC 1.2.4), and so what distinguishes intentional manipulation of symbols from mere movements of the body is that in the intentional case the bodily motion is an effect of internal mental representations.[6]

The quoted passages from *De Corpore* and *Leviathan* clearly show that Hobbes believed that some mental operations are indeed computations. However, we must be careful about how much we can legitimately infer from these passages. In these passages Hobbes is only maintaining that human *reasoning* is computation, and this does not

---

calculation are numerals and other symbols used in the calculation. The indirect objects of the calculation are the numbers and functions that are represented by the symbols used in the calculation.

6. See Dascal (1987: 32–6) on the secondary role public symbols seem to play in Hobbes's theory of thinking. Pécharman (1992) also arrives at the conclusion that Hobbes believes that reasoning is not just a sequence of names but consists of internal mental states.

show that all human thinking is computation unless Hobbes also identifies thinking and reasoning. So we need to take a closer look at the
relation between thinking and reasoning for Hobbes. It turns out that
for Hobbes, reasoning is a species of thinking, namely, rule-governed,
purposeful, and voluntary mental activity.

This really should not be surprising, because Hobbes's discussion
of reason as computation is his contribution to the 17th-century discussion of the proper method for discovering new knowledge. He is
laying out "the shortest way of finding out effects by their known
causes, or of causes by their known effects" (DC 1.6.1). Ratiocination
or computation is a method, that is, a procedure or art whose application leads to new knowledge, and philosophy is knowledge acquired
with this method. Knowledge that is not acquired by computation but
that is "given us immediately by nature," as in the case with sense
experience, is not philosophy (DC 1.1.3). Hobbes, as Leibniz well
understood, was making a contribution to the art of discovery and
demonstration by tying it to the combinatorial arts, whose roots lie in
the 13th-century combinatorial figures of Ramón Llull.

The attempt to mechanize reasoning and logical derivation can be
traced to Llull's *Ars demonstrativa* (1283), where he describes several
combinatorial devices to aid reasoning. One model consists of a list
of sixteen basic predicates arranged in a circle. Lines connect each
predicate with all the others in order to indicate that they all can be
combined with each other (Llull 1985: 320). Another model is a
figure that

is composed of six revolving circles along with a wheel situated in the middle.
. . . It is made up of circles, each inside the other, like weights inserted one
in another, with a pin in the middle, which keeps the circles in place. (Llull
1985: 333–4)

The central wheel contains five triangles for the relations, and the
concentric circles are marked off with letters for the sixteen basic
properties and some of the combinations of those properties. By
moving the revolving circles, different combinations of the basic
elements are generated mechanically.

A problem with this mechanical model is that the basic predicates
are combined without a set of rules or operations that determine
the combinations. Hobbes's contribution was to substitute simple
mechanical association with a finite set of operations that determine

each step. Each step of reasoning ultimately had to be one of two operations, addition or subtraction. This is what Leibniz found noteworthy in Hobbes, and what Leibniz develops in *De Arte Combinatoria* (1666), where he suggests that we assign numerical values to all the simple concepts, and compound and decompose concepts using addition and subtraction (GP IV: 64–75).[7]

Reasoning and Thinking in *Leviathan*

Nevertheless, for Hobbes not all thinking is computation. To see this, let us first look at the *Leviathan*, where Hobbes gives a taxonomy of thinking from which it is clear that he is committed to the view that only reasoning is computation, not thinking in general.

According to Hobbes, thinking is *"Mentall Discourse,"*[8] namely, a "TRAYNE of Thoughts" or a "succession of one Thought to another" (L 1.3/94).[9] He distinguishes between two kinds of trains of thoughts: mental discourse that is *"unguided, without design*, and inconstant" and mental discourse that is *"regulated* by some desire, and design" (L 1.3/95). Unguided thoughts are a stream of consciousness "in which . . . the thoughts are said to wander, and seem impertinent to one another."[10] Our unregulated mental meandering is constrained only by past associations in experience. In regulated mental discourse, the sequence of thoughts is generated not only by past associations, but also by a "Passionate Thought" of an object of desire (ibid.).

A passionate thought can determine two kinds of trains of thoughts. (1) A train can be guided by a passion or desire, together with past associations which will bring to mind a chain of means to

---

7. Also see Pombo (1987: 89–90).
8. In *Elements of Law* Hobbes preferred "DISCURSION" because "discourse is commonly taken for the coherence and consequence of words" (EL 1.4.1).
9. In *De Corpore*, Hobbes uses "phantasm" to cover all thoughts. A phantasm belongs to sense as long as the object is present producing it, and it belongs to imagination when it is weakened by the absence of the object (DC 4.25.7). There is a noticeable shift in terminology from *The Elements of Law* to *De Corpore*. In *The Elements of Law*, Hobbes clearly limits phantasms to the imagination (EL 1.3.5). Hobbes's usage of "phantasm" in the *Leviathan* seems to waffle between the usages in the *Elements of Law* and *De Corpore*. I follow Hobbes's usage of "phantasm" in *De Corpore*.
10. See Hobbes's vivid example in *The Elements of Law*: "the mind runneth" from St. Andrew to St. Peter, a stone, a foundation, a church, people, a tumult (EL 1.4.2).

satisfying this desire that terminates in a thought of something one can do that will be a means to satisfying the ruling desire (ibid.); (2) a train can also be regulated by the search for "all the possible effects" of some event or action (L 1.3/96). This search is also guided by passion, namely, curiosity or prudence, that is, a desire for the pleasure of the mind that comes with the "foresight of the End, or Consequences of things" (L 1.6/122).

Both of these types of regulated trains of thoughts are, in and of themselves, not cases of reasoning.[11] They become reasoning when they are improved by an acquired and artificial method, namely, reason (L 1.8/138). Reason is acquired through "study and industry" and it depends on the "invention of words, and speech" (L 1.3/98–9). Reason is "consequent to the use of Speech" (L 4.46/683), and so children who are not yet speaking "are not endued with Reason at all" (L 1.5/116). We reason when we regulate our search for causes and effects with an acquired method, embodied in a system of sensible symbols, that guides us from one specific thought to the next (L 1.5/31).[12] The result of such a methodical search for causes and effects is science or natural philosophy (L 1.5/115 and 4.46/683).

In *Leviathan*, then, reasoning is a species of regulated thinking, namely, thinking regulated by the use of public language. The centrality of language to reasoning is expressed in Hobbes's explicit definition of "reason":

Out of all which we may define . . . what that is, which is meant by this word *Reason*, when wee reckon it amongst the Faculties of mind. For REASON, in this sense, is nothing but *Reckoning* (that is, Adding and Subtracting) of the Consequences of generall names agreed upon, for the *marking* and *signifying* of our thoughts. (L 1.5/111)

Unfortunately, he also seems to deny that reasoning is limited to words. In *De Corpore* he writes that we can compute "in our silent thoughts, without the use of words" (DC 1.1.3) and in *Leviathan* he writes that to reason, "*if* it be done by Words, is conceiving of the consequence of names" (my emphasis), leaving open the possibility that there are other objects of computation (L 1.5/110–11). Hobbes

---

11. For example, Hobbes writes that "prudence . . . is not attained by Reasoning" (L 4.46/682).

12. The method includes "the making of syllogisms," which in *The Elements of Law* is identified with reasoning (EL 1.5.11).

in fact goes on to list other objects of computation: numbers, lines, figures, degrees of force and power, contracts, laws, and facts. Logicians teach how to compute the "Consequences of words," while Arithmeticians, Geometricians, and Lawyers are concerned with computing over the other objects.

The fact that Hobbes appears contradictory on the role of language in reasoning does not affect the conclusion that in the *Leviathan* Hobbes distinguishes thinking and reasoning. Even reasoning without words requires a method, and hence is, for Hobbes, not the only kind of thinking. Consider Hobbes's example in the *Leviathan* of reasoning without words, namely, a speechless geometrician who has "set before his eyes a triangle, and by it two right angles" (L 1.4/103).[13] Hobbes writes that without the use of words "he may *by meditation compare and find*, that the three angles of that triangle, are equall to those two right angles that stand by it" (my emphasis). The speechless geometrician's thoughts must be guided by more than his desire to compare the angles. The sequence of thoughts leading to the discovery of the identity will need to be guided by a method for calculating the identity. So this will be a case of thinking that is regulated by desire and method, and for Hobbes not all regulated thinking needs a method.

Incidentally, the silent geometrician will need words if he wants to generalize his result to other triangles. Without words, he would have to calculate anew every time he encounters a triangle that the sum of its three angles are equal to the sum of two right angles. With words, however, the geometrician "will boldly conclude Universally, that such equality of angles is in all triangles whatsoever" (L 1.4/104).

This suggests a way of resolving the apparent inconsistency about language and reasoning in the *Leviathan*. Hobbes allows for reasoning without words, but only words or other sensible marks allow us to refer to "divers particular things" (L 1.4/103). Without the use of words we can reason only about particular things and particular causes (L 1.5/112). Hobbes's nominalism precludes there being any real universals, kinds, or properties we can use to refer to several distinct individuals. Consequently, words or some other sensible symbols are needed for science because science is concerned with general-

---

13. See Tom Sorell's discussion of this example and the problem of common names in Sorrell (1986: 40–41).

izations about causal relations (L 1.5/115).[14] The fact that reasoning about general kinds and causal relations requires words suggested to Hobbes a stipulative definition for the word "reason." Although reason, as a matter of fact (that is, "*Reason what it is*"), does not require words,

> we may define . . . what . . . is . . . meant by this word *Reason*, when wee reckon it amongst the Faculties of the mind (to be) *Reckoning* . . . of the Consequences of generall names agreed upon, for the *marking* and *signifying* of our thoughts. (L 1.5/111)

Scientific reasoning begins with the defining of words (L 1.5/115), and Hobbes is stipulating that the meaning of the word "reason" in our scientific reckoning about the faculties of the human mind be limited to reasoning with general terms. After all, that is the sort of reasoning necessary for science itself.

Reasoning and Thinking in *De Corpore*

The apparent inconsistency of Hobbes's story about reasoning and language in the *Leviathan* is absent from *De Corpore*. Here Hobbes writes clearly: "philosophy, that is *natural reason*, is innate in every human being; for each and everyone reasons continuously" (DC 1.1.1). Human beings can reason without words and other sensible devices, and thus in *De Corpore*, the discussion of words comes *after* he has defined reason in terms of computation.

Although words are not constitutive of reasoning, they do improve it. Without words or some other sensible marks for our thoughts, "whatsoever a man has put together in his mind by ratiocination without such helps, will presently slip away from him, and not be revocable but by beginning his ratiocination anew" (DC 1.2.1). It follows that any reasoning about general causal relationships (that is, the sort of reasoning that is required by science and that goes beyond immediate and singular causes and effects) will require some sensible marks.

Nevertheless, Hobbes describes in some detail "reasoning in silent thought without words" (DC 1.1.3). For example, when observing a

---

14. "It is the duty of philosophy to establish universal principles [*regulas*] about the properties of things" (DC 1.4.7).

human being from a great distance, we might only have the phantasm of a body. As we get closer, we might get the phantasm of something animate, and if we get still closer, we might also get the phantasm of something rational (e.g., something speaking and exhibiting "other things which are signs of a rational mind"). We can then add these ideas together into a single new idea of a "*rational animate body* or *man*" (DC 1.1.3). By the same token, we can take a complex idea and subtract its parts to get new ideas.

In the chapter titled "Of Method," Hobbes labels the operations of addition and subtraction "composition" and "division or resolution" (DC 1.6.1).[15] Composition (i.e., synthesis) and resolution (i.e., analysis) of phantasms are the only methods available for coming to know causes and effects, and applying these methods is the job of reason. Hobbes writes that "the work of ratiocination . . . consists" in the composition and division of phantasms, and there is no other method available to us for discovering the causes and effects of things (DC 1.6.1).

So, in *De Corpore* (where thinking is, as in *Leviathan*, mental discourse or "the perpetual arising of phantasms" (DC 4.25.8)) reason is also thinking that is regulated by a method, and Hobbes leaves plenty of room for thinking that is not guided by method. He maintains that the sensations and memories that are "given to us immediately," as well as our immediate expectations of future events, are not gotten by ratiocination (DC 1.1.2). Mental discourse that is generated by sense, memory, or expectation without the aid of method will not be a reasoned mental discourse.

This conclusion is corroborated by Hobbes's discussion of "discourse of the mind" in the fourth part of *De Corpore* (called "PHYSICS, or the *Phenomena of Nature*"). Although by not explicitly discussing reasoning in this part of *De Corpore* Hobbes misses an important opportunity to classify reason as a phenomenon of nature, he discusses cases of thinking that clearly are not cases of reasoning.

In dreams, our phantasms succeed each other without order or coherence, and the explanation for this is that "in sleep we lose all thought of the end," and so "our phantasms succeed one another, not in that order which tends to any end" (DC 4.25.9). Dreams in *De*

---

15. This discussion in Hobbes is often linked to Galileo and the School of Padua (Watkins 1965: 28–54). For a dissenting view, see Gilbert (1963).

Corpore, then, are very much like unregulated thoughts in *Leviathan*. He also distinguishes the succession of phantasms generated simply by past associations from the succession of phantasms generated by "the thought or phantasm of the desired end" (DC 4.25.8). The latter train of thoughts is regulated by a desire in that it causes thoughts of the means to satisfying the desire, but it need not be ordered by a method. The desire itself is sufficient to generate the train of thoughts.

Moreover, thinking requires that we are in a position to compare phantasms with respect to their similarity and differences: "For he that thinketh, compareth the phantasms that pass, that is, taketh notice of their likeness or unlikeness to one another" (DC 4.25.8), and the result of this comparison is a judgment (DC 4.25.5). Such a judgment involves a sequence of phantasms, namely, the two being compared, but it cannot always be a case of reasoning. Reasoning involves adding thoughts to each other to make new thoughts or subtracting thoughts from a complex thought, but this presupposes some judgments about the likeness of the thoughts (just as one cannot perform arithmetic operations without being able to distinguish numerals).

Finally, there are the series of thoughts Hobbes calls "deliberation" (DC 4.25.13; EW I: 408–9). This is a sequence of thoughts that can be generated by the "vicissitude of appetites and aversions" with respect to some object. I see an apple, and it stimulates memories of past apples and simple pleasures, which generates a desire for the apple. But this is an apple on a tree in a new place, and new places remind me of dangers, and so now I have an aversion to it. But I see no other apple trees, and I am getting increasingly hungry and thirsty, so my aversion yields to appetite. Such a sequence of thoughts is driven only by sense, memory, association, and passion, but not by method.

However, deliberation can become a case of reasoning when the desire for a better life drives us to more reliable deliberation. We seek generalizations about causes to improve our lives, expand our power, and, most important, avoid the calamities and the causes of calamities that can be avoided by human industry: "war,... slaughter, loneliness, and want of all things" (DC 1.1.7; EW I: 8). Reasoned deliberation is what allows us to avoid calamities such as civil war because "the cause ... of civil war is, that men know not the causes neither of war nor peace" (DC 1.1.7; EW I: 8) and knowledge of causes and effects requires reason.

Hobbes's Objects of Computation

Hobbes, then, does not hold that all thinking is computation, and this is sufficient to show that Hobbes does not offer us a computational approach to human thinking. But perhaps he gives us a computational account of reasoning, and this might be sufficient to vindicate a computational reading of Hobbes.[16] To evaluate this claim we have to turn to the objects of reason's computations and examine if they are language-like symbols. A computational reading of Hobbes's theory of reasoning must not only show that reason is computation, but also must show that it is computation over language-like symbols.

Language-like symbols have three properties. In addition to having semantic properties and nonsemantic properties, language-like symbols are arbitrary "in the sense that there is no intrinsic reason for them to be one way rather than another: our word 'squid' could just as well have meant what 'squalid' does, and so on" (Haugeland 1985: 91).[17] The nonsemantic properties of an arbitrary symbol are not natural causal effects of the symbol's semantic properties or the properties of what the symbol represents. The properties of squids do not causally determine the nonsemantic properties of tokens of the English word "squid." The uninterpreted input and output states of a calculator are also arbitrary in this sense. There is no intrinsic reason why the plus function should be represented by one sequence of button-pushings rather than another, or why the displayed numeral "10" represents the number 10 rather than the number 2.

In Hobbes's discussion of thinking, there are only two objects of computation available to reasoning: names and phantasms. When reasoning computes over words, it obviously computes over language-like symbols. Hobbes, however, allows for reasoning without words, namely, with phantasms. Are phantasms language-like symbols?

16. For example, one might argue that what Hobbes meant by "reasoning" is what we today mean by "thinking." I owe this point to Rob Cummins.
17. Haugeland (1985: 27) maintains that for Hobbes thoughts "were composed of distinct, arbitrary symbols."

Hobbes's phantasms have semantic properties. They are representations of things. In the *Leviathan*, Hobbes writes that every sense or phantasm is "a *Representation* or *Apparence*, of some quality, or other accident of a body without us" (L 1.1/85; L 4.45/669). In *The Elements of Law* he writes that "an obscure conception is that which representeth the whole object together, but none of the smaller parts" (EL 1.3.7). In *De Corpore* "apparitions" are "patterns . . . of things" by means of which "we know all other things" (DC 4.25.1). In other words, phantasms must have enough semantic content to allow us to make judgments about objects (DC 4.25.5).

Hobbes does not explicitly dwell on the nature of the relationship of representation, and instead he dwells on the causes of sensation (Peters 1956: 109), but the reason for this is that for Hobbes representation in the case of phantasms is a species of causality. In his discussion he quickly identifies a crucial semantic fact about sensation, namely, what it is to be an *object of sense*, with a causal fact. He writes: "bodies . . . are the efficient causes or objects of sense" (DC 4.26.1). Earlier he wrote that the object of sense "is the thing received," namely, the thing whose motion by "perpetual propagation" causes the internal reaction of our senses (DC 4.25.3). Thus it is not true that Hobbes had nothing to say about "original meaning" (Haugeland 1985: 27–8). The meaning of public symbols, such as found in discourse and books, rests on thoughts, but the content of thoughts rests on natural causes.

Hobbes, by the way, is very clear about what the objects of our experiences and judgments are (Barnouw 1980: 123). Except in the case of memory (DC 4.25.1), phantasms are not the objects of perception. Phantasms are states of the sense organs, but the objects of sensing are the objects that cause the phantasms:

> The object is the thing received; and it is more accurately said, that we see the sun, than that we see the light. For light and colour, and heat and sound, and other qualities which are commonly called sensible, are not objects, but phantasms in the sentients. (DC 4.25.3; also see 4.25.10)

We make judgments about objects by means of "their phantasms," but our judgment is not about the phantasms (DC 4.25.5). The fact that we make judgments about objects by means of phantasms is also further evidence that for Hobbes phantasms have semantic properties.

In addition to semantic properties, phantasms have nonsemantic properties. They are "divers motions" in us (L 1.1/86). A phantasm is "some internal motion in the sentient" (DC 4.25.2; EW I: 391) and it is "determined, and made to be of such quality and quantity by compounded motions" (DC 1.6.6; EW I: 73).[18] The compounded motions include "*the reaction and endeavour outwards in the organ of sense, caused by an endeavour inwards from the object, remaining for some time more or less*" (DC 4.25.2; EW I: 391). This motion appears in a certain way, such as light, color, heat, sound, and other sensible qualities (DC 4.25.3; EW I: 391–2; L 1.1/86). Seeing light is a motion within us, but we experience this motion as a luminous sensation. A phantasm appears to be external to us "by reason of the endeavour outwards" in response to the incoming motion from the perceived object (DC 4.25; EW I: 406); the endeavor "*Outward*, seemeth" to us in a certain way, namely, as "some matter without" (L 1.1/85–6). However, these seemings or fancies do not constitute the semantic content of the phantasm. For example, when I perceive the sun, I have a phantasm with the sensible qualities of light, color, and heat, but my perception is not of these sensible qualities. As we just saw, for Hobbes, "the object is the thing received; and it is more accurately said, that we see the sun, than that we see the light" (DC 4.25.3). The phantasm is light and warm, but it is about the sun, not its own light and warmth.

So phantasms have semantic and nonsemantic properties. What remains to be seen, however, is whether phantasms are arbitrary in the sense characterized above. They are not arbitrary in Hobbes's sense of "arbitrary [*arbitraria*]" because the relation between a phantasm and its object is not a product of a voluntary decision or convention (DC 1.2.2). In this respect, phantasms are different from public language symbols because the names in a public language are the products of human decisions. However, this does not preclude that they are arbitrary in the sense that there is no intrinsic connection between the nonsemantic properties of phantasms and the properties of what they represent. It is this sort of arbitrariness that is required if Hobbes is an ur-computationalist.

Unfortunately, Hobbes did not explicitly discuss this sense of "arbitrary" and nothing Hobbes writes suggests he had some considered

---

18. Hobbes distinguishes simple and compound motions at DC 3.15.4/EW I:216.

views about it.[19] Consequently, the claim that Hobbes believed that thoughts as the objects of reasoning are arbitrary language-like symbols is, strictly speaking, unwarranted. Moreover, there are good reasons for thinking that, for Hobbes, thoughts cannot be arbitrary.

This is already suggested by the fact that Hobbes appears to believe that representation in the case of phantasm is a species of causality. This seems to make phantasms into natural signs, which are defined in terms of causal relations (EL 1.4.9; L 1.3/98; DC 1.2.2; EW I: 14). However, a causal account of representation is not sufficient to make representations into natural, nonarbitrary signs. We need to distinguish two ways in which a representation can be causally related to what it represents.

Case (1): x represents y, x is a regular and causal effect of y, but the nonsemantic properties of x are not causally dependent on the properties of y. In other words, although occurrences or tokenings of x causally depend on occurrences or tokenings of y, the characteristics x has are not determined by the characteristics of y.[20] For example, suppose that in some system tokens of the letter "o" nomically covary with the presence of oranges. It is a law in situ that whenever an orange is present, that system exhibits a token of o.[21] Although these two entities causally covary, the intrinsic properties of o are independent of the intrinsic properties of oranges. Only the occurrences or tokenings of o are causally determined by the presence of oranges.

Case (2): x represents y, x is a regular and natural effect of y, and the nonsemantic properties of x *are* causally dependent on the properties of y. In other words, not only do occurrences of x covary with occurrences of y, but the intrinsic properties of x are themselves determined by the causal powers of y. Here is an example of case (2).

---

19. Hobbes appears to be running at least two notions of "arbitrary," namely, the sense specified here according to which names are arbitrary if there is no intrinsic connection between word and referent, and the sense in which the combination of concepts that defines a word is arbitrary (Dascal 1987: 61–2).

20. This is the view defended by contemporary covariance theories of content. For a critical overview of covariance theories, see Cummins (1989: 35–75). On another fault of covariance theories, see Losonsky (1993a).

21. This is a law that does not hold universally, but holds for particular organisms or systems. The notion of a law "in situ" is due to Millikan (1984: 20).

Fire and smoke covary, but the intrinsic properties of smoke are causally dependent on the properties of fire. Not only is the occurrence of smoke causally dependent on fire, but the very properties of smoke are causal effects of the properties of fire for which smoke is a natural sign.

Case (1), but not case (2), is a case of an arbitrary symbol that is nevertheless causally connected to what it represents.[22] For Hobbes, phantasms belong to the second case. The properties of the phantasm depend on the properties of the object. For Hobbes, the object's "diversity of working" is responsible for the "diversity of Apparences" (L 1.1/85). The motion of the external object is not just the occasion for the occurrence of a phantasm, but it determines the properties the phantasm has. The phantasm that is made by seeing the sun is light, which is a product of the motions of a lucid body together with our reaction to it. The motions of a lucid body are responsible not just for the tokening of a phantasm, but for the sensible properties of the phantasm, namely, that it is experienced as light.

So for Hobbes there is a natural reason why light represents a lucid object. Any other phantasm could not do just as well because its properties could not be the effects of the motions appropriate to a lucid body (EL 1.2.7–8). It is the nonarbitrary nature of phantasms and conceptions that leads Hobbes to refer to them loosely as images, even though he is aware of the fact that they need not resemble their objects (L 1.1/86; L 4.45/668). They are like images in that their semantic properties are products of the properties of the objects they represent. Hobbes's phantasms, then, are not arbitrary, language-like symbols.

A consequence of this is that for Hobbes thinking is not medium-independent. Not any medium that preserves the same functional relations would constitute a mind for Hobbes. The physical properties of mental states, and not just their occurrences, will depend on the properties of the objects in the environment they represent. For Hobbes this meant that a mind had to have sensations, such as the luminescence brought about by the perception of light. Everything in the mind is "totally, or by parts . . . begotten upon the organs of

---

22. Language of nature doctrines are committed to the view that linguistic signs are not arbitrary in that the symbols of the language of nature would fall under case 2. On language of nature doctrines, see Coudert (1978) and Losonsky (1992).

the senses," and sensations, seemings, fancies, or phantasms belong to these organs (L 1.1/85–6). For Hobbes, a sensation "consisteth, as to the Eye, in a *Light*, or *Colour figured*; To the Eare, in a *Sound*; To the Nostrill, in an *Odour*; To the Tongue and Palat, in a *Savour*; And to the rest of the body, in *Heat, Cold, Hardnesse, Softnesse*, and such other qualities, as we discern by *Feeling*" (L 1.1/86). The other faculties of minds, such as imagination, memory, understanding, and reason, all depend on these medium-dependent sensations.

Passionate Thought

The final piece of evidence for Hobbes's alleged computationalism is that he seems to explain all human action in terms of internal mental representations. As we saw earlier, Hobbes writes that actions such as "*going, speaking* and the like Voluntary motions depend alwayes upon a precedent thought of *whither, which way*, and *what*," and thus "the Imagination is the first internall beginning of all Voluntary Motion" (L 1.6/118). Thus for Hobbes a voluntary action is not simply the product of the last appetite in deliberation – it must be an appetite in a deliberative series that proceeds from imagination (Pécharman 1990). Nevertheless, Hobbes's explanation of voluntary action appeals not just to the representations of imagination, but also its endeavors: "These small beginnings of Motion, within the body of Man, before they appear in walking, speaking, striking, and other visible actions, are commonly called ENDEAVOUR" (L 1.6/119). Endeavors play a key role in Hobbes's theory of mind and action (Barnouw 1980, 1989; Rudolph 1989).

Endeavors are not just the causes of visible voluntary motions that involve the motion of "any of our limbs," but are the causes of all voluntary acts, including invisible acts such as reasoning. For Hobbes, "a *Voluntary Act* is that, which proceedeth from the *will*, and no other," and the will is simply "the last Appetite, or Aversion in Deliberating" (L 1.6/128). For Hobbes, there is no special faculty of will distinct from appetite or aversion (EW 5: 82–91). However, acting on an appetite is not sufficient to make the action voluntary. What is required is that the effective appetite be part of deliberation or a "vicissitude of appetites and aversions" (DC 4.25.13; EW I: 408–9). Only in the context of deliberation will an appetite be a will and the ensuing action a voluntary action.

Appetites and aversions are endeavors, and as such they are motions. It has been argued that this is not to be understood literally (Barnouw 1980), but in the *Leviathan* Hobbes explicitly denies this. He writes that an endeavor is not a "Metaphoricall Motion" of "the Schooles" but an "actuall Motion" toward a body or withdrawing from it (L 1.6/119; also see DC 4.25.12; EW I: 407).[23]

The notion of an endeavor (*conatus*) is first introduced by Hobbes in terms of psychological appetites (EW 4: 31), but endeavors come to play a central role in his physical as well as psychological explanations (Brandt 1928: 300). Hobbes believes that endeavors are essential to all motion and that an endeavor is to motion what a point is to a line: it is the "*motion made in less space and time than can be given; ... that is, motion made through the length of a point, and in an instant or point of time*" (DC 3.15.2; EW I: 206). However, this characterization is incomplete. For Hobbes, an endeavor is not just instantaneous motion or speed, but it is a vector quantity and a motive force (Brandt 1928: 299–300; Watkins 1965: 124). An endeavor has a velocity (DC 3.15.2; EW I: 207), which is a "*power by which a body moved may in a certain time transmit a certain length*" (DC 3.15.1; EW I: 204–5). "For simply to endeavour is to go," Hobbes writes, and when resistance is met, the endeavor "is that which we call pressure" (DC 3.22.1; EW I: 333). Already in the *Elements of Law* Hobbes writes that an aggregate of endeavors "presses" and "tend" in a certain direction (EW 4: 351).

Hobbes has been criticized for using endeavors in both his physical and psychological explanations (Brandt 1928: 355; Peters 1956: 99–100). Since endeavors are both powers in inanimate objects and psychological powers, Hobbes needs to find a way to distinguish the mental from the nonmental endeavors. He needs to do this even if we grant him his materialist metaphysics and recognize that Hobbes's endeavors allow him to overcome Cartesian dualism (Watkins 1965: 123; Lott 1982). After all, there is a difference between the weight of a beam and an animal's search for food, and if Hobbes cannot make this difference, he is open to the objection that his universe is haunted with psychic endeavors (Watkins 1965: 124 and 127–8) or

---

23. Compare Leibniz (GP IV: 468–70), who also rejects the Scholastic notion of a bare power or logical disposition. However, for Leibniz thought is not motion (A VI.3: 586).

that his minds really are just thoughtless mechanisms (Peters and Tajfel 1957).

This issue is not explicitly treated by Hobbes, but perhaps this is because the answer was obvious to him. The "very first endeavors of animal motion" (as opposed to inanimate motion) are appetite and aversion (DC 4.25.12), and although these belong to the same genus as the endeavors of inanimate objects, they comprise a distinct class or species because they together with other motions are constitutive of mental representations. The "small beginnings of Motion, within the body of Man" that "are commonly called ENDEAVOUR" are also the "precedent thought[s] of *whither, which way,* and *what*" that Hobbes identifies as the "first internall beginning of all Voluntary Motion" (L 1.6/118). Hobbes goes on to attribute semantic properties to human endeavors: desires "signifie that Absence of the Object" toward which it endeavors, while "by Aversion, we signifie the Absence; and by Hate, the Presence of the Object" from which it endeavors to withdraw (L 1.6/119).

Psychological endeavors, then, are endeavors or motive forces of motions that are constitutive of the motion of phantasms. As we have seen, phantasms or sensations are compound motions that consist of the motion caused by the object and the reactions of the subject. One such reaction is the endeavor outward that causes the appearance of something external to us. The resistance that explains the external appearance is an outward "endeavour of the heart, to deliver it self" (L 1.1/85). But "the motions of the heart are appetites and aversions" (DC 4.259; EW I: 401). In *Leviathan* Hobbes writes:

When the action of the same object is continued from the Eyes, Eares, and other organs to the Heart; the reall effect there is nothing but Motion, or Endeavour; which consisteth in Appetite, or Aversion, to, or from the object moving. (L 1.6/121)

The resistance of the heart to deliver itself of the incoming motion is an aversion, and so the experience of externality is due to our aversion to intrusive motion and to "shun what is troublesome" (DC 4.25.12; EW I: 407).

Thus, as Hobbes remarks in *De Corpore*, the "heart . . . is the fountain of all sense" (DC 4.25.4; EW I: 392). If the motion from the object is "intercepted between the brain and the heart . . . there will be no perception of the object" (DC 4.25.4; EW I: 393). The reaction of the sentient is not subsequent to the phantasm but happens in the same instant as the phantasm (DC 4.25.3; EW I: 392) and the phantasm is partly "made by reaction" (DC 4.25.4; EW I: 393). "So reciprocal," Hobbes writes, "are the motions of the heart and brain" (DC 4.25.9; EW I: 401). In *De Homine* Hobbes writes that "all sense is conjoined [*conjuncta*] with some appetite or aversion" (DH 2.11.15; LW 2: 103). The constitutive role of endeavors is already suggested in *The Elements of Law* (EW 4: 32), but the role of conation in cognition is developed only in the later work (Rudolph 1989). So phantasms, the basic elements of all thinking, are the products of interaction between external forces and human passion. In this sense, human beings are sentient creatures that are "Makers of Images" (Sacksteder 1982: 88) and more: they are passionate makers of their thoughts.

Appetite and aversion are the fundamental human passions, and Hobbes believes that all other passions are varieties of these first endeavors.[24] For example, hope is an "*Appetite* with an opinion of attaining" while "the same, without such opinion" is despair (L 1.6/123). Confidence in ourselves is constant hope, while constant despair is diffidence. Pusillanimity is also a fear, and it causes irresolution because the "weighing of trifles" prevents one from choosing between what seem to be equally good alternatives (L 1.11/164; cf. EW 4: 52). Curiosity is an appetite or "Lust of the mind," and the expectation that this curiosity will be satisfied is a kind of joy, namely, admiration.[25] It is noteworthy that for Hobbes the passion of curiosity is strong enough to compete with other passions: the "delight in the continuall and indefatigable generation of Knowledge, exceedeth the short vehemence of any carnall pleasure" (L 1.6, 26).

But the passion of curiosity also has a darker side (James 1997: 210–15). Curiosity seeks causes, and in this search we realize that

---

24. Gert (1989: 88–9) argues that Hobbes distinguishes desire and passion. Gert's primary concern is to distinguish rational from emotional desires, and he identifies passions with emotions. It is true that for Hobbes an aversion to death and desires for "commodious living" are rational, but for Hobbes these are "Passions that encline men to Peace" (L 1.13/188).

25. In *Elements of Law* Hobbes describes admiration as an "expectation of future knowledge from anything that happeneth new and strange" (EW IV: 50), and so Descartes's fundamental passion of wonder is a derived passion in Hobbes.

there are causes that escape our inquiry (L 1.11 and 12/51–2). Consequently, we realize that we are not able to ensure that we will escape evil in the future and ensure only good results for us. Thus overly prudent people will become anxious, and in them the pursuit of knowledge will create a fear that actually stifles the pursuit of knowledge (L 1.12/52). It is also the seed of religion and the postulation of invisible agents and spirits that play a role in human superstitions. Although religion will never be "abolished out of human nature" because the search for causes will always end with the need for deities and invisible powers, religions are determined to change and replace each other (L 1.12, 58). One reason for this is that there will always be "men of judgment" who will desire evidence, and this inevitably will weaken the faith in any particular religion (L 1.12, 59). This desire for evidence is just the passion of curiosity at work, and thus more curiosity is the cure for the anxiety caused by our pursuit of knowledge.

Curiosity and admiration are significant because when we are motivated by the appetite for knowledge, we are acting voluntarily, but in this case the voluntary animal motion is not a movement of the limbs, but a movement of the mind. Curiosity can motivate a "chain of Discourse" that is "meerly Mentall" (L 1.7/130). This mental discourse consists of a sequence of thoughts about the consequences of alternative possibilities: "if This be, That is; if This has been, That has been; if This shall be, That shall be" (L 1.7/131). The last thought in this chain is judgment. When this chain of discourse relies on language and method, the final thought is a conclusion, and science consists of conclusions of this sort.

The first thought in such a chain, however, will be a passionate thought. The motion that constitutes a chain of thoughts needs an endeavor to generate the progression of thoughts. Without a passionate thought, thinking cannot be regulated:

This Trayne of Thoughts, or Mentall Discourse, is of two sorts. The first is *Unguided, without Designe,* and inconstant; Wherein there is no Passionate Thought, to govern and direct those that follow, to itself, as the end and scope of some desire, or other passion: In which case the thoughts are said to wander, and seem impertinent one to another, as in a Dream. Such are Commonly the thoughts of men, that are not onely without company, but also without care for anything. (L 1.3/95)

Unregulated thoughts are "one kind of Madnesse" that those with the virtue of discretion keep to themselves (L 1.8, 139, and 142).[26] Moreover, those without great passions "cannot possibly have either great Fancy, or much Judgment" because thoughts are the "Scouts and Spies" for our desires (L 1.8/139).

Guided thoughts are *"regulated* by some desire" from which "ariseth the Thought of some means we have to produce the like of that which we ayme at" and so on until we think of some means of getting what we want that is within our power (L 1.3/95–6). The same holds for fears because they can also guide our thoughts. A passionate thought, then, is a desire or fear that regulates thinking, that is, it is an endeavor. But it is also an "impression made by such things wee desire, or fear" that "is strong, and permanent, or . . . of quick return" (L 1.3/95). Here it seems that for Hobbes the endeavor is not just a constituent motion of a thought, but is itself also a representation of the desired end.

Since regulated thoughts are motivated by appetites and aversions, they can also be voluntary actions insofar as the motivating appetite or aversion is the last one in a chain of deliberation. It seems that Hobbes is committed to the view that regulated thinking can itself be a product of deliberation and hence voluntary. Our very constitution, as Hobbes understood it, ensures that as a matter of fact regulated thinking will usually be voluntary activity. Our appetites and aversions are not constant; our passions are a source of "immediate quandary" (Spragens 1973: 164). "The constitution of a mans Body," Hobbes writes in *Leviathan*, "is in continuall mutation" and so "it is impossible that all the same things should always cause in him the same Appetites, and Aversions" (L 1.6/120; also see L 1.15/216). Usually we are not simply driven by a single particular desire, but we have conflicting desires that drive us to deliberation. We always desire power, but there are different kinds of powers and different means for acquiring power (L 1.8/139 and L 1.10/150). These will come into conflict, and, to make matters worse, our desire for power comes into conflict with our desire to avoid death. So when we finally do have an effective desire, it will be the product of deliberation.

26. However, having strong passions that are not shared by others is also a kind of madness (L 1.8/139).

This is certainly true of knowledge and reasoning. We need to be convinced that regulating our thoughts with a method is a good thing, and Hobbes argues for this on many occasions, but most eloquently in the discussion of the "*utility* of philosophy" in the first book of *De Corpore*. This is where Hobbes writes that philosophy (which for Hobbes includes all methodical knowledge, including the natural sciences) is the cause of many benefits and the lack of philosophy is the cause of calamities such as war, massacres, and hunger (DC 1.1.7; EW I: 8).

Nevertheless, in the third part of the *Leviathan*, devoted to the "Christian Commonwealth," Hobbes writes:

For Sense, Memory, Understanding, Reason and Opinion are not in our power to change; but alwaies, and necessarily such, as the things we see, hear, and consider suggest unto us; and therefore are not effects of our Will, but our Will of them. (L 3.32, 410)

The context of this passage is a discussion of the "Captivity of Our Understanding" wherein our speech conforms to the commands of authority even "though the mind be incapable of any Notion at all from the words spoken" (L 3.32, 410). We cannot make ourselves believe something at will in response to the commands of authority, but we can make our visible actions (including our speech) conform to the requirements of authority.

The context of this passage suggests that the issue here is not volition, but liberty. Our reasoning is not free in the sense of being independent of external determination: the motions of external objects force themselves on our senses and we cannot simply make ourselves see or hear what is not there. For Hobbes, our memories "frame and make us to the election of whatever it be that we elect," but memory is determined by the senses, which in turn are determined by "agents . . . externall to us." Consequently, Hobbes adds, "all actions, even of free and voluntary agents, are necessary" (EW 5: 328–9). Even free agents, that is, agents who on Hobbes's view can act on their wills without external impediments blocking their action (L 1.14, 189), are subject to external determination. So this passage does not preclude that some instances of thinking, for example, a regulated chain of reasoning, are products of deliberation because for Hobbes deliberation and external determination are compatible. All it precludes is that thinking is free of external necessity.

In sum, the role of passion in Hobbes's theory of thinking is clear. Thinking, when it is more than just free association, is a procession of phantasms constituted by an endeavor or motion toward an object of desire or a withdrawal from an object of aversion. Accordingly, it is not quite right to say that for Hobbes "thinking comes down to a procession of phantasms or images" (Sorell 1986: 85). It is a train of phantasms guided by desire. Moreover, human action is not a stepchild of theory. Human action requires internal representations as well as endeavors. For Hobbes, all cognitive processes, from individual phantasms through trains of thought to scientific knowledge, involve human endeavor.

Mind and Environment

Endeavors sometimes appear to us as pleasure or delight, in the case of appetite, and trouble of mind or displeasure, in the case of aversion (L 1.6/121). However, they need not be visible or conscious (L 1.6/118–19). Human beings do not always know what motivates them, and thus in Hobbes we find the outline of a conception of unconscious thought and action that is developed by Leibniz (Watkins 1965: 128). Although not necessarily conscious, endeavors nevertheless are object-directed on Hobbes's view. Appetites are endeavors "toward something" and aversions are endeavors "fromward something" (L 1.6, 119).

Hobbes does not explain the object-directedness of endeavors in terms of the content of internal representations. Endeavors are constituents of all motion, and all of these endeavors are vectors or physical magnitudes with a direction. Hobbes's basic idea was that the highly complex motions that constitute human activity and human intelligence are built out of simple motions and endeavors that we can find in animate as well as inanimate objects. In this respect, the mind was no different than any other complex physical phenomenon.

However, the vector quality of endeavors as conceived of by Hobbes has an important consequence. Endeavors are physical magnitudes that direct us to the environment. Appetites and aversions point to external objects. Although these motions are initially the invisible and minute internal beginnings of action, Hobbes always characterizes these first-minute endeavors in terms of gross objects in the environment. An endeavor is a motion toward objects such as food (L 1.6/119). An appetite (or aversion) is the pursuing (or avoiding) of pleasing (or troublesome) objects (DC 4.25.12; EW I: 407). In fact, the endeavor continues to propagate outward because "all endeavour, whether strong or weak, is propagated to infinite distance" (DC 3.15.7; EW I: 216).

Just as the passions are propagated outward, the endeavors of the objects in our environment that we experience are propagated inward. The motion of both the external object and the sentient creature "will be continued every way, especially to the confines of both the bodies" (DC 4.25.10; EW I: 405). The "mutual action and reaction" of these "two endeavours opposing one another" will be a phantasm of "external things" (DC 4.25.10; EW I: 405). A phantasm is a "concourse of two movements" in which the motion is compounded because the "lines" projected by the individual endeavors are not the same (DC 3.15.6; EW I: 215): the inward endeavor is from the outside toward the heart, while the outward endeavor opposes it and propagates into the environment. Although phantasms are internal to the sentient, they are nevertheless examples of interaction between two vectors, both of which involve the environment.

The role of the environment is especially vivid in the case of reasoning with external symbols. The reasoning process consists of the interaction between internal states (the trains of internal phantasms) and the trains of marks on paper, and the external symbols are part of the computation. Reason requires "a good and orderly method in proceeding *from the Elements, which are Names*, to Assertions made by Connexion of one of them to another; and so to Syllogismes, which are the Connexions of one Assertion to another, till we come to a knowledge of all the Consequences of names appertaining to the subject in hand" (L I.5/115, my emphasis). The external markers are the elements of reasoning; they are the objects that are manipulated by the computation that constitutes reasoning.

Reasoning with words, like any use of language, is to transfer the "Trayne of our Thoughts, into a Trayne of Words" (L 1.4/101), but the sequence of external symbols can itself order our thoughts. One case of this was already discussed above, namely, thinking about abstract and universal properties. He writes that without abstract names we could not "reason, that is, compute the properties of bodies" (DC 1.3.4; EW I: 33). For example, language allows us to abstract and reason about heat apart from hot bodies and "consider thinking without considering [the thinking] body" (DC 1.3.4; EW I: 33–4). Another example is the thoughts generated by syllogisms. For Hobbes a syllogism is a type of ordered speech or verbal discourse (DC 1.4.1; EW I: 44), and "the thoughts in the mind answering to a . . . syllogism, proceed in this manner" (DC 1.4.8; EW I: 49). After a general description he gives the following example:

When this syllogism is made, *man is a living creature, a living creature is a body*, therefore, *man is a body*, the mind conceives first an image of a man speaking or discoursing, and remembers that, which so appears, is called *man*; then it has the image of the same man moving, and remembers that, which appears so, is called *living creature*; thirdly, it conceives an image of the same man, as filling some place or space, and remembers that what appears so is called *body*; and lastly, when it remembers that thing, which was extended, and moved and spake, was one and the same thing, it concludes that the three names, *man*, *living creature*, and *body*, are names of the same thing, and that therefore *man is a living creature* is a true proposition. (DC 1.4.8; EW I: 50)

The syllogistic thought in this case depends on the syllogism made with external symbols. Without the syllogism, the syllogistic train of thoughts could not exist:

From whence it is manifest, that living creatures that have not the use of speech, have no conception or thought in the mind, answering to a syllogism made of universal propositions; seeing it is necessary [in the course of doing the syllogism] to think not only of the thing, but also by turns to remember the divers names, which for divers considerations thereof are applied to the same. (Ibid.)

A significant feature of this description is that the thought is generated by alternating between words and thoughts. The train of thoughts answering to the verbal discourse constituting the syllogism is generated by moving back and forth between thought and language, putting thoughts in place that answer to the names of the syllogism.[27]

---

27. The interpretation of this passage is disputed. Laird (1934: 154) claims, without any argument, that names do not do any work in this passage, while Brandt (1928: 233–4) correctly argues that the names generate the syllogistic train of thoughts. Dascal seems ambivalent. Dascal (1987: 35–6) argues that for Hobbes words and verbal discourse do *not* play an "important role in the constitution of thought itself, especially in the performance of reasoning," but later he argues that for Hobbes public symbols are "the stuff out of which judgment, reasoning, and science are made" (1992: 147).

Thus for Hobbes public symbols are constitutive of thinking in two ways. First, they are needed to structure certain thoughts answering to a syllogism. The external symbols make it possible for us to order our thoughts in new ways (Sorell 1986: 31). Second, the reasoning process itself is constituted by the external symbols. The external symbol manipulation is not simply a consequence or trigger for scientific reasoning, but constitutive of scientific reasoning. The reasoning is a sequence that involves a train of thoughts and words, and this is also incompatible with the individualism associated with classical computationalism.

Individualism in psychology, as we saw in the introduction, is the view that "no psychological state, properly so called, presupposes the existence of any individual other than the subject to which the state is ascribed" (Putnam 1975: 220). Computationalists take this to imply that psychological states are individuated only by their formal or computational properties, and that the computational states that play a role in any adequate explanation of individual behavior do not include environmental structures (Fodor 1980, 1987). In other words, the individual embedded in the environment does not make up an integrated computational system (Segal 1991). Hobbes's reasoning with external markers is a computation that involves internal thoughts as well as external markers. The computational system is the thinker embedded in a symbolic environment, and so reasoning, on Hobbes's view, does presuppose the existence of symbol structures in the environment.

Nowhere is Hobbes's commitment to the belief that the causal powers of the environment are constitutive of the nature of mind more evident than in his own treatment of the threat of Cartesian solipsism. This argument survives in *De Corpore*, although it can be found in a more compact form in Hobbes's earlier writings (Tuck 1989: 41–5). In *De Corpore* the argument begins in Book II with Hobbes "feigning the world to be annihilated" except for one man, and Hobbes wonders, "if such annihilation of all things be supposed, it may be asked, what would remain" for this man "to consider as the subject of philosophy, or at all to reason upon" (DC 2.1.1; EW I: 91). Hobbes then proceeds to lay out at great length his philosophy of space, time, and motion, and the argument is not picked up until Book IV, where he discusses humans and other animals.

The crucial premise in this argument is that it is the nature of thought to be constantly changing: "our phantasms or ideas are not always the same; but that new ones appear to us, and old ones vanish. . . . And from hence it is manifest, that they are some change or mutation in the sentient" (DC 4.25.1; EW I: 389). Hobbes writes that "the nature of sense . . . is some internal motion in the sentient" (DC 4.15.2; EW I: 390). But "no motion is generated but by a body contiguous and moved" (DC 4.25.2; EW I: 390). Hobbes refers to his earlier discussion of the nature of motion, which can be known without knowing that there is a world (DC 2.9.7–9; EW I: 124–6).

Given these facts about the nature of thought and motion, which can be discovered by reason,

It is manifest, that the immediate cause of sense or perception consists in this, that the first organ of sense is touched and pressed. . . . And thus also the pressure of the uttermost part proceeds from the pressure of some more remote body, and so continually, till we come to that from which, as from its fountain, we derive the phantasms or idea that is made in us by our sense. (DC 4.25.2; EW I: 390)

This cause is "*the object*" and it is only after this argument that Hobbes characterizes sense as an internal motion that is generated by the action of an external object and the reaction of the sentient.

In sum, self-movement is impossible, and hence the solitary man's motion, which, after the world's annihilation, is just the motion of his own thinking, proves to him that at least once upon a time there were other moving bodies. This he can discover just using his reason. Thus Hobbes, like Descartes, thought that the very nature of his thinking required an external world, except that for Descartes this world was in the first instance divine, while for Hobbes it was a material world in motion. This was guaranteed by what Descartes and Hobbes took to be the nature of their psychological states.

Conclusion

The interdependent role of internal mental representation and external bodily behavior in Hobbes's theory of mind suggests a resolution to the conflict between action-based theories of mind that take *knowing how* or *ways of being in the world* to be basic to the nature of the mind and theory-based accounts that make all action a stepchild

70

of theory. The Hobbesian resolution may be expressed by the following variation on a Kantian theme: Behavior without internal information processing is empty, but internal states without behavior are blind. Behavior requires appropriately complex internal mental representations; we know how to do something only if what we are doing depends on inner thoughts. But internal states by themselves (no matter how complex and fine-grained) are mental states only if they are embedded in a natural and social environment.

Examples in which the inner and the outer conspire to produce cognition are writing, speaking, calculating, solving a puzzle, or finding your way about town. In these cases, the behavior is not just a consequence of a cognitive process, but constitutive of the cognitive process itself. Hobbes's discussion of vision also suggests that vision itself is such an interaction of the external and the internal. Hobbes recognizes that perception is made possible by eye movement (DC 4.25.5; EW I: 394; see Barnouw 1980 and Losonsky 1993a). Hobbes compares perception to reading, which involves the movement of the eye so that it can scan the letters of the page one by one (DC 4.25.6; EW I: 395). The motion necessary for visual perception is not just the motion of the seen object and the endeavor of the heart outward, but bodily behavior such as eye movement. Our changing sensations are caused in part by how "we apply our organs of sense, now to one object, now to another" (DC 4.25.1; EW I: 389), and this will need bodily motion. Therefore, seeing is not just something the eye does: "We speak more correctly, when we say a living creature seeth, than when we say the eye seeth" (DC 4.25.3; EW I: 391).

The unity of the inner and outer achieved in Hobbes's philosophy was an extremely significant achievement of 17th-century philosophy, and it surely contributed to at least the philosophical development of the idea of the public exercise of reason. From Locke to Leibniz, we see an increasingly greater recognition of the role of the public exercise of reason in the attainment of enlightenment.

4

Locke: Uneasy Thinking

Mental Action

The long chapter on power and liberty in John Locke's *Essay Concerning Human Understanding*, a topic which was treated only briefly in earlier drafts of the *Essay* and troubled him enough to revise it substantially for the second edition of the *Essay*, concludes with an observation about the relation between perception and action. He observes that although the language of perception is grammatically active, such propositions do not always refer to actions. For example:

This Proposition, I see the Moon, or a Star, or I feel the heat of the Sun, though expressed by a *Verb Active*, does not signify any *Action* in me whereby I operate on those Substances; but the reception of the *Ideas* of light, roundness, and heat, wherein I am not active but barely passive, and cannot in that position of my Eyes, or Body, avoid receiving them. (E 2.21.72)

Unlike Hobbes, Locke does not make action a prerequisite for all perception. While for Hobbes all phantasms involve some action on the part of the sentient creature, Locke here states that with respect to simple ideas sentient creatures can be passive.

Although Locke usually thinks of simple ideas as passive, in a few places he recognizes that the perception of simple ideas can involve bodily action. When we "bring into view *Ideas* out of sight, at one's own choice, and to compare which of them one thinks fit, this is an *Active Power*" (E 2.21.72). For example,

When I turn my Eyes another way, or remove my Body out of the Sun-Beams, I am properly active; because of my own choice, by a power within myself, I put my self into that Motion. Such an *Action* is the product of *Active Power*. (E 2.21.72)

In this case the ideas are caused not just by external objects, but by the sentient being's willful bodily movements. The role of willful bodily motion in determining what we know and see is mentioned again in Book 4, where Locke explains why knowledge and perception are "*neither wholly necessary, nor wholly voluntary*" (E 4.13.1).

Moreover, as we see below, for Locke our use of language, and hence the bodily activity involved in language, play an important role in the structuring of our thoughts. Nevertheless, the role of voluntary bodily action in human thinking is not treated in any great detail in the *Essay*. Instead, in the *Essay* Locke continues the Cartesian tradition of focusing on voluntary mental activity abstracted from its physical aspects. The making of complex and abstract ideas as well as reasoning and belief fixation are all voluntary mental actions, that is, they are activities generated by the will and motivated by desire. The upshot of Locke's account is that the developed mind is literally the product of intellectual labor, and in this respect, Locke, like both Hobbes and Descartes before him, thinks of the mind as a human artifact for which we have to accept responsibility (Yolton 1985: 138).

To see this, it is best to begin with a look at Locke's account of mental activity. Locke distinguishes between active and passive power. An active power is the ability to make changes, while a passive power is the ability to receive changes (E 2.21.2). The having of simple ideas is an example of the mind's passive "Power to receive *Ideas*, or Thoughts, from the operation of any external substance" (E 2.21.72). The activity of thinking with those ideas, as well as the willful movement of our bodies, are the best sources of our idea of an active power. Locke writes that it is

evident, That we find in our selves a *Power* to begin or forbear, continue or end several actions of our minds, and motions of our Bodies, barely by a thought or preference of the mind ordering, or as it were commanding the doing or not doing such or such particular action. (E 2.21.5)

This power is the will, the exercise of this power is volition, and a voluntary action is an action that is brought about by volition (E 2.21.5).

Mental as well as bodily acts can be voluntary. We not only have a power to move or rest our bodies "as we think fit," but "the infinite Wise Author of our being" has "given a power to our Minds, in several Instances, to chuse, amongst its *Ideas*, which it will think on, and to pursue the enquiry of this or that Subject with consideration and attention" (E 2.7.3). Although some thinking is passive, Locke writes that "Thinking, in the propriety of the *English* Tongue, signifies that sort of operation of the Mind about its *Ideas,* wherein the Mind is active; where it with some degree of voluntary attention, considers anything" (E 2.9.1). Prominent examples of voluntary mental activity in the *Essay* are exercising the "ability in the mind, when it will, to revive" ideas it previously received (E 2.10.2) and the activity of comparing, composing, enlarging, and abstracting our ideas, all of which play a role in the making of complex ideas (E 2.11.4–9).

In his 1676 journal entries Locke illustrates mental actions as follows:

> Thus a man finds that he can rise out of a seat where he sat still and walk, and so produce a motion that is not before, and can also at pleasure, being in France, think of England or Italy, of respiration, playing cards, the sun, Julius Caesar, anger, etc., and so produce in his mind thoughts that are not there before. (LN 271)

Locke distinguishes these thoughts, which are a product of will, from thoughts that we have in dreams or right after we wake up, which are "without choice or deliberation and not consequent to any precedent thought" and thus "cannot be ascribed to the will or be counted voluntary" (LN 272).

Mental actions, then, are like bodily actions in that they are the products of antecedent thoughts, deliberation, and volition. In other words, they are intentional actions as much as deliberate bodily actions such as getting up for a walk (pace Yolton 1985: 135). It follows that we can also be morally responsible for our mental actions. Ignorance, error, and infidelity are all faults for which, Locke believes, we can and will be held accountable (E 4.20.16). For Locke the only difference between mental and bodily actions is that mental actions, unlike bodily activity, seem "to take up no space, to have no extension; so its actions require no time, but many of them seem to be crouded in an Instant" (E 2.9.10).

Not only can thinking be voluntary, it can also be free. The improvement of human knowledge depends on freedom of thought: "Humane Knowledge . . . may be carried much farther, than it hitherto has been, if Man would sincerely, and with freedom of Mind, employ all that Industry and Labour of Thought, in improving the means of discovering Truth, which they do for the colouring or support of Falsehood, to maintain a System, Interest, or Party, they are once engaged in" (E 4.3.6). However, there are obstacles to the "liberty of thought" (E 2.21.53). These obstacles and their remedies are discussed at length in *Of the Conduct of the Understanding*, especially the last section (WL II: 395–401). The "liberty of mind" consists in being a "master of his own thoughts" and having the ability "to transfer our minds from one subject to another" (WL II: 400), but sometimes a thought becomes "a clog [that] . . . hangs upon the mind" (WL 396) so much that we cannot think about other things even though we recognize that they are "fitter for our contemplation" (WL II: 397). The main cause of this condition is that a certain passion comes to rule our minds like a "sheriff" and his "posse" (WL II: 396). The remedy for this "tyranny" (ibid.) is to find another counterbalancing passion, "which is an art to be got by study and acquaintance with the passions" (WL II: 400).

Sometimes this condition occurs spontaneously without a passion or design on our part. We find ourselves entertaining certain thoughts despite our efforts to stop them. Locke's remedy is to try harder to keep those thoughts out. Sometimes we must work at it and "introduce new and more serious considerations, and not to leave till we have beaten [the mind] off from the pursuit it was on." Other times this is easier because what intrudes is a "noise in the head" and any idea whatsoever is better than "the insignificant buzz of purely empty sounds" (WL II: 401). For Locke, "it is best that [the mind] should be always at liberty, and under the free disposal of the man, and to act how and upon what he directs" (WL II: 397). That is, we should try to cultivate and exert our power to think or not to think as we will, which is just how Locke characterizes freedom in the *Essay* (E 2.21.56). If we deliberate about what we should think, then thinking is also free according to the richer conception of freedom Locke introduces in the second edition of the *Essay*, where freedom is the suspension of our desires' influence on the will so that we may examine the consequences of the action (ibid.).

The Need for Uneasiness

Although for Locke freedom is something we need to cultivate, voluntary actions come naturally to us: "the greatest part of our Lives is made up" of voluntary actions (E 2.21.33). What determines the will in voluntary actions is "the *uneasiness* of *desire*" (E 2.21.33), which for

Locke is not just a representation, but a causal power. Uneasiness "is the great motive that works on the Mind to put it upon Action" (E 2.21.29; also 2.20.6) and it is a "*spring of Action*" (E 2.21.34). Locke describes uneasiness as a "disquiet of the mind" (E 2.21.31) and "a state" that exerts "pressure" (E 2.21.32). As such it comes in degrees. The lowest degree of desire for something is velleity, where "there is so little uneasiness . . . that *it carries a Man* no further than some faint wishes for it, without any more effectual or vigorous use of the means to attain" the desired object (E 2.20.6; my emphasis). Even in this weakest case there is more than representation; there is also an uneasiness which causes a certain state of mind, namely, having a wish for the object.

Locke needs mental powers because the mere idea of a desired object will not spur us to action. Without the accompanying uneasiness of desire, "the *Idea* in the mind of whatever good, is there only like other *Ideas*, the object of bare unactive speculation; but operates not on the will, nor sets us on work" (E 2.21.37). Representations are not enough to motivate people to act, even when these are "representations set before their minds of the unspeakable joys of Heaven, which they acknowledge both possible and probable" (E 2.21.37). Only ideas that come with uneasiness can determine the will and bring about action, including mental action.

Locke allows for a role for delight, which he contrasts with uneasiness.[1] For example, the passion of "*Joy* is a delight of the Mind" at the presence or prospect of some good, while "*Sorrow* is uneasiness in the Mind, upon the thought of a Good lost . . . or the sense of a present Evil" (E 2.20.7–8). These passions themselves can operate on the body and cause various changes in it (E 2.20.17). However, uneasiness is always needed to determine the will and spur us to action (E 2.21.34–5).[2]

Uneasy ideas, then, are Locke's passionate thoughts. In Book 2 of the *Essay*, after he has described reflection as "the *Perception of the Operations of our own Minds* within us" (E 2.1.4), Locke writes:

1. Delight and uneasiness also need to be distinguished from bodily pleasure and pain, which are only species of delight and uneasiness (E 2.20.15).
2. This seems to be a shift from his earlier views found in his 1676 journal entries, where Locke gives love a motivating power without making desire a necessary part of love (LN 269–70). There is no discussion of pleasure and pain in the 1671 drafts of the *Essay*.

The term *Operations* here, I use in a large sence, as comprehending not barely the Actions of the Mind about its *Ideas*, but some sort of Passions arising sometimes from them, such as is the satisfaction or uneasiness arising from any thought. (E 2.1.4)[3]

Later Locke makes the stronger claim that almost all ideas involve delight or uneasiness:

Delight, or *Uneasiness*, one or two of them join in themselves to almost all our *Ideas*, both Sensation and Reflection: and there is scarce any affection of our Senses from without, any retired thought of our Mind within, which is not able to produce in us *pleasure* or *pain*. (E 2.7.2)

A function of the associated pleasures and pains is to motivate us to regulate our thinking as well as bodily action. Without delight or uneasiness "to excite us to these Actions of thinking and motion," we would not have a "reason to preferr one Thought or Action, to another; . . . And we should neither stir our Bodies, nor employ our Minds" (E 2.7.3).

The result would be that "our Thoughts (if I may so call it) run adrift, without any direction or design." We would have to "suffer the *Ideas* of our Minds . . . without attending to them." Without passion "Man . . . would be a very idle unactive Creature, and pass his Time only in a lazy lethargic Dream." This is why "it has . . . pleased our Wise Creator to annex to . . . *Ideas* . . . as also to several of our Thoughts, a concomittant pleasure" (E 2.7.3). Pain has the same effect on our minds and bodies as pleasure because in order to avoid it, we move our bodies and engage our thoughts (E 2.7.4). Without passion, to borrow Hobbes's words, our thoughts wander, and seem impertinent to one another, as in dreams and in those that are idle and without care (L 1.3/95).

However, there are important differences between Hobbes and Locke on passionate thoughts. Hobbes is quite clear about the relation between desire, uneasiness, and will. As we saw, for Hobbes the will is just the last appetite in deliberation, and uneasiness, or what Hobbes calls "trouble of mind," is just how the appetite appears to us (L 1.6, 121). Unlike Hobbes, Locke distinguishes between desire and will because we can will something we do not desire (E 2.21.30). To

---

3. While the characterization of reflection is found in both of the earlier drafts for the *Essay*, this addition does not include it (DE 7 and 129).

will is to direct one's thought to the production of an action and exerting one's power to act (E 2.21.28). It is the "power of directing" (E 2.21.29) and endeavor to do something (E 2.21.30). We can have a desire to do something without directing ourselves and endeavoring to the production of that action.

Moreover, unlike Hobbes, Locke is ambivalent about the relation between desire and uneasiness (Schouls 1992: 128–9). In his summary of his position he writes that what determines the will "is some present uneasiness, which is, or at least is always accompanied with that of desire" (E 2.21.71). This ambivalence about whether uneasiness is identical to desire or is accompanied by desire runs throughout his discussion of power and liberty. For instance, he writes, on the one hand, that uneasiness and desire are always conjoined and "scarce distinguishable" from each other (E 2.21.31), but on the other hand he writes that desire is a type of uneasiness, namely, "an uneasiness of the Mind for want of some absent good" (E 2.21.31). Perhaps Locke was being ambivalent because his empirical reflection did not show him how they were related. For Locke pain, trouble, uneasiness – "call it how you please" – cannot be defined or described because it is something that you simply know by experience (E 2.20.1), and the uneasiness of desire is simply something "Man finds in himself" (E 2.20.6). So perhaps Locke would attribute this ambivalence not to any conceptual confusion, but to the fact that the resolution of reflection in this case was not sharp enough to perceive the relation between pain and desire.

Finally, Locke is also ambivalent about whether passion requires consciousness. While Hobbes believes that we do not need to be conscious of the endeavors that motivate human action, Locke devotes much space to arguing that all thinking requires consciousness (E 2.1.10–19). What seems especially absurd to Locke is the notion of unconscious pleasure or pain (E 2.1.11). One of the problems is that unconscious misery or happiness wreaks havoc for personal identity. A conscious Socrates would know or care as little about his unconscious pleasures and pains as he does "for the Happiness, or Misery of a Man in the Indies" (E 2.1.11). Without this continuity of concern it is "hard to know wherein to place personal Identity" (E 2.1.11). Locke also argues that the bodily changes caused by the passions, for example, the blushing caused by shame, are not part of the idea of the passion because we need not be conscious of these bodily changes (E 2.20.17).[4]

On the other hand, Locke admits, although not at great length, that some of the mind's actions occur "without our taking notice of it," just as sometimes habitual bodily actions escape our notice (E 2.9.10). An example of this is making judgments on the basis of perceptions. When looking at a globe we actually first perceive a flat circle shaded and colored in various ways, but on the basis of past experience, according to Locke, we judge that this variously shaded and colored object is a convex object, and this judgment "alters the Appearances" and "frames to it self the perception of a convex figure" (E 2.9.8). This is an action of the mind in which the mind changes "the *Idea* of its Sensation, into that of its Judgment . . . without our taking notice of it" (E 2.9.10).

Making Ideas

A product of this kind of action are complex ideas, which are "*voluntary Combinations*" of simple ideas (E 2.30.3). Locke first discusses complex ideas in Book 2 of the *Essay* where he refers to three kinds of mental actions, namely, "combining," "bringing two ideas . . . together," and "abstraction" (E 2.12.1). These actions produce, respectively, complex ideas, ideas of relations, and general ideas.

Let us first turn to general ideas. General ideas, he writes, "*are the Inventions and Creatures of the Understanding*, made by it for its own use" (E 3.3.11); they are the "Workmanship of the Understanding" (E 3.3.13–14). All "General *Ideas* are made," and to illustrate the making of ideas Locke compares manual and intellectual labor. Locke distinguishes between "bare naked *Perception*," which was passive, and an "operation of the Mind about its *Ideas*, wherein the Mind is active; where it with some degree of voluntary attention, considers any thing" (E 2.9.1). Contemplating, remembering, discerning, comparing, composing, enlarging, and abstracting are all examples of such operations that involve some degree of voluntary attention.

---

4. In his journal Locke writes about the unobserved "motion of the blood and the spirits" that accompanies passions but is not part of the idea of any passion (LN 265).

Abstraction is "the *way* which *Man first formed general* Ideas *and general names of them*" (E 3.4.9), and for Locke abstraction is a mental action. Beyond that, Locke is not always clear about what he took abstraction to be. Sometimes abstraction involves attending to one idea in a complex idea and separating it out of the complex, for example, considering only the color of an object and separating this feature from the other features (E 2.11.9).[5] However, Locke also suggests (in the very same section) that abstract ideas are formed by attending to a particular idea in a complex idea and making that particular complex idea a "general Representative of all of the same kind" (E 2.11.9; also 3.3.11).[6] In either case, however, abstraction involves voluntary attention, namely, the "partial Consideration" of a certain feature in the whole complex (E 2.13.13).

Complex ideas are also artifacts of voluntary mental activity. When Locke writes that "all Complex *Ideas* are made" (E 2.12.1), he is being careful and deliberate. As with general ideas, he illustrates his claim with an analogy between manual and intellectual labor:

> This shows Man's Power and its way of Operation to be muchwhat the same in the Material and Intellectual World. For the Materials in both being such as he has no power over, either to make or destroy, all that Man can do is either to unite them together, or set them by one another, or wholly separate them. (E 2.12.1)

This is not the first time he has made such a comparison. When discussing the given nature of simple ideas Locke also compares intellectual artifice to physical artifice:

> The Dominion of Man, in this little World of his own Understanding, being muchwhat the same, as it is in the world of visible things; wherein his Power, however managed by Art and Skill, reaches no farther, than to compound and divide, the Materials, that are made to his Hand. (E 2.2.2)

Locke is fond of this comparison, and it underlies his frequent use of the words "work" and "make" when writing about complex ideas. Complex ideas are the "Workmanship of the Understanding" (E 3.3.14 and 3.5.13). Ideas of mixed modes, for instance, "are made *by the Understanding*" (E 3.5.2); they are "the Workmanship of the Mind"

---

5. This is the view Berkeley attributed to Locke and criticized (P II: 27–40).
6. This view does not suppose that we can have an idea of color without an idea of a particular color, and so it avoids Berkeley's problems (Ayers 1991: I: 250–4).

(E 3.5.2 and 14); they "are of Men's making" (E 3.5.4); they are "an Artifice of the Understanding" (E 3.5.9). But our complex ideas of natural sorts or kinds are also "Collections of *Ideas,* as Men have made" (E 3.6.1). For Locke "our *ranking,* and distinguishing of natural *Substances into Species consists in the Nominal Essences* the Mind makes" (E 3.6.10). Although "in making its complex ideas of substance" the mind "never puts any [ideas] together that do not really, or are not supposed to co-exist[,] . . . Yet *the number* it combines, *depends upon the various Care, Industry, or fancy of him that makes it*" (E 3.6.29). For Locke "the boundaries of species . . . are made by men; . . . [s]o that we may truly say, such manner of sorting of Things, is the Workmanship of Men" (E 3.6.37).

Locke's use of the verb "make" in all these passages is not metaphorical. In the index that Locke himself assembled for his *Essay* he includes "MAKING" as a main entry, and it refers to a passage where Locke characterizes the way in which "artificial things" are produced (E 2.26.2). We also need to keep in mind the importance of labor in Locke's political philosophy. Moreover, the question of the value and nature of intellectual vis-à-vis manual labor had divided English society during the revolution and was one of the issues that divided radical critics such as John Webster from the moderates in the Royal Society, including John Locke (Debus 1970).

The trend in recent scholarship has been to downplay this feature of Locke's philosophy and argue that for him not all complex ideas are constructed (Woolhouse 1983: 51; Alexander 1985: 106–13). The following passages are evidence for this: "As simple *Ideas* are observed to exist in several Combinations united together; so the Mind has a power to consider several of them united together as one *Idea*" (E 2.12.1). At one point Locke writes that we get ideas of mixed modes "By Experience and Observation" (E 2.22.9), and about our ideas of substances he writes:

the Mind, in making its complex *Ideas* of Substances, only follows Nature; . . . No body joins the Voice of a Sheep, with the Shape of a Horse; nor the Colour of Lead, with the Weight . . . of Gold, to be the complex *Ideas* of any real Substances; unless he has a mind to fill his Head with Chimaera's, and his Discourse with unintelligible Words. Man, observing certain Qualities always join'd and existing together, therein copies Nature; and of *Ideas* so united, made their complex ones of Substances. (E 3.6.28)

Such passages might suggest that for Locke some complex ideas are given to us passively.[7]

But they show this only if we equate "several Combinations united together" or "certain Qualities join'd and existing together" with complex ideas. Clearly, our experience is complex in that many simple ideas occur together at the same time, for example, "the coldness and hardness, which a Man feels in a piece of Ice" (E 2.2.1), but this is not the complexity Locke has in mind when he is thinking about complex ideas. The many simple ideas given in our immediate experience are not united or connected in any way. What we are confronted with is only an aggregate of distinct ideas.

But for Locke a complex idea is not just an aggregate of simple ideas.[8] This is stated quite clearly, for instance, when Locke writes that the complex idea of an army of men or a flock of sheep, namely, "*collective* Ideas *of* several *Substances* thus put together[,] are as much each one of them one single *Idea*, as that of a Man, or an Unite" (E 2.12.6). On the ideas of mixed modes he writes that "Men have put together such a Collection into one complex Idea" (E 3.5.3). When a combination or collection is made into a complex idea something new is added to the collection. In Book 2 he writes that our ideas of substance are "complex and compounded" (E 2.23.14). Later in Book 3 he writes that the mind in making a complex idea first takes a number of ideas and then "gives them connexion, and makes them into one *Idea*" (E 3.5.4).

In sum, the collection of ideas must be connected together in certain ways and turned into one single idea. Locke does not dwell on what must be done to turn a collection into a complex idea, but in an earlier draft to the *Essay* he wrote that in the case of our ideas of substances what is added is an affirmation on our part that all the ideas out of which the complex idea is formed in fact belong together in one substance (DE 8). This suggestion that complex ideas involve a proposition does not survive in the *Essay* (Ayers 1991: I: 24), but what does survive is that a complex idea is more than a collection of ideas.

7. For a discussion of other evidence, see Losonsky (1989).
8. Thus the view that Locke was wedded to the view that "a complex whole . . . [is] the mere sum of its constituent parts" (Gibson 1917: 47) is false. This seems to be the root assumption behind contemporary interpretations of Locke's views on complex ideas.

The distinction between a collection of ideas and a complex idea is relevant to the distinction between ideas of mixed modes and ideas of substances. In the case of mixed modes we not only turn collections of ideas into complex ideas, but usually we make the collections themselves. We put together "several scattered independent Ideas, into one complex one" (E 3.5.6).[9] Ideas of substances, however, are complex ideas made out of simple ideas that "we find to be united together" (E 3.6.21); the simple ideas that go into the making of a complex idea of a substance must "have ... Union" or at least "are ... supposed to have an union in Nature" (E 3.6.28). Ideas of substances, then, have some foundation in reality because they are based on combinations of simple ideas that are given to us. On the other hand, ideas of mixed modes are not grounded in such given collections. For this reason they are much more difficult to make and public language plays a role in their making.

Language and Mind

Locke follows Hobbes in assigning to language a role in the constitution of mind (Yolton 1970: 197–8; Aarsleff 1982: 54; Formigari 1988: 133). Ideas of mixed modes are moral ideas, such as murder, sacrilege, justice, gratitude, triumph, or ambition, and so forth, and, as we just saw, their unity is not based in nature. Consequently, an idea of a mixed mode requires something that will "hold it together, and keep the parts from scattering." What holds the idea with "loose parts" together is a word: "'Tis the Name which, is, as it were the Knot, that ties them fast together" (E 3.5.10; also see 4.5.4).

For example, if there were no name for triumph, we would only have ideas of the various parts of what we take to be triumph, but not the complex idea of triumph. It is not simply that these ideas are annexed to a name that contributes to their unity, but "the Name in common use" is needed if these ideas are to exist.

In fact, *"for the most part the Names of mixed Modes are got, before the* Ideas *they stand for are perfectly known"* (E 3.5.15). Locke argues that

9. At E 3.4.17 Locke seems to suggest that the ideas in the idea of a mixed mode are "perfectly *arbitrary*," but at (E 3.5.7) he writes that although they are "made ... with great liberty; yet they *are not made at random*, and jumbled together without any reason at all." Locke writes that practical reasons determine how we make ideas of mixed modes.

this is especially true of children: "What one of a thousand ever frames the abstract *Idea* of *Glory* or *Ambition*, before he has heard the Names of them[?]" (E 3.5.15). Language also plays a role in the constitution of propositions, namely, the *"joining or separating of Signs"* (E 4.5.2). Locke distinguishes between mental and verbal propositions, but it is difficult to separate the two. First, any discussion of mental propositions will rely on words, and so all examples of mental propositions in such a discussion will really be verbal propositions (E 4.5.3). Second, language also plays a role in the constitution of mental propositions. Locke writes that "most Men, if not all, in their Thinking and Reasonings within themselves, make use of Words instead of *Ideas*, at least when the subject of their Meditation contains in it complex *Ideas*" (E 4.5.4).

Whatever ideas are produced by our use of language are the products of voluntary activity, because for Locke language is a human artifact (Aarsleff 1982). Names signify ideas, Locke writes, "not by any natural connexion, that there is between particular articulate Sounds and certain Ideas . . . but by a voluntary Imposition, whereby such a word is made arbitrarily the Mark of such an Idea" (E 3.2.1).[10] In fact, Locke argues that we can immediately signify our own ideas only because signification is the product of a voluntary act. "Words being voluntary signs," he writes, "they cannot be voluntary Signs imposed by him on Things he knows not," and since ideas are the immediate objects of knowledge, this is what we signify (E 3.2.2).[11]

---

10. Locke does not say much about this "voluntary Imposition" whereby a name is made to signify an idea. It seems that Locke has in mind a decision to make a word signify an idea. He suggests that individuals "arbitrarily appoint, what *Idea* any Sound should be a Sign of" for themselves (E 3.2.8). We do this because we either wish to communicate our ideas to others (presumably because of our "inclination" to be social (E 3.1.1)) or because we have a desire to record our own thoughts (E 3.9.1). In either case, making words stand for ideas must, on Locke's view, be a mental act. Although the word is nonmental in the sense that it is written or spoken, the idea is a mental entity "within [one's] own Breast, invisible, and from others" (E 3.2.1), and making the connection between word and object must at least involve some mental attention to each and some sort of resolution to make the one signify the other. Of course, with time and constant use the connection becomes involuntary and words "readily excite" ideas (E 3.2.6). On meaning and signification in Locke, see Losonsky (1990).

11. On this passage and in what sense ideas are the objects of knowledge, see Alexander (1985: 135).

Locke even suggests that it is our *right* to make such connections: "And every Man has so inviolable a Liberty to make Words stand for what *Ideas* he pleases" (E 3.2.8). He writes that "no one has Authority to determine the signification of the Word *Gold* . . . more to one collection of *Ideas* to be found in that Body, than to another" (E 3.9.17). Even Adam had the "Liberty . . . of affixing any new name to any *Idea*" (E 3.6.51). Of course, practical considerations, such as a desire to be understood and not ridiculed, will lead us to conform to what other people do, but the liberty to conform is still ours.

These practical considerations are given a central role in Locke's discussion of what he calls "rectification," namely, the adjusting of our ideas in order to facilitate communication.[12] Locke believed communication was fraught with pitfalls. The "very nature of Words, makes it almost unavoidable, for many of them to be doubtful and uncertain in their significations" (E 3.9.1; also 3.9.4 and 3.10.1). This is not an idle observation on Locke's part. If we were more aware of the

imperfections of Language, . . . a great many of the Controversies that make such a noise in the World, would of themselves cease; and the way to Knowledge, and, perhaps, Peace too, lie a great deal opener than it does. (E 3.9.21)

The remedy to this is rectification, by which we try to adjust our ideas so that they conform with our communicants.

Although the intelligibility of language depends on this conformity (E 2.32.8), our judgments about the likeness our ideas have with the ideas of other people are all fallible (E 2.32.9). We make hypotheses about what other people signify with their words, and these we can test in various ways. Once we have good supporting evidence for our hypothesis, we can adjust our ideas and enter agreements about the signification of our words. Thus rectification is significantly similar to what we do in "natural" and "experimental" philosophy, where we try to find out what "secret reference" our words have to "*the reality of Things*" (E 3.2.5 and 3.11.24).

12. Aarsleff (1982: 375–6) recognizes that a process of rectification is central to Locke's theory of language, but for some odd reason he attributes the term to Destutt de Tracy. Ashworth (1984: 64–5) notices several crucial passages that belong to Locke's theory of rectification, but dismisses them only as "practical hints" and not central to his theory of meaning.

In the case of simple ideas Locke thinks that we "are *least* of all *liable to be so mistaken*" because "every Day's Observation" gives us some reason to believe that you and I are seeing the same color when looking at, say, a yellow marigold. If a person doubts this conformity "he may easily rectify by the Objects they are to be found in" (E 2.32.9). The way to "mak[e] known the signification of the name of any simple *Idea*, is *by presenting to his Senses that Subject, which may produce it in his Mind*, and make him actually have the *Idea*, that Word stands for" (E 3.11.14).

What makes rectification of simple ideas relatively easy is that their meaning or content is determined by their external causes (Ayers 1991: I: 40). Locke says as much when he writes:

Our simple *Ideas*, being barely such Perceptions, as God has fitted us to receive, and given Power to external Objects to produce in us by established Laws, and Ways, . . . their Truth consists in nothing else, but in such Appearances, as are produced in us, and must be suitable to those Powers, he has placed in external Objects, or else they could not be produced in us: And thus answering to those Powers, they are what they should be, *true Ideas*. (E 2.32.14)

This causal account of content for simple ideas is suggested earlier in Locke's discussion of primary and secondary qualities, where he maintains that two people have the same kind of simple idea if their perceptions are brought about by the same causal powers, both the powers of the objects as well as the powers of their sensory organs (E 2.8.4; also see Losonsky 1990).

Rectification for names of complex ideas of mixed modes is more difficult because they "for the most part, *want Standards* in Nature, whereby Men may rectify and adjust their significations" (E 3.9.7; also 3.9.5). They are "assemblages of *Ideas* put together at the pleasure of the Mind, pursuing its own ends of Discourse" (E 3.9.7). Locke is assuming that voluntary activity is not subject to lawlike regularities, and so we cannot rely on causality to classify our ideas as we do in the case of simple ideas. The only way to rectify the names of mixed modes is to explicitly define the word in terms of the simple ideas that constitute the signified complex idea.

However, substance or natural kind terms do have natural standards that can be used for rectification. These terms signify complex ideas that we have constructed on the basis of passively given patterns of simple ideas. We are not only given individual simple ideas; they are given to us in groups, and these we form into complex ideas of substances (E 3.6.28). For example, Locke claims that our "simple ideas of Bright, Hot, Roundish, having a constant regular motion, at a certain distance from us, and, perhaps, some other" coexist in our experience (E 2.23.6). Out of these coexisting ideas we construct a complex idea which we give a name (E 3.6.28). Regularly coexisting simple ideas are the patterns or the archetypes we can use for the rectification of the signification of natural kind terms (E 3.11.13).

For Locke, then, the mind's interaction with language is a source of internal mental structure. Just as for Hobbes reasoning was physical interaction with symbols in the environment that structured our internal trains of thought, for Locke language and communication, which rest on the use of external symbols (E 3.2.1; Yolton 1970: 213–14), structures the mind's ideas. Sometimes even our thinking and reasoning within ourselves depends on words instead of ideas (E 4.5.4), and "making *Inferences in Words* [is] a great part of Reason" (E 4.17.18).[13]

Knowledge as Work

Since volition plays a crucial role in the construction of our ideas, it is not surprising that Locke gives it a major role to play in human cognition. For Locke human knowledge is *"partly necessary, partly voluntary"* (E 4.13.1), and Locke's conception of knowledge acquisition as voluntary activity is clearest when he speaks of knowledge as work. We are condemned to hard labor in the acquisition of knowledge just as we are condemned to work to make a living:

We are born ignorant of everything. The superficies of things that surround them, make impressions on the negligent, but nobody penetrates into the inside without labor, attention and industry. Stones and timber grow of themselves, but yet there is no uniform pile with symmetry and convenience to lodge in without toil and pains. God has made the intellectual world harmonious and beautiful without us; but it will never come into our heads all at once; we must bring it home piece-meal, and there set it up by our own industry, or else we shall have nothing but darkness and a chaos within, whatever order and light there be in things without us. (WL II: 385, sec. 38)

---

13. However, for Locke "the principle Act of Ratiocination is finding the Agreement, or Disagreement of two *Ideas*" and the inferential relations of words is parasitic on the inferential relations of ideas (4.17.18).

What is involuntary and passive is the receiving of simple ideas, remembering ideas we had, and perceiving the disagreement and agreement of the ideas immediately present to us. These operations are easy and require no work on our part. Here knowledge is like vision: that we see black as black, rather than yellow, is due to an involuntary process with respect to which we are passive. So unlike Descartes, Locke believes that perception itself can constitute knowledge without any contribution of the will (Ayers 1991: I: 107).

However, what we look at and how closely we look at it is a voluntary action: "All that is *voluntary* in our Knowledge, is the *employing*, or with-holding any of *our Faculties* from this or that sort of Objects, and a more, or less accurate survey of them" (E 4.13.2). For example, we cannot help but perceive that 3 + 4 + 7 is less than 15 if we compute those numbers. In the same way, if we have an idea of ourselves as "frail and weak . . . made by and depending on another, who is eternal, omnipotent, perfectly wise and good" we will know that we should obey this being. Nevertheless, we need to pay attention and apply our minds to be able to know these propositions: "these Truths, being never so certain, never so clear, he may be ignorant of either, or all of them, who will never take the Pains to employ his Faculties, as he should, to inform himself about them" (E 4.13.3). The employment of one's faculties on this subject – starting to reason about these propositions as well as the continued and orderly reasoning about this subject – is a willful activity.

It is important not to underestimate what is involved in "the *employing*. . . of *our Faculties* from this or that sort of Objects, and a more, or less accurate survey of them." What we have before our minds determines what we know and we can decide what we do have before our minds (Passmore 1986: 30), but what we have before our minds is not just a function of where we decide to look. We must reason with complex and abstract ideas, and all of these are, as we saw, the "workmanship of the understanding." Sometimes we will rely on words in our reasoning, especially if the train of reasoning is long or involves difficult moral ideas, and here again volition will play a role.

The reasoning needed to set up a properly ordered train of thoughts that constitutes a demonstration is voluntary mental labor. Reason "searches" for agreement or disagreement between ideas where they cannot be compared directly using intuition (E 4.2.2 and 4.17.1–2). It does this by finding one or more intermediate ideas that it can compare using intuition, and then it draws an inference. Inference "when it is rightly made" involves "finding out the intermediate *Ideas*, and taking a view of the connexion between them" (E 4.17.4). The "Labour of strict Reasoning" is not only tedious, but it is "not always successful" (E 4.19.5). Sometimes we draw an inference without a view of the connection between two ideas or propositions. We may do this when we have a desire that the conclusion be true (E 4.17.4). Many other things can go wrong in our reasoning: reason can fail us because we use bad methods, false principles, or defective ideas (E 4.17.4 and 9–12). We may also be incapable of the attention needed in long chains of reasoning (E 4.14.3).

Love and Belief

Volition also plays a role when we aim for something less than knowledge, namely, judgment, assent, belief, or opinion.[14] Although reason may fail to perceive a necessary connection between ideas, it may still perceive a probable connection (E 4.17.2) or presume that there is a necessary connection between two ideas (E 4.15.3), and think assent is due on account of this perception or presumption.[15] Such assent is a belief or judgment, and here too Locke assigns a role to volition. An important piece of evidence of why belief can be voluntary for Locke is that he devotes much discussion to the role of desire and other motivations in belief formation.

On Locke's view, a voluntary act is an act of will motivated by desire, and so if belief formation is voluntary for Locke, he needs to assign to belief a motivating desire. In Locke's later writings it is clear that belief formation is driven by desire. In the discussion of religious enthusiasm added to the *Essay* in 1700, Locke distinguishes between the "lovers of Truth for Truths sake," who regulate their assent according to the evidence available to them, and others whose assent is motivated by other passions and interests (E 4.19.1). Love of truth

---

14. Although Locke believes that, strictly speaking, judgment is mental while assent is verbal, for the purposes of his discussion Locke identifies judgment, assent, belief, and opinion (E 4.14.3 and 4.15.3).

15. Locke's discussion of the perception of probable connections is rare and typically he speaks of the presumption of a connection (Ayers 1991: I: 316n87). However, I do not think this is a reason for discounting Locke's claim that there are probable connections between ideas that we sometimes perceive.

keeps our degree of assent to a proposition regulated by its manifest probability.

Love of truth plays a prominent role in Locke's posthumously published practical guide to better thinking: *Of the Conduct of the Understanding*. Assent that exceeds the available evidence is motivated by prejudice, which is to love something more than truth. A "lover of truth" avoids prejudice by "being in love" with true propositions simply for the sake of truth and remaining indifferent to a proposition until we know its truth value (WL II: 346, sec. 10). Remaining indifferent in this way is a mark of "the love of [truth], as truth, but not loving it for any other reason" (WL II: 347, sec. 12). The love of truth is also a constituent of the "freedom of the understanding" (WL II: 347, sec. 12), and the task of education is to give the mind such freedom (WL II: 348, sec. 12).

Although the most difficult task in the conduct of the understanding appears to be "to know when and where, and how far to give assent," we nevertheless have a "natural relish" for truth that will regulate our assent (WL II: 379, sec. 33). Unfortunately, we can lose this natural desire, for example, by regularly arguing for both sides of a proposition even against our own persuasion. Also, interests and passions for other things besides truth can "dazzle" us.

The remedy for this situation is to "keep a perfect indifferency for all opinions, not wish any of them true" and to "receive and embrace them" according to their evidence, that is, to love truth. Those who "keep their minds indifferent to opinions, to be determined only be evidence, will always find the understanding has perception enough to distinguish between evidence and no evidence, betwixt plain and doubtful" (WL II: 380, sec. 34). However, love of truth is not sufficient for the proper conduct of the understanding. For example, "Lovers of truth" err when "they canton out to themselves a little Goshen, in the intellectual world . . . , but the rest of that vast expansum they give up to night and darkness" (WL II: 327, sec. 3). That is, good conduct involves pursuing truth into new and unfamiliar territory.

Although the love of truth is highlighted in the added chapter on enthusiasm, it also plays a role in earlier versions of the *Essay*. In his revision of the chapter on power for the second edition of the *Essay* (1694), Locke identifies himself "as a Lover of Truth, and not a Worshipper of . . . Doctrines" (E 2.21.72). The first edition (1690) already mentions the love of truth in his criticism of scholastic disputation. Arguing on both sides of a proposition, even after conviction, is "a strange way to attain Truth and Knowledge: And that which I think the rational part of Mankind not corrupted by Education, could scarce believe should ever be admitted amongst the Lovers of Truth" (E 4.7.11). This sort of disputation is "likely to turn young Men's Minds from the sincere Search and Love of Truth; nay, and to make them doubt whether there is any such thing."

Perhaps Locke did not intend "love of truth" to be taken literally, and what he had in mind was a kind of intellectual respect for truth (Ayers 1991: I: 111). This is supported by the fact that sometimes Locke contrasts passion, inclination, and interest with reason and the love of truth (E 4.19.1, 4.20.12 and 14; WL II: 326, sec. 3). But there are many more passages where Locke writes of the love of truth as a desire or passion.

For instance, in *Conduct* we saw that he writes about the "natural relish" for truth. There he also writes that if people were to assent to a proposition without any evidence, they "would be intolerable to themselves" because the mind is "unquiet and unsettled" when it entertains a proposition without any evidence (WL II: 335, sec. 6). This unease of the mind is due to an unsatisfied desire, namely, our natural desire for truth: "our tempers dispose us to right use of our understandings if we would follow, as we should, the inclinations of our nature" (WL II: 335, sec. 6). We have an "eagerness and strong bent of the mind after knowledge," Locke writes a little later in the *Conduct* (WL II: 366, sec. 25).

Locke also explicitly classifies love as a passion, and to my knowledge he never discusses a kind of love that is not a passion (E 2.20.4). In his brief survey of the passions in the *Essay*, Locke mentions "the pleasure of . . . well directed study in the search and discovery of Truth" (E 2.20.18). Truth, like all desired objects, gives us pleasure. Here Locke appears to follow Hobbes, who, as we saw in the previous chapter, in his discussion of the passions in the *Leviathan*, refers to our desire to know, or curiosity, as one of the appetites. If Locke had in mind a purely intellectual attraction to truth, it seems that he would have made this explicit to his readers because this sort of purely intellectual respect for truth was not an unfamiliar notion to his contemporaries.[16]

In sum, Locke's discussion of the inclination and love of truth should be taken literally. After all, Locke himself urges that "philosophers and lovers of truth" should first understand things literally before they rely on figures of speech (WL II: 378, sec. 32).

The State of Mediocrity

If taken literally, Locke's discussion of judgment repeatedly suggests that human assent or judgment is an act of will motivated by desire. He assumes that human judgment requires an "inducement" (E 4.15.1 and 4, 4.16.5) or motive (E 4.20.1). We do not simply find ourselves believing something, but evidence "persuades" us to assent to a proposition (E 4.15.3). He also writes that evidence operates on the mind that "searches after Truth, and *endeavours* to judge right" (E 4.16.1; my emphasis).

For Locke all industry and work is primarily driven by the uneasiness of desire (E 2.20.6 and 2.21.34), and Locke discusses assent in terms of work. We "exercise" (E 4.14.3) and "form" (E 4.16.3) judgments. Sometimes this is easy, but at other times "Diligence, Attention, and Exactness is required, to form a right Judgment, and to proportion the *Assent*" to the available evidence (E 4.16.9). In fact, Locke describes judgment based on probability as one of the "labours" of our "State of Mediocrity" (E 4.14.2). In this state "every day's Experience" makes us "sensible of our short-sightedness and liableness to error," and this serves as "constant Admonition to us, to spend the days of this our Pilgrimage with Industry and Care, in the search, and the following of that way, which might lead us to a State of Greater Perfection." This view of human beings working with industry and care in improving their judgments in order to minimize their short-sightedness and liableness to error is made explicit in the *Conduct*, where Locke describes assent as a species of "conduct of the understanding" that is difficult for us. It is not easy to "know when and where, and how far to give assent" (WL II: 379, sec. 33).

---

16. The Cambridge Platonists endorsed such a purely intellectual attraction for truth. For example, Henry More (OO I: 24–5).

The work involved in proper assent is "the putting *Ideas* together, or separating them from one another in the Mind, when their certain Agreement or Disagreement is not perceived, but *presumed* to be so" (E 4.14.4). For Locke, judgments, strictly speaking, are not "thoughts ...run a drift, without direction or design" (E 2.7.3), or what in *Conduct* Locke describes as "wandering" thoughts (WL II: 373, sec. 30). Judgment requires that we direct our ideas and this means we have some power over our ideas. We can determine what to think and in what order, and this power is just the capacity of volition (E 2.21.5). One way in which we order our ideas is by preferring some ideas over others.

For Locke the mind's resolute "*Ordering, Directing, Chusing, Preferring*, etc." are all examples of volition (E 2.21.15). In his discussion of our judgments about happiness Locke even seems to identify preference with judgment. His heading for a section discussing preferences states: "*Preference of Vice to Vertue a manifest wrong Judgment*" (E 2.21.70). He writes in this section that "Morality, established upon its true Foundations, cannot but determine the Choice in any one, that will but consider," and this choice is the judgment to prefer the endless happiness of afterlife to earthly happiness. God's rewards and punishments "are weight enough to determine the Choice, against whatever Pleasure or Pain this Life can shew" (E 2.21.70; also see 2.21.65). In this case the choice would not be free because it would be determined by our rational understanding of how earthly and heavenly happiness compare, but it would nevertheless be a volition.

A source of such wrong judgments is "heat and passion" (E 2.21.67). Present pains that one actually feels can be so strong that

> Our whole Endeavours and Thoughts are intent, to get rid of the present Evil, before all things.... Nothing, as we passionately think, can exceed, or almost equal, the uneasiness that sits so heavy upon us. (E 2.21.64)

Here the preference is described as a passionate thought or judgment that anything is better than the present pain.

That judgment is voluntary is also suggested by Locke's discussion of the precipitancy of judgment. To judge "is, as it were, balancing an account, and determining on which side the odds lies," and we overlook relevant factors when we rush, which happens when we are concerned with present pains and pleasures (E 2.21.67).[17] The cure for such errors of judgment due to precipitancy is liberty: "To check this Precipitancy, our Understanding and Reason was given to us . . . to search, and see, and then judge thereupon" (E 2.21.67). We can suspend our judgment and examine more thoroughly the evidence, but this suspension is just an exercise of our liberty. Locke writes that "the first . . . and great use of Liberty is to hinder blind Precipitancy" (E 2.21.67), and hasty judgments are examples of blind precipitancy that can be hindered by the exercise of liberty. But if judgments or beliefs can be suspended in order to examine the evidence more carefully before we judge, they are free, and consequently they are also volitions because liberty presupposes volition (E 2.21.8).

If beliefs involve volition, they are subject to conflicting desires, and this in fact is a major concern for Locke. Although probability is the "proper Object and Motive of our Assent" (E 4.20.1), our assent can be motivated by other objects besides the force of evidence. Probabilities can "cross Men's Appetites, and *Prevailing Passions.*" The force of evidence, for example, can come into conflict with avarice in the process of belief formation:

Let never so much Probability hand on one side of a covetous Man's Reasoning, and Money on the other; and it is easie to foresee which will outweigh. Earthly Minds, like Mud-Walls, resist the strongest Batteries. (E 4.20.12)

In the avaricious mind good evidence crosses a prevailing passion for money and loses to it. Here assent is motivated not by good evidence, but by the passion for money. Since for Locke the primary causal power of desire is its power over our volition, the conflict Locke envisions between evidence and the passion for money must be at the point of volition, which in this case is our will to judge or assent. Evidence and money are vying for influence on our will to believe or assent to a proposition.

This also means that the force of evidence operates on the mind *via* uneasiness because for Locke "*uneasiness* alone determines the *will*" (E 2.21.36–7). As we saw, in order to assent to a proposition, we need to be persuaded and have some inducements to receive it as

17. This passage also suggests that Locke did not sharply distinguish inquiry from judgment. The judgment includes the balancing, which is the inquiry. See Ayers (1991: I: 109).

true (E 4.15.3–4), and this suggests that assent is an act of will. But since uneasiness alone operates on the will, the inducement of evidence must involve some uneasiness, that is, there must be a desire for good evidence that persuades the rational person but in the avaricious man loses out against the prevailing desire for money. This desire for good evidence is nothing else but the desire for truth.

If we suppose that the desire for truth is always a passion akin to the pangs of first love – a reigning passion of which we are constantly conscious – then the doctrine that rational belief is motivated by the love of truth might seem implausible. However, just as love can take more subtle and mature forms, so can the desire for truth. When I seem to see a friend on a busy street and the evidence is not sufficient for knowledge, for a brief moment I need to think about the evidence and whether or not to assent to the proposition that my friend is here on this street. It is during such brief moments that the desire to have my beliefs conform to the evidence can come into play, and perhaps also come into conflict with other desires, such as my strong desire to see a friend.

The Freedom of Belief

For Locke, as for Descartes, an action may be voluntary without being free.[18] To be free with respect to a thought or action is to have the "power to think, or not to think; to move, or not to move, according to the preference or direction of his own mind" (E 2.21.8). Locke adds: "Where-ever any performance or forbearance are not equally in a Man's power; where-ever doing or not doing, will not equally follow upon the preference of his mind directing it, there he is not *Free*, though perhaps the action may be voluntary" (E 2.21.8). An action is voluntary if it is simply wanted, preferred, or willed, and this for Locke involves a power, namely, "the power of the Mind to determine its thought, to the producing, continuing, or stopping any Action" (E 2.21.15).[19] Locke illustrates the distinction between free

18. Both Ayers's and Passmore's discussions of the role of will in Locke's account of belief formation seem to ignore this distinction.
19. So for Locke to prefer an action is not just to have a mere preference, but to have what might be called an "effective preference" because it is a preference that directs action.

and merely voluntary actions with the example of a man who is in a room that (unbeknownst to him) he cannot leave but that also contains his good friend with whom he wants to converse (E 2.21.10). So he stays in the room, which is a voluntary action because he is doing what he wants to do without impediment, but he is not free because there is no choice but to stay in the room.[20]

If we apply this distinction to beliefs, then beliefs are voluntary but not free if they are products of will and desire, but we do not have the ability to believe or forbear believing. A belief would be free if not only would it be the product of desire, but we would also have a choice about whether to believe. Is belief acquisition ever free for Locke?

Locke's position is unclear. In the *Essay* there are many suggestions that belief is not only voluntary but free. Toward the end of Book 4 of the *Essay*, Locke writes that "Assent, Suspense, or Dissent, are often voluntary Actions" (E 4.20.15), and what he has in mind here is freedom and not mere volition. The case he discusses is one where we have the power to refuse assent and suspend judgment because we can be suspicious of the evidence or the words used to state the evidence. He contrasts voluntary assent with situations where the evidence is such that a man "cannot refuse his Assent" and "it is not in any rational Man's Power to refuse his Assent." In the section that follows this discussion Locke again contrasts the situation *"Where it is in our power to suspend"* assent and where it is not in our power (E 4.20.16). If we use Locke's discussion of power in Book 2 where he distinguishes freedom and volition as the standard for his best views on this issue, then his concern here is whether beliefs can be freely chosen, not whether they are voluntary.[21]

Locke's discussion of how we can sometimes "resist the force of manifest Probabilities" (E 4.20.12) also suggests that sometimes we

---

20. On Locke's revised view in the second edition of the *Essay*, an action is free if we have the power to suspend our desires before they determine the will to act (E 2.21.47).

21. It is not surprising that Locke does not incorporate the results of his discussion of liberty and volition in chapter 21 of Book 2 of Locke's *Essay* in the discussion of belief in chapter 4 of the *Essay*. Chapter 21 of Book 2 was thoroughly revised by Locke for the second edition, while the discussion of belief in Book 4 relies heavily on the earlier drafts of the *Essay* where this distinction between volition and freedom is not to be found.

are free to believe. This discussion of the freedom to resist evidence is a stable and old part of the *Essay*. In Draft A Locke writes that "men may and doe often where upon the whole matter the affirmative and the negative appears by the arguments to be more probable . . . suspend their assent, or sometimes give it to the lesse probable opinion" (DE 70). He also considers the situation where "probabilitys . . . crosse mens appetites" and he discusses how we can resist or evade apparent and manifest probabilities and withhold our assent in these situations because there is some evidence "to suspect that there is either a fallacy in words or contrary proofs as considerable to be produced on the contrary side" (DE 73; E 4.20.13–14). Of course, sometimes there is very little reason to suspect a fallacy or that there are unknown arguments that have yet to be considered. In these situations the evidence is overwhelming and we do not have the power to resist it (DE 74). However, in "lesse clear cases I thinke it is in a mans power wholy to suspend & perhaps is some cases imbrace either side."[22]

We are forced to choose even when we are not in the crossfire of love of truth and baser inclinations. We encounter "lesse clear cases" in which we have a choice of beliefs when we deal with probabilities under less than ideal circumstances:

Who almost is there, that hath the leisure, patience, and means, to collect together all the Proofs concerning most of the Opinions he has, so as safely to conclude, that he hath a clear and full view; and that there is no more to be alledged for his better information? And yet we are forced to determine ourselves on the one side or other. The conduct of our Lives, and the management of our great Concerns, will not bear delay: for those depend, for the most part, on the determination of our Judgment in points, wherein we are not capable of certain and demonstrative knowledge, and wherein it is necessary for us to embrace the one side, or the other. (E 4.16.3)

It is a fact about our "state of mediocrity" that usually we simply cannot complete our inquiries far enough to alleviate our worries that

---

22. Locke's manuscript shows several deletions before he settled on the phrase "& perhaps in some cases imbrace either side." Clearly Locke was unsure about how precisely to characterize free assent not determined by evidence. This is also shown by how tentative his language is when he writes sometimes we cannot resist the evidence. For example, in the *Essay* he writes, "I think, *a Man*, who has weighed [the probabilities] *can scarce refuse his Assent* to the side, on which the greater Probability appears" (E 4.20.15). Also see E 4.20.16, to be discussed below.

there may be "evidence behind, and yet unseen, which may cast the Probability on the other side, and outweigh all, that at present seems preponderate with us." Locke believes that these second-order worries about the completeness and balance of our inquiry leave the degree of belief underdetermined by the evidence, and hence belief is open to choice.

Locke has been criticized for not considering the possibility that these second-order worries could be automatically reflected in the manifest probability of a proposition (Ayers 1991: I: 108). Perhaps what Locke had in mind are second-order worries that undermine confidence in the very process that fixes all manifest probabilities. It seems plausible to suppose that the anxiety that comes with lack of leisure, patience, and means can extend to the cognitive processes that yield all our manifest probabilities, and this anxiety cannot be reflected in the degree of manifest probability. In this situation, the manifest probability, no matter what it takes into account, is subject to doubt. Consequently, this doubt blocks automatic assent to the manifest probabilities, and the force of volition is needed to generate assent. If we cannot inquire anymore and we must make a judgment, we will have to make a choice for or against the manifest probabilities. We have to make a choice and determine ourselves to believe, say, on the basis of the evidence as we see it, and ignore our anxiety.

At one point Locke suggests that if a proposition is important to our concerns, then we will overcome our second-order worries and our assent will cease to be a matter of choice. He writes:

Where the Mind judges that the Proposition has concernment in it; where the Assent, or not Assenting is thought to draw Consequences of Moment after it, and Good or Evil to depend on chusing, or refusing the right side, and the Mind sets it self seriously to enquire, and examine the Probability: there, I think, it is not in our Choice, to take which side we please, if manifest odds appear on either. The greater Probability, I think, in that Case, will determine the Assent. (E 4.20.16)

In these serious moral conditions our residual worries about the results of future inquiry would vanish because we would simply make a judgment on the basis of the available evidence what the likelihood is that future inquiry will undermine what presently seems preponderate to us.

Locke's suggestion is tentative, as indicated by his frequent use of "I think" in this passage. I believe that this hesitation should be taken seriously, especially in light of the fact that in his earlier discussion of faith and reason Locke discusses a case that seems to have great moral consequences, but nevertheless he maintains we should decide against the manifest probabilities. Locke writes that when revelation contradicts probable propositions that are less than certain, the "evident *Revelation* ought to determine our Assent even against Probability" (E 4.18.9). In sum, faith can be "above" reason where reason falls short of certainty.[23]

However, even if we strip this suggestion of Locke's apparent hesitation, belief fixation is still not a passionless intellectual operation for Locke. A person can choose to believe, Locke writes, where assent "is of no Importance to the Interest of any one, no Action, no Concernment of his following, or depending thereon" (E 4.20.16). But if our assent has consequences for people's interests and good and evil depend on our assent, then belief is determined by and proportioned to the available evidence. The serious pursuit of happiness turns belief formation into a purely intellectual operation in which assent is inevitably determined by the available evidence. We love truth when our happiness is on the line.

Nevertheless, there is a passage in the *Letter on Toleration* where Locke seems to deny that belief is voluntary. He writes that beliefs cannot be imposed by governments because "to believe this or that to be true does not depend on our will [*in nostra voluntate situm non est*]" (ET 120).[24] This passage has been taken to be an explicit denial of the view that beliefs are voluntary actions and that Locke changes

---

23. Whether something is a revelation reason must decide, according to Locke (e.g., E 4.18.8), but what is crucial here is that although reason has determined that it is true or probable that *the proposition that p is divinely revealed*, the evidence for the proposition that p (which is distinct from the proposition *the proposition that p is divinely revealed*) can still be outweighed by the available contrary evidence. For Locke, if this available evidence is less than certain, we should let revelation trump rational evidence, and that is why in such cases faith, according to Locke, is "above *Reason*" (E 4.18.9). If such cases were simply cases in which the proposition that p has a probability on account of its source in revelation that trumps the contrary evidence, there would be no need to characterize this as a case in which faith trumps reason.

24. Also see WL V: 40, where Popple's 17th-century translation is in this isolated case more accurate than Gough's translation.

his mind between the writing of this letter and the later revisions of the *Essay* (Passmore 1986). It seems to me that this conclusion is not justified. Before we draw this conclusion, we must decide whether "*voluntas*" refers to free will or mere volition. Given that Locke is discussing political freedoms, particularly, the freedom of religion, it seems that at best the issue here is whether believing something is not free, not whether believing something is voluntary.

Moreover, it is not obvious that this passage is about whether one's own beliefs depend on one's *own* will. Right after this passage about will and belief in the *Letter* Locke writes: "But on that I have already said enough" (ET 120). This claim is very surprising if we take Locke to have claimed that a person's own belief formation does not depend on her own will, because the rest of the *Letter* does not discuss this issue at all. The discussion so far in the *Letter* is not about the role of one's own will in one's own belief formation; it is about whether *another* person can impose his will on you and make you believe something. Locke's concern throughout the *Letter* is people's "dominion over one another in matters of religion" (ET 101). His main point in the *Letter* is that "no man . . . can believe at another's dictation" (ET 67) and that "such is the nature of the human understanding, that it cannot be compelled by any *outward* force," no matter how brutal it is (ET 69; my emphasis).[25] This suggests that the point in this passage is that beliefs cannot be commanded because a person's beliefs cannot depend on the will of *another.*

Passion and Enthusiasm

People have to guide their own cognitive activities according to their own desires and passions. Lovers of truth proportion their belief to the available evidence simply because they have a desire for truth, and Locke believes, as we saw, that all people have a "natural relish" for it. Locke contrasts lovers of truth with enthusiasts, whom he discusses in some detail in a chapter he adds to the fourth edition of the *Essay.*

Locke characterizes enthusiasm as a condition in which the mind is guided by the "ungrounded Fancies of a Man's own Brain" (E

25. This point of the *Letter* is echoed in the *Essay* when Locke writes that the understanding cannot "blindly submit to the Will and Dictates of *another*" (E 4.16.4; my emphasis).

4.19.3). Enthusiasts do not "regulate their Conduct" by "the tedious and not always successful Labour of strict Reasoning" (E 4.19.5). Instead, "the Conceits of a warmed or over-weening Brain" give rise to Enthusiasm, which "works . . . powerfully on the Perswasion and Actions of Men" (E 4.19.7). In fact, it seems that the primary focus of Locke's discussion of enthusiasm is not unreasonable passion for something other than truth but these misconceptions or conceits that we fail to examine (Ayers 1991: I: 112). The nature of the enthusiastic imagination and its physiological causes was a standard feature of 17th-century medical discussions of enthusiasm (Heyd 1981: 258–80).

However, for Locke there are important connections between enthusiasts' passions and their conceits and misconceptions. First, enthusiasts are "freed from all restraint of Reason, and check of Reflection," and consequently they act simply on the basis of the strength of their impulse or inclination (E 4.19.7). That is, to quote R. A. Knox, enthusiasts make "intuition (a hunch, if we are talking American)" a primary determinant of our conduct (1950: 154). The reason they do this is they have come to believe that their impulses or inclinations are the work of God (E 4.19.5).

For example, they follow their impulses to believe and affirm propositions without search, proof, or examination (E 4.19.8). The strength of an enthusiast's propositional attitude is based not on the propositional content and its evidence, but simply on the initial and unreflected degree of confidence, assurance, or persuasion the enthusiast has toward the proposition. As Locke writes, an enthusiast is sure that a proposition is true simply because he has a strong inclination to believe it (E 4.19.9 and 11).

This distinguishes enthusiastic assent to a proposition from intuitive knowledge of self-evident propositions. In the case of intuitive knowledge, our attitude is grounded in properties of the known proposition itself, namely, its self-evidence. In the case of enthusiastic beliefs, the affirmation is grounded in the properties of the attitudes toward it, namely, the strength of one's inclination or desire to believe it (E 4.19.12–13).

The second important connection between passion and misconception is that the desire to believe something, when it is not the love of truth, can actually be responsible for misconceptions. Locke writes that if I enthusiastically affirm a proposition, say, that I am divinely inspired, it is possible that this proposition was not "put into my Mind" by God, but that it is "an Illusion drop'd in by some other Spirit, or *raised by my own phancy*" (E 4.19.10; my emphasis). I suggest that the meaning of "phancy" in this context is distinct from Locke's earlier use of the term "Fancy," which refers to an idea or phantasm that is produced purely by the imagination. In this sense a fancy is a mental delusion or what Locke also calls a "Phantom" (E 4.11.6–7), and this was a standard use of the term in the discussion of enthusiasm.[26] However, as Peter Nidditch notes under "Fancy" in his glossary to the *Essay*, this term can also refer to a capricious or arbitrary preference, and to illustrate this Nidditch cites a passage in the chapter on Enthusiasm where Locke refers to "the ungrounded Fancies of a Man's own Brain" that ground an Enthusiast's "Opinion and Counduct" (E 4.19.3). When Locke a little later in the same chapter writes about propositions "*raised by my own phancy*" I believe he is again referring to one's preferences.

This mechanism by which our desires cause misconceptions is treated explicitly in the *Conduct*. People who do not pursue truth and are not indifferent about a proposition that they have not yet examined for the available evidence – who have a desire to believe it apart from the available evidence – "put coloured spectacles before their eyes, and look on things through false glasses, and then think themselves excused in following the false appearances, which they themselves put upon them" (WL II: 380, sec. 34). If we have a desire that a proposition be true, then we are in danger of changing and adding to our ideas so that they will support the truth of the proposition (WL II: 391, sec. 41). This influence of desire can escape our awareness. When you take a side on an issue before the evidence has been examined, "the mind is insensibly engaged to make what difference it can, and so is unawares biassed" (WL II: 382–3, sec. 35).

Moreover, habitual associations of ideas, which can be brought about voluntarily and hence different people will have different associations depending on their "different Inclinations, Educations, Interests, *etc*" (E 2.33.6), can "by an instantaneous legerdemain" substitute one idea for another "often without perceiving it themselves" (WL II: 390, sec. 41). In the *Essay* Locke gives an example of how a person's "wanton Phancies," that is, capricious or arbitrary preferences, can

---

26. For example, Henry More (ET). Also see Crocker (1990: 137–55).

determine such associations. A grown person suffering the effects of overeating honey, presumably because he had a wanton desire for honey, will dislike honey so much that the very idea of it makes him sick. Just hearing the word "honey" will evoke his dislike for it, and this "Phancy immediately carries Sickness and Qualms to his Stomach, and he cannot bear the very *Idea* of it; other *Ideas* of Dislike and Sickness, and Vomiting presently accompany it" (E 2.33.7). This is not a case of enthusiasm, but it is a case where preferences cause us to have ideas, and it is this very same process that is at work in enthusiasm. People imagine that they are hearing God because they have an overpowering desire to hear God.

Passion, then, can be the source of error not only because it keeps us from examining our ideas and searching for the available evidence, but because it can cause us to have misconceptions. This is the reason why Locke is so insistent on the need for our indifference before we examine the evidence. In the conduct of the understanding we need to work hard at not wanting a proposition to be true unless we have evidence for it. When we are guided by a love of truth and properly indifferent, we are less likely to suffer from misconceptions.

Conclusion

It is not uncommon to place Locke's *Essay* in the context of the rise of corpuscular science and Newton's mechanics, but it must not be forgotten that Locke also plays a role in the political, economic, and cultural revolution of the 17th century. In this latter revolution conceptions of free, active, and working human beings who fashion the world around them to satisfy their needs and desires, *homo faber*, play a leading role. Clearly Locke's political writings must be read in this context, and the same is true of Locke's philosophy of mind and knowledge.[27]

Locke stands at the beginning of a period that leads to the philosophy of Kant, where the mind's constructive activity is the key player in Kant's Copernican Revolution. After all, in the introduction to his Transcendental Deduction Kant himself maintains that he is "indebted to the celebrated Locke for opening out this new line of

---

27. For a recent attempt to paint a more integrated picture of Locke's *Essay*, see Jolley (1999).

enquiry" (Ak VIII: 100). In particular what he has in mind is the distinction between "the *matter* of knowledge" and "a certain *form* for the ordering of this matter" that is due to the action of our own understanding. Of course, in this context Kant is referring not to voluntary activity of the understanding, but to its involuntary activity where it functions, to borrow a phrase we will encounter in Spinoza, like a spiritual automaton. However, as we saw in the introduction, for Kant, voluntary activity, namely, public activity, also plays a role in improving the mind, and this idea also has a place in Locke's theory of the mind when Locke argues that we can use language to structure our minds.

Nevertheless, this idea does not have a firm place in Locke's philosophy of mind and it would be an exaggeration to say that for him the voluntary activity that leads to the improvement of the understanding is public and bodily activity. As we have seen, Locke often speaks of voluntary mental activity as if it alone can at times change our minds. It seems that a greater appreciation of the automatic functions of the human mind – an appreciation we will encounter in Spinoza and the Enthusiasts – will heighten the awareness of the importance of language and other bodily activities in the mind's pursuit of self-improvement.

5

Enthusiasm: Inspired Thinking

Webster–Ward Debate

One of the central issues that separated enthusiastic writers in the 17th century from their critics was the proper role of human volition in cognition. Enthusiastic writers saw the human will as primarily a source of sin and error, and consequently the attainment of truth, virtue, and salvation required the renunciation of will. They believed that inspired and involuntary human activity directed by divine powers is to be preferred over our deliberate and willful conduct. Inspiration, in the words of Henry More, is *"to be moved in an extraordinary manner by the power or Spirit of God to act, speak, or think what is holy, just and true"* (ET 2), and the legitimacy and even superiority of inspiration in all areas, including cognition, is a central feature of enthusiasm. This assessment of the role of will in the human understanding is a stark contrast to the views of the critics of enthusiasm, such as Locke, who we just saw had a high regard for human voluntary activity, including voluntary intellectual activity and its products, but felt that unthinking and impulsive activity places the human understanding, as Locke writes, "in the dark, or in the power of the Prince of Darkness" (E 4.19.13).

The dispute over the role of human volition and its merits is especially vivid in the so-called Webster–Ward debate, which primarily consists of two pamphlets.[1] The first pamphlet, published in 1653, was *Academiarum Examen, or the Examination of the Academies*, a call for university reform written by John Webster (1610–82), a chaplain and

---

1. For a reprint of these pamphlets and a useful introduction, see Debus (1970).

medic in Cromwell's army.[2] The response – *Vindiciae Academiarum* (1654) – was commissioned by John Wilkins (1614–72), who wrote a preface for it, and it was written by Seth Ward (1617–89), who was also involved in the well-known acrimonious dispute with Thomas Hobbes over the squaring of the circle. Both Wilkins, who was its first secretary, and Ward were prominent founding members of the English Royal Society.

John Webster's critique of the academies was part of the Learned Ministry Controversy about the training of preachers (Webster 1975: 178). Webster reproaches the universities for their emphasis on "humane knowledge," which is "good and excellent . . . while moving in its own orb," but it is bad when it is extended either to theology or to "the things of nature" (AE 3). Humane knowledge is a product of "proud, and towering imagination" and it is, in Webster's words, one of man's "acquisitions." The acquisitions of the human understanding are the target of Webster's critique. These are made by "the light of his own sparks, and by the fire that he hath kindled unto himself," but religious knowledge is not a "humane acquisition" (AE 4) or "gotten learning" (AE 6). This knowledge is given and infused into human beings by God: it is a product of divine grace, not human works.

In his *Saint's Guide; or, Christ the Rule, and Ruler of Saints* (1654), Webster continues his attack on "acquired Knowledge." Humane learning is "Science or knowledge that is or may be acquired by Natural power, capacity and industry" (SG B2), and it must be distinguished from infused knowledge. Infused knowledge is "evidential and experimental knowledge, which men partake of, by the sending in, inflowing, and indwelling of the Spirit of Christ" (SG 1). The only way to know "the things of the Spirit of God" is by divine "infusion" because "natural man cannot know them by any natural power or acquisition" (SG 2). Although acquired knowledge has its proper

---

2. John Webster is also known for his enlightened views on witchcraft in *The Displaying of Supposed Witchcraft*. Webster "utterly denied and disproved" that "there is a *Corporeal League* made betwixt the DEVIL and the WITCH." This is a critique of Joseph Glanville's views, which were republished in an expanded form in *Saducissmus Triumphatus* (London, 1681) together with a very intemperate response to Webster by Henry More. Webster is also known in the history of science for his *Metallographia; or, An History of Metals* (London, 1671), which has been described as competent and "arguably the most effective work in its area produced by any English writer before 1700" (Webster 1982: 71).

place, it must always be supplemented with infused knowledge because "acquired learning by it self, and of its own nature is nothing else but sin" (SG 3). It is "fleshly, earthly, deadly and destructive" (SG 4). Since humane knowledge by itself is sinful, Webster's criticism extends beyond the training of ministers and applies to the university curriculum in general (Debus 1970: 33–56).[3]

Webster's broad attack on the training of ministers, the university curriculum, and the privileges of academic clergy was met headlong by Wilkins and Ward, who, among other things, worried that if Webster's "reformation shall take place, we must be put shortly to work for our livings" (VA 48). A major aim of Wilkins's preface is to defend the products of intellectual labor. He rejects the claim that infused or given ideas are sufficient for attaining knowledge, even on theological subjects. In addition to being "infused by the Spirit of God," a good minister needs "naturall abilities" and "something to be acquired by our own industry" (VA 3). It is no hindrance to the study of God, Wilkins writes, to depend on "notions . . . put together . . . by the labours of many wise and good men" (VA 4).[4]

Human industry in knowledge acquisition plays an important role in Wilkins's *Essay Toward a Real Character and Philosophical Language* (1668), which is one of the first attempts to develop an unambiguous artificial language (Salmon 1966). The human understanding is a natural power, according to Wilkins, and we must distinguish "Infused Habits" from "ACQUIRED Intellectual Habits" (RC 204–5). Infused habits require "Divine favour and assistance . . . which are therefore styled by the general name of GRACE, *Gift.*" Acquired intellectual habits, on the other hand, "may be gotten by Industry, and tend to the perfecting of the Mind or Understanding." Speculation is the first acquired intellectual habit that Wilkins lists, and according to him, speculation improves our thinking and "furnishes the mind with due Notions and conceptions conceiving the Nature of things, their Causes, Differences, Relations, and Dependencies." So

---

3. Nevertheless, it must be noted that Webster argues that universities should not be seminaries (SG B2 and AE 11–12), and that there should be no "National Ministry" (SG 21). Ministers should be supported by the voluntary contributions and academic clergy should not receive "publick salaryes" (AE 2). Moreover, Webster argues for a sharp division between church and state (SG 32).

4. See Shapiro (1969: 101–10) and Debus (1970: 33–56) on the religious, pedagogical, and scientific dimension to Wilkins's critique of Webster.

our ideas about the nature of reality are "gotten by Industry," not by "Divine favour and assistance." Consequently, "Science, Wisdom, Craft, Art, Experience, Learning, Literature, Scholarship, Scholastics, Liberal Science" all turn out to be acquired intellectual habits for Wilkins (RC 205).

Wilkins and Ward become viscious when they turn to the topic of the language of nature. Wilkins writes that Webster "doth give me the freest prospect of his depth and braine, in that canting Discourse about the language of nature" (VA 5). The debate about whether there was a language of nature independent of human volition emerged in the 16th century, in part due to the rediscovery of Plato's dialogue *Cratylus* (Ashworth 1981: 307), and it remains an important topic throughout the 17th century. Webster not only believed that there was a language of nature, but he even urged that it be taught in the universities, and this was intolerable to Wilkins and Ward (AE 26).[5]

Webster describes this language as "the language of nature infused into [Adam] in his Creation, and so innate and implantate in him, and not inventive or acquisitive, but merely dative from the father of light" (AE 29). In creation God spoke "this characteristical word," and "this outflown language of the father . . . is the procedure of the all-working and eternal *fiat*, in which all things live, stand, operate and speak out" (AE 27). Created objects "live in" this language because in creation this divine language becomes the essence or nature of created things: from "that generative and faetiferous word . . . sprung up the wonderfull, numerous and various seminal natures, bearing forth the vive and true signatures of the divine and characteristical impressions" (AE 27).

What is infused into Adam are notions or "images or *ideas* of things themselves reflected in the mind." These given notions are such that there is an "absolute congruency betwixt the notion and the thing, the intellect and the thing understood" (AE 29–30). He compares this congruency to a face and its reflection in a mirror and to a seal and its wax impression. This similarity, according to Webster, is not arbitrary or conventional, but a natural relation. Every mind has such notions that naturally and unequivocally represent, and these notions are naturally connected to certain sounds:

5. Webster was not alone in making this recommendation. See Hutton (1990a: 157n8).

No truly, the mind receiveth but one single and simple image of everything, which is expressed in all by the same motions of the spirits, and so doubtlessly in every creature hath radically, and naturally the same sympathy in voice, and sound.

This is what needs to be recovered:

but men nor understanding these immediate sounds of the soul, and the true *Schematism* of the internal notions impressed, and delineated in the several sounds, have instituted, and imposed others, that do not altogether concord, and agree to the innate notions, and so no care is taken for the recovery and restauration of the Catholique language in which lies hid all the rich treasury of natures admirable and excellent secrets. (AE 32)

These "internal notions impressed" on every mind and their natural audible signs are obscured by ordinary, conventional languages.

Although Webster is primarily interested in humans, he does not exclude animals from the language of nature. He writes that "the voices of birds, and beasts (though we account them inarticulate) are significative one to another, . . . I cannot but believe that this is a part of the language of nature" (AE 31). Webster repeats his commitment to animal intelligence later in his discussion of logic, where he maintains that humans "maintain [an] unjust tyranny over the other fellow creatures" (AE 101). Humans claim "the title of being Rational, and excluding all other living Creatures from that prerogative," although "if it be diligently searched into, it will be found that there is not specifical but a gradual difference" (AE 102).

Since the language of nature is a language common to all people, it would "repair the ruines of *Babell*" (AE 24–5). Disputes about facts would also be eliminated because this language was a "real character" that accurately represented the natures of all things. Wilkins and Ward were also interested in universal language schemes, which were intended as remedies for the linguistic diversity in educated circles that ensued after the demise of Latin, the ascendance of the vernacular and the recognition, as a consequence of European colonial expansion, of the great variety of cultures and languages beyond Europe's borders (Knowlson 1975). In fact, Ward uses his discussion of the language of nature as an opportunity to develop his own ideas on universal language. He rejects the proposal that such a language will contain "Symboles for every *thing* and *notion*" on the grounds that "the number of severall Characters will be almost infinite" (VA 21). Instead, he suggests that the universal language have a compositional structure: a finite set of simple signs will be combined with other signs to form new complex signs.[6]

The point of contention between Webster, on the one hand, and Wilkins and Ward, on the other, was whether the universal language would be a product of human industry or a divine gift. Ward believes that the universal real character will be a language that is acquired and not simply given to us (VA 22). A language of nature is impossible, Ward argues, and he offers a parody of enthusiastic writing as a demonstration of its impossibility (VA 22–3). In the course of this parody, Ward writes:

> But where . . . the *Phantasmaticall* effluviums checked by the tergiversation of the *Epiglottis*, from its due subserviency to that concord and harmony which ought to have been betwixt lapsed man and his fellow strings, . . . no perfect tone could follow. And consequently this Language of nature must needs be impossible. (VA 22–3)

It seems that Ward is making a point with this parody. Henry More discusses the inspired and illuminated state as one in which our own individual wills die and there is "no room left for any *Tergiversation*" in our conduct. We cannot disobey because we lack our own wills. So Ward's point appears to be that it is the fact that we can disobey, especially in our speech, that makes a language of nature impossible. A language of nature requires that we are wholly determined by external forces, but this is not to be had in willful creatures.

Jakob Boehme's Language of Nature

In his defense of the language of nature Webster refers to the "mysterious and divinely inspired *Teutonick*" Jakob Boehme (1574–1624), who was a major source for language of nature doctrines in 17th-century Europe, (AE 26).[7] The idea of a language of nature has roots

---

6. Ward does not confuse the composition of sentences out of words with the composition of words out of letters. Also see Wilkins (RC 45–6). *The Port Royal Grammar* fails to distinguish between generating an infinite variety of words out of a finite class of letters and the composition of an infinite variety of sentences out of a finite vocabulary (Kretzmann 1975: 178–9).
7. Between 1612, when *Morgen Röte im Auffgang (The Aurora)* was completed and his first publication in 1624, the year of his death, Boehme's works circulated widely in manuscript form. After his death, his works were first published in Amsterdam. A German anthology was published in 1631 and an anthology in Dutch was

in late 15th-century Neo-Platonists, Hermeticists, and Kabbalists, who all believed that there are natural and divine symbols with magical powers, but Boehme's account in 1612 of a religious experience he had twelve years earlier revitalized that doctrine for his century (Kayser 1930; Benz 1936, 1970; Koyré 1968). Boehme influenced Francis Mercury Van Helmont (Coudert 1978), who discussed Boehme with the circle of intellectuals around Anne Conway (CL 381–2), and the Cambridge Platonist Henry More maintained a steady interest in Boehme's writings throughout his career (Hutton 1990a). He had followers in France (Knox 1950: 354; Meyer 1985: 74), one of whom – André Morell – engaged Leibniz in a long correspondence about the nature of Boehme's philosophy (Gr I: 101–46).

Although the language of nature was supposed to be the Adamic language (see Leibniz, NE 281), namely, the language of Adam in Genesis, this was not its most important feature, at least not for Boehme. In Boehme's first work, *The Aurora* (1612), the language of nature (*Natursprache*) is identified with Adam's language, which he believes is the root of all human languages, but this is only a secondary fact about the language of nature. Boehme's primary concern is with a language that is not conventional but a divine creation, and whose intrinsic properties, specifically, its sounds, accurately express the natures of all created objects in such a way that we can know the properties of things simply by knowing the sounds of their names (Au 19.76–7/Ur I: 208).

In Boehme's later work, *De Signatura Rerum* (1622), the language of nature is first characterized without mentioning Adam or the origins of languages. All objects have an inner essence or form and an outer form accessible to the senses. An important feature of this outer form is sound, which expresses the internal essences.[8] The

<hr />

published in 1634, which was followed by at least eighteen Dutch translations of Boehme's works. The first collected works of Boehme were also published in Amsterdam in 1682, apparently financed by Spinoza's friend Konrad van Beuningen. All of Boehme's writings were published in English between 1644 and 1662. For his reception in the Netherlands and England, see Struck (1936), Hutin (1960), and Petry (1984). Stoudt (1957) is still the best introduction in English to Boehme's doctrines.

8. "*[D]ie Natur hat jedem Dinge seine Sprache nach seiner Essenz und Gestaltniss gegeben, dann aus der Essenz urständet die Sprache oder der Hall . . . Ein jedes Ding hat seinen Mund zur Ofenbarung*" (SR 1.16/Bo VI, p. 7). For Boehme, all sounds signify inner forms, not just Adam's sounds (see SR 1.4/Bo VI: 4; Au 6.5–9/Ur I: 58–9).

outer sensible form, according to Boehme, "is the language of nature, with which everything speaks according to its properties, and reveals itself" (SR 1.16/Bo VI: 7). In the case of human beings, the language of nature consists of the sounds we make that express our own inner natures, namely, our souls or minds (*Gemüth*). What is special about human beings is that our minds contain "signatures" for all things because we are made in the image of God (SR 1.6–7/Bo VI: 4–5). Thus, by knowing ourselves and these signatures, a human being "not only comes to know himself, but also recognizes in it the being of all being" (SR 1.16/Bo VI: 7).

Boehme's discussion of inner nature shows that the language of nature doctrine is not just a doctrine about language, but is also a philosophy of mind. This is especially clear in Boehme's mature writings. While in *Aurora*, nature is both an immediate expression of God and the body of God (Ur I: 31), in *De Signatura Rerum* and *Mysterium Magnum* (1623), he interposes a spiritual and eternal nature between God, on the one hand, and sensible and temporal nature, on the other. This distinction between eternal and temporal nature applies to human beings as well. Our outward appearance, including our spoken language, is an expression of our soul, but our soul itself contains internal, mental, or spiritual words that themselves are expressions of God's mind. The sensible expression is part of the "sensual language [*sensualische Sprache*]," but the spiritual words are part of "mental speech [*mentalische Zunge*]" (SR 9.22–3/Bo VI: 102; also see MM 35.57/Bo VII: 333 and 52.43/Bo VIII: 554). The sensible expression has a corresponding nonsensible inner form: "the formed thought [*den gefassten Gedanken*]" (MM 35.54/Bo VII: 332).

The distinction is stated with relative clarity in Boehme's preface to the *Mysterium Magnum*, his most systematic work. There Boehme compares the relation between the visible, sensible world and the spiritual world with the relation between body and mind. The human mind (*des Menschen Gemüthe*), which for Boehme is the seat of not just thinking but also of will and desire, is an invisible fire that in itself is nothing but a power to bring about bodily states (MM Preface, sec. 2; Bo VII: 1). We are like God in this respect because the states of the external world of sensible objects are outer expressions of God's inner nature (sec. 3). But this inner nature contains inner, spiritual words. "The invisible, spiritual word of God's power acts with and through visible beings, as does the soul with and through the body," and it acts by speaking or enunciating (sec. 4). The inner human soul or understanding is brought about by God speaking or blowing the invisible word of God's power into the visible being, and thus the human understanding contains the science and knowledge of the visible and invisible world (sec. 5). "The human soul is a spark of the eternally speaking word of God's wisdom and power [that is, the *Mysterium Magnum*] . . . , so it has the power to speak of the *Mysterium Magnum*, the source of everything" (sec. 9).

In other words, humans have the power to speak the sounds that express the natures or essences of things because the eternal word in us is an expression of God's eternal word that created and individuated all things. Boehme writes:

So a person has received the power from the invisible word of God to say it again, so that he can say the hidden word of God's wisdom [*Scientz*] . . . in the manner of temporal creatures; and this same spiritual word makes the living and growing things, through which God's invisible wisdom [*Weisheit*] is modelled in different formations [*Formungen*], as it is before our eyes, so that the human understanding can . . . name all things according to their properties. (sec. 6)

The sensible language of nature is an expression of the language of God that human beings have in their understanding, and that allows them in principle to understand the true nature of things.

God "in itself is not a being [Wesen], but merely . . . an eternal will" (MM 6.1/Bo VII: 29; also see MM 1.4/Bo VII: 6). The relation between will and desire in Boehme is unclear, but it appears that he distinguishes the two (Ur II: 14). The will initially appears to be free in the sense of not determined by anything, and it is also without an object. However, it determines an object for itself, and once it has an object, the will becomes a desire (MM 3.5–7/Bo VII: 12; Elert 1973: 35). God's first desire is to be manifested, particularly to itself (MM 6.1/Bo VII: 29), and this desire is revealed in the command to make something:

This hunger . . . is the first *Verbum Fiat*, or Make, because the desire has nothing that it could make or grasp. It grasps only itself, impresses itself, that is, it coagulates itself, and creates itself . . . with the magnetic pull that the nothing become full. (MM 3.5/Bo VII: 12)

This desire for self-manifestation itself needs to be manifested and it is manifested in a spoken command "Make." The reason this desire is manifested in a verbal command is that God wants to be manifested to the senses; God has a desire to see itself (*Selbst-Schauen oder Sehen*) (MM 3.4/Bo VII: 11), and thus the desire itself must be manifested as something that can be perceived.

God's verbal fiat is at the beginning of all creation (MM 3.8; Bo VII: 13). God's words created the objects and impressed upon them their essential natures, and this command still individuates objects: "We can say truthfully that the *Verbum Fiat* is still in creation today. Although it does not create stars and the Earth, it still has an effect in that it forms and coagulates [*formet und coaguliert*]" (MM 11.9/ Bo VII: 68–9).[9]

In *De Signatura rerum* Boehme writes that the nature of a corporeal object depends on the qualities that were "imprinted on it at creation with the *Verbo Fiat*" (SR 14.3/Bo VI: 194), and this "impression" left on the object is a nature (SR 14.7/Bo VI: 195). The idea that God's command literally individuates creation is already found in *Aurora*, where he writes: "the sound that comes through the word executes the Father's mandate that was uttered with the word" (Au 6.3/ Ur I: 58).

Since creation is a product of desire, Boehme believes that each created essence is characterized by hunger (SR 9.24) or desire (MM 6.1–2/Bo VII: 29–30). God's desire makes itself essential (*wesentlich*) in creation (MM 3.8–9/Bo VII: 13). For example, when God said, "Let there be light," the power of God's desire and hunger passed into the power of light (MM 12.13–14/Bo VII: 76–7). The same applies to earth, grass, herbs, and trees (MM 12.38/Bo VII: 82). If everything is a manifestation of God, it is difficult to see how things can be distinct from each other, but it is one of Boehme's central tasks to account for difference. In *Mysterium Magnum* distinct external objects are needed to satisfy God's love (*Liebe-Begierde*) and they are nothing but the love-play (*Liebes-Spiel*) of God's powers (MM 5.3/Bo VII: 24 and MM 6.1–3/Bo VII: 24). Difference is achieved by letting different objects be manifestations of different aspects of their essences. If objects would manifest their whole nature, "all things and essences would only be one thing or essence," but it is the fact that objects manifest different aspects of their essence to themselves and to others that we have a world of varied and distinct objects (MM

9. Also see MM 52.5/Bo VIII: 543–4 and MM 26.31/Bo VII: 204.

13.9/Bo VII: 85 and MM 13.12/Bo VII: 86). It is a world of distinct and discordant desires in search of harmony and tranquility.

Boehme's Will and Enthusiasm

Since Boehme's God is not disinterested (unlike, for instance, the God of Meister Eckhart), Boehme's conception of the mystical union with God does not reject will and desire. Human beings, as manifestations of God, have a divine will and desire, and thus Boehme extends the doctrine of the omnipresence of God to our conative natures (Weeks 1991: 46–7). Divine will and desire is immanent in human beings, and inspired conduct is conduct that is determined by one's divine will and desire.

Boehme came to accept this view as a result of an experience he had in 1600 that concluded a period of deep melancholy due, according to Boehme, to the problem of evil (Au 19.8–9/Ur I: 199). He remembers this twelve years later in *Aurora* as follows. At the end of his wits about why there is evil, he resolved with "his whole heart and mind together with all my other thoughts and will . . . to wrestle with God's love and mercy" until he would "understand God's will and get rid of my sadness" (Au 19.10/Ur I: 200). He "stormed" God repeatedly until he broke through to "the innermost birth of the deity [*die Innreste geburtt der Gottheit*]." He was then as if "resurrected from the dead" and "in this light" he was able to see through everything and understand God's will (Au 19.13/Ur I: 200). His will also "grew with the drive [*Trieb*]" to describe God. The source of his knowledge, as well as his will and drive, he writes, is the light he experienced in 1600 (Au 19.17/Ur I: 200–1).

What he came to know, he writes, is that "real heaven is everywhere" (Au 19.24/Ur I: 202). Nature in "its innermost birth" shares qualities (*Inqualiret*) with what is taken to be "heaven above" and together they are "one heart, one being, one will, one God, all in all" (Au 19.26/Ur I: 202). Boehme argues that God is present in this world because there is nothing that could have banished God from it, and if that is the case, then God dwells here, and consequently "God is indeed in his heaven" here on Earth (Au 19.42–3/Ur I: 204).

Evil also turns out to be a feature of God. He writes that "the whole deity has in its innermost . . . birth at its core a . . . terrifying sharpness" or astringency (Au 13.55/Ur I: 135). This astringency draws and coagulates into distinct creatures that are self-willed (Au 13.94/Bo I: 140). These self-willed beings contain to some degree the powers of God, they comprehend God, and they subsist in God or even in God's body (Au 13.97–100/Ur I: 140–1; Au 13.115/Ur I: 143). However, these self-willed beings, among which he counts Lucifer, are the sources of evil. Evil occurs when a feature or part of God aims to be like the whole. This causes these self-willed bodies to harden, and the friction between these self-willed bodies generates heat, which is God's wrath (Au 13.116–130/Ur I: 143–4). Human beings are also self-willed bodies in God, and contain in their own degree all divine powers (Au 26.46–7/Ur I: 290). Consequently, human beings recapitulate in and amongst themselves the divine conflict of powers that generates evil.

Later in life, Boehme explains the source of wrath in terms of God's desire for self-manifestation and the love-play discussed above. To manifest divine love and joy, God needs fear and wrath. It is significant that God needs this not in order to manifest love for other creatures, but to manifest divine love to itself (MM 3.21–2/Bo VII: 16). As a consequence, there are three realms, worlds, or principles: divine love, divine wrath, and the arena where love and wrath conflict (MM 15.18–20/Bo VII: 96–7; also Ur II: 40). The third realm of interaction between love and wrath is the realm of the "external world [*äussern Welt*]," or sensible nature. These principles are in all creation, including human beings, and initially these powers were engaged in harmonious love-play (MM 17.17/Bo VII: 110–11). But each sought to be manifested in Adam at the expense of the other powers, and this caused Adam to have his own imagination and his desire "to live in his own will," and imagination and this desire are the sources of evil (MM 17.37/Bo VII: 115).[10]

With his own will, Adam was able to "sample, feel, taste, hear, smell and see" the world's qualities (MM 17.37/Bo VII: 115). Adam's own volition made this experience possible because the will directs the

---

10. Hence the claim that the critique of enthusiasm was also a critique of the orna-mental literary style and the imagination must be carefully qualified (Heyd 1981: 265). Boehme and Webster are paradigm enthusiasts, and both considered the "towering imagination" to be a source of sin and error. Moreover, both associate ornamental speech with cultivation and education that is incompatible with the virtue of humility.

senses in pursuit of the different qualities in the world. In fact, for Boehme, not only is volition necessary for experience, but the will is also the source of belief, including religious faith, and it is what survives death (Elert 1973: 25 and 34–5). Thus, will appears to play a central role in Boehme's conception of cognition. Since the will plays such a central role, it is tempting to characterize him as a voluntarist (Elert 1973; Weeks 1991). This is true insofar as for Boehme God's will has dominion over reason, but Boehme's voluntarism about God is not duplicated for human beings. As is characteristic for enthusiasm, Boehme condemns human volition. Illumination consists in the rejection of our own wills and the finding of another will, which is not our own, "deeply buried within us" (Ur II: 167).

The low esteem for human volition and its products is expressed with relative clarity in Boehme's short work called *Von der Wahren Gelassenheit* (1622). "*Gelassenheit*" refers to a calm, tranquil, or relaxed state of mind in which there are no strong passions. This term is a nominalization of the verb "to leave" (*lassen*), and Boehme has in mind not only inner peace, but a state in which a person has left or abandoned her selfhood and her own individual will so that she is guided by God's will. Boehme writes that the "natural will [*Naturliche wille*]" (Ur I: 333) or our "own will [*eigne wille*]" is only a source of sin (Ur I: 335). When this will, along with our "selfhood [*selbstheit*]," perishes, we have no desires save those that are divine. We are then guided by the "tranquil will [*gelassene wille*]" and become "only tools of conduct with which God does what he wills" (Ur I: 335). This state of indifference and abandonment plays a central role in 17th-century Quietism (Knox 1950: 254–63) as well as earlier German mysticism (Völker 1972).

So what Locke extols as "the workmanship of the understanding" for Boehme is the work of selfhood (*Selbstheit*) and individual volition, which are a source of sin, even when applied to the conduct of the human understanding. Lucifer and Adam, Boehme writes, are examples of what "selfhood does when it gets the . . . light for its own conduct so that it in the understanding may behave by its own rule" (Ur I: 329). The educated and cultivated person also exemplifies the consequences of getting the light of one's own reason: pride and arrogance. Even people who claim to be guided by God succumb to pride insofar as they follow the light of their own reason, which is only a mirror of divine reason (Ur I: 330). In fact, selfhood and reliance on reason's conclusions as guides for our conduct are responsible for the conflict and confusion in Christendom, Boehme writes (Ur I: 331).

Boehme considers the objection that it is only proper that human beings as God's creatures use the light of their own reason, which was given to them by God, to guide their own lives wisely and according to Scripture (Ur I: 332). He responds that he grants that the light of reason is a great gift and treasure of this world, but it has to be ignited by the inner light of God. When reason is ignited by this inner light, reason will reject itself. Boehme writes that with this proper illumination, a person will desire that his own reason and desire perish, and instead that his conduct becomes God's own conduct.

Boehme's views on *Gelassenheit* must be seen in the context of the 17th-century revolt against the standardization and regimentation of prayer and meditation (Knox 1950: 231–2 and 245–6). A formal meditation was an act of will regulated by a method or a set of rules in which the mind was directed either inward to one's soul or outward toward God, depending on the needs of the meditator. But formal meditation could fail to achieve its object, and in such cases an alternative was prescribed, namely, suspending the mind's faculties and making them passive. The idea was that such a suspension of will would "open a window outwards upon God" and we would "forget ourselves in the exercise" (Knox 1950: 248). In forgetting ourselves, we suppress our own willful activity, and the mind sees itself as if it were an automaton driven by larger forces. Conscious intellectual activity, discursive reasoning, and rational reflection on one's own activities, including self-consciousness, were excluded from this kind of unregulated contemplation (Knox 1950: 252–78). The 17th-century revolt against formal prayer elevated unregulated contemplation into the primary mode of prayer, instead of being a fall-back for the times formal meditation fails.

Boehme's *Gelassenheit* was a form of unregulated contemplation. In this state, a human being did not reflect, reason, or deliberate, and instead acted on impulse and intuition. Boehme recommends this stance not only in religious matters, but for all knowledge. All real knowledge is infused or inspired, and not something acquired by intellectual labor. Knowledge is the result of the influence of larger forces for which individual human beings are mere conduits or tools. Our own individual will, passion, reflection, and deliberation are sources of error in all human activity and must be suppressed. This ideal of knowledge as involuntary, inspired, and the product of impulse, that is, an ideal of cognition as primarily a product of passive contemplation and submission to uncontrollable forces acting in and upon us rather than our own voluntary and methodical meditation, is, in my view, the defining philosophical feature of enthusiasm.

Henry More's Enthusiasm

The Cambridge Platonist Henry More appears as a severe critic of enthusiasm (e.g., Heyd 1981). Certainly More would not classify himself as an enthusiast. He published both an antienthusiastic manifesto – *Enthusiasmus Triumphatus* – and a detailed rebuke of Boehme's views in *Philosophiae Teutonicae Censura*. Nevertheless, his relationship to enthusiasm was sufficiently ambiguous that he was classified with them by both critics and sympathizers (Henry 1990: 57; Hutton 1990a: 157–8). This classification is essentially accurate because More endorses enthusiasm's cognitive ideal. More shares with Boehme and Webster a low esteem for human volition and its products and a high regard for the role of inspiration, impulse, and illumination in cognition. These commonalities clearly overshadow the ontological differences that More emphasizes, such as whether there are seven basic divine qualities, God has a body, or metals have an imagination (ET 30–1 or PTC 3.5/OO II.1: 542–3). They also overshadow the differences More sees in their respective stands on human reason. Although More extols human reason and rejects enthusiasm's critique of human reason, his conception of reason is essentially enthusiastic. As we see later in this section, More simply turns enthusiastic inspiration and illumination into a principle of human reason, a not uncommon move in enthusiastic circles.

More's affirmation of the existence of inner divine illumination – the "celestial flame" and "vestal fire of divine love in your heart's temple" (EE 3.8.8/OO II.1: 86) – is very explicit. He writes that he was influenced by Neo-Platonic writers such as Ficino, Plotinus, and "the *Mystical Divines*," all of whom "frequently mention the *Purification* of the *Soul* and the *Purgative* Course that is previous to the *Illuminative*" (OO II.1: vii).[11] More himself claims to have achieved some

---

11. The preface is translated in Ward (1710), and I follow Ward's translation.

degree of illumination, and this is the impulse behind his early poetry, especially his *A Platonick Song of the Soul.* He writes that his poetry was incited by "some *Heavenly Impulse* of *Mind* [*mentis instinctu*]" (OO II.1: viii).

Action based on such an impulse cannot be voluntary given More's account of voluntary activity. A voluntary action, which More distinguishes from a free action, is one whose principle is in the agent and the agent is cognizant of this principle and the circumstances relevant to the action (EE 3.1.9/OO II.1: 68). For More, whatever is done under external compulsion goes against the will, and hence impulsive conduct is involuntary. But *"the way of Enthusiasm,"* he writes, referring to Aristotle, is to act without having a reason on "a blind and determinate impulse" (EE 1.12.1–2/OO II.1: 37–8). He goes on to claim that impulses, inward propensities, or strong inclinations are all imposed or implanted in us by either nature or God.

More's affirmation of divine impulse is coupled with a critique of human volition that is characteristic of enthusiasm. Referring to a classic work of German mysticism, the anonymous *Theologia Germanica*, edited and published by Martin Luther in 1516 and 1518, More maintains that "we should thoroughly put off [*exuamus*], and extinguish our own proper Will; that being thus Dead to ourselves, we may live alone unto God, and do all things whatsoever by his Instinct [*instinctu*]" (OO II.1: vii). Obedience to God should be such that there is "no room left for any *Tergiversation*" and "our *own Will* is *"oppos'd, destroy'd, annihilated"* so that the *"Divine Will* alone . . . may *revive* and *grow up* in us." More believes that he himself was freed in this way from the "sordid Captivity of my *own Will*" and achieved a *"Joyous* and *Lucid* State of *Mind."*

In his discussion of Genesis, More interprets the fall of Adam as a triumph of human will over divine light. The divine prohibition to eat the "luscious and poisonous fruit of *the Tree of Knowledge of good and evil"* is, according to More, a prohibition to eat the fruits "of *thine own Will"* (CSP CC 23). "We are only forbidden to feed on *our own Will*," More has Adam telling the Serpent (CSP CC 26). Thus More precludes knowledge from being a product of will, and what happened when Adam ate the fruit from this tree is that Adam, whom More now characterizes as a *"feminized Adam"* (CSP CC 26), was "forsaking the *divine Light,* and letting his own Will get head against it" (CSP CC 27).

Accordingly, More's critique of enthusiasm in *Enthusiasmus Triumphatus* is not a general rejection of enthusiastic or inspired and involuntary knowledge, but a critique of false inspiration (cf. Popkin 1992: 97). Early in this pamphlet More identifies enthusiasm with "a misconceit of being *inspired*" or a "*full but false, perswasion in a man that he is inspired*" (ET 2). This formulation preserves the possibility of true inspiration and identifies enthusiasm with false inspiration. However, later in the essay More even rejects the identification of enthusiasm and false inspiration. True inspiration, he writes, is "a presage in the spirit of a man that is to act in things of very high concernment" and this "*Presage of a mans own heart from a Supernatural impulse sensible to himself, but inexplicable to others.*" This "is *Enthusiasm* in the *better* sense, and therefore not so proper for our Discourse, who speak not of that which is true, but of that which is a mistake" (ET 21). Those who have a "*true* and *warrantable Enthusiasm*" are "strangely transported in that vehement *Love* they bear towards God, and that unexpressible *Joy* and *Peace* they find in him" (ET 45).

True enthusiasm consists of "the triumph of the Soul of man inebriated, as it were, with the delicious sense of the divine life," and More proclaims himself "a friend" of this kind of enthusiasm (ET 45). Impulse, as long as it is divine, leads us to truth as well as virtue, and this can be achieved only if we suppress our wills. According to More, humility, which is "an entire Submission to the will of God in all things" (ET 37), cures false enthusiasm, which elsewhere More characterizes as a product of "wilfull Imagination" (MG 4.3.3/221). Not only is it a remedy against enthusiasm, but humility also leads to knowledge (ET 37). The humble man who subdues his will, More maintains, "cannot avoid being the *most knowing man* that is." Humility not only leads to knowledge in religious matters, but "all manner of *Wisdome*, as well *Natural* as *Divine*" (ET 38).[12]

Another cure for false inspiration is reason. More extols reason, and in fact thinks that the virtue of Christianity is that it can appeal

---

12. Hence, it is not surprising that More shared the enthusiasts' reservations toward human education. For example, the moral knowledge with which we are born and which God and nature implanted in us is perverted by education. More writes that those who have been corrupted by education would have been better off if nature had been their only instructor "because then the sparks of virtue and truth" in our souls would not have been extinguished (EE 1.13.7/OO II.1: 40). Also see CSP IS 1.2.2–4/3–4.

to reason (CSP vi). However, for More, as was the case for all the Cambridge Platonists, human reason is something quite extraordinary (Hutton 1984). The *"Spirit of Illumination* which resides in the Souls of the faithful, is a Principle of the *purest Reason* that is communicable to the humane Nature" (ET 39). He adds that it comes from "the all-comprehending Wisdom and Reason of God" and it allows us to see "through the Natures and *Ideas* of all things." Whatever *"Intellectual light"* we have "is derived" from this spirit of illumination, he writes (ET 39). In the *Divine Dialogues,* More distinguishes between *"dry Reason* unassisted by Spirit" and reason that comes with the *"Spirit of Life in the new Birth,* which is a discerning Spirit, and makes a man of *a quick understanding in the fear of the Lord."* When guided by the Spirit, "a man shall either immediately feel and smell out by an holy Sagacity what is right and true, and what is false or perverse, or at least he shall use his Reason aright to discover it" (DD 2: 404). Unassisted reason is capable only of "Humane certainty," but *"illuminated Reason"* has superior "Divine Certainty" (DD 2: 484). This dependence of the human intellect on divine illumination is something we have already encounted in the discussion of Boehme, for whom the light of human reason must be ignited by the divine light if it is not to be a source of evil.

In effect, More simply expands reason to include divine illumination. This move was not unfamiliar to the enthusiasts More was attacking, especially people in and around the Society of Friends. For example, in 1662 one of Spinoza's closest friends, the Mennonite Pieter Balling, wrote a Spinozist tract, *The Light on the Candlestick* (*Het Licht op den Kandelaar*), which was thought to have been written by the Quakers and was translated into English in 1663 by the prominent English Friend Benjamin Furly (Struck 1936: 119; Hubbeling 1984: 155–8; Petry 1984: 112). The light, "within the understanding [*verstant*] of everyone," allows us to know truth not only of good and evil, but all things (LK 4). This light, which can also be thought of as Christ, soul, or the word within, is also the source of true religion and leads a person to unity with God (LK 5). Outward signs, whether words or events (e.g., miracles) cannot be sources for knowledge of God because we would first have to know that we are dealing with events caused by God and not something else, and this knowledge we just do not have (LK 8).

Not only is reason for More something extraordinary in that it can incorporate enthusiastic elements, but the ordinary reason itself is primarily a "Composure of Mind" or passive attitude, rather than a mental activity (ET 38). The only activity More assigns to reason is deduction. He writes that reason is limited to *"Common notions, . . . Evidence of outward Sense,* or else a *clear and distinct Deduction from these"* (ET 38). More does not have much to say about the nature of deduction, but it seems that for him it is a succession of conceptions that are connected and cohere with each other (CSP IS 1.2.4/17–8). Reason enlarges "her sphere of Intellectual light, by laying open to her self the close connexion and cohesion of the Conceptions she has of things" (MG 2.11.1/51). How reason "opens to her self" these connected conceptions is not clear, but it seems that for More they are simply given to reason rather than constructed by ratiocination.

The individual conceptions of a deduction of reason are wholly passive. External evidence is the passive reception of ideas from sense perception (CSP IS 2.10.4/102). Our common notions, namely, our innate ideas, are conceptions that, according to More, are "jogg'd and awakened by the impulses of outward Objects" (CSP AA 1.5.3/17). Although on More's view they do not exist in our minds as *"Starres* in the Firmament" or *"Characters* in an *Almanack,"* they are also not the achievements of mental labor. They involve only perception and no discourse or reasoning (CSP IS 1.2.4/17–18). In fact, More writes that our recognition of these innate conceptions are "the dictating of Truth unto us" and the reception of a person's "Naturall Emanations of his own Mind" (CSP AA 1.7.1/20).

Thinking as a natural emanation, rather then a product of willful endeavor, is an important feature of More's theory of mind. More endorses the idea, traceable to Pseudo-Aristotle's explanation of Plato's divine mania and revived by Marsilio Ficino in the late 15th century, that inspiration has a basis in the body's natural constitution and is necessary for making outstanding contributions to the arts and sciences.[13] Inspiration is true or false, depending on whether it has a

---

13. For Plato, see, for instance, *Ion* (533e–534e), *Meno* (99c–d), and *Phaedrus* (244c). Pseudo-Aristotle's discussion of Platonic frenzy is in *Problemata,* Book 30.1, 953a–955a. The classic work on the influence of Pseudo-Aristotle's text, especially in the 15th and 16th centuries, is Klibansky, Panofsky, and Saxl (1964).

divine cause or is merely caused by our natural "complexions" (ET 44–5). True inspiration has divine origins, whereas false inspiration has only natural causes, specifically, the overheating of melancholy (ET 17). Nevertheless, melancholy has a positive role to play in true enthusiasm (ET 46–7). A person's natural complexion disposes them to find and assent to certain truths and makes other truths "lie not within their prospect or the limits of their natural *Genius.*" While mathematical truths can "spring from" a *"Mathematicall Complexion,"* religious truths can spring from a *"Religious* complexion," which involves melancholy (ET 46). The atheists' problem, More believes, is that they lack the natural genius and complexion for religious insight.[14]

For More, the highest form of knowledge involves divine impulse, and he characterizes these impulses as passions (EE 1.12.1/OO II.1: 37). Thus for More, as for Boehme, passions have a cognitive role: they drive us to accept divine truths. Inspiration is not the only case where the passions have a cognitive role to play. More believes that all human passions are from either God or nature without the admixture of human volition, and thus they indicate to us what is good and just (EE 1.12.1/OO II.1: 38 and EE 1.12.9/OO II.1: 39). With the help of reason, which needs to interpret them, the passions are a source of moral knowledge. Referring to Plato's *Phaedrus*, he compares the passions to the wings or steeds of the soul,[15] and he maintains that a mind without passion is like a harp without strings (EE 1.6.11/OO II.1: 27). They spur the mind toward truth and virtue, and without them we would "stagnate and decay" (EE 1.6.3/OO II.1: 26).

In sum, human cognition, at its best, is not a product of human volition. Truth is acquired not by meditation and other willful activity: "The souls most proper food is verity Got and digest by Contemplation" (CP 64). Nothing illustrates this better than More's account of his own thinking. More describes his thinking as the "easie springing up of coherent Thoughts and Conceptions" from which he receives great pleasure (MG v).[16] In fact, More claims that since his

---

14. The psychological and physiological foundations of true enthusiasm are discussed by More in his poems (Crocker 1990: 139).
15. In the *Phaedrus* (251–5c) the "flood of passions" actually only water the wings and make them grow. They are not the wings themselves.
16. These observations apply only to thinking. For More, the writing down of his thoughts was a painful chore.

"natural Constitution" was not to be ambitious, he was either going to "lie fixt for ever in an unactive idleness, or else be moved by none but very great Objects." But the "Contemplation of the Outward world" did not move him, and so More was going to be either idle or moved by a "*Heavenly Impulse*" (MG v). In either case, he does not mention voluntary, deliberate mental labor as an alternative for him.

Since the mental conduct of an inspired mind is an involuntary process, we can think of such a mind as an automaton, albeit a spiritual automaton. The idea of such an automaton, which, as we see below, is mentioned explicitly in the philosophies of Spinoza and Leibniz, is suggested by More's discussion of the spirit or soul of the world. More thought that certain natural phenomena (including magnetism, gravity, and air pressure) are the effects of an "*Immaterial* Principle, (call it *the Spirit of Nature* or what you will) which is the Vicarious Power of God upon this great *Automaton*, the World" (CSP AA 2.2.13/46). The motion of matter follows the blind and mechanical laws of motion unless these laws are trumped by the Spirit of Nature (Gabbey 1982; Henry 1986). The Spirit of Nature is "a pre-emptory, and even forcible, execution of an *All-comprehensive and Eternal Counsel* for the *ordering* and the *guiding* of the Motion of the *Matter* in the Universe to what is for the *best*" (CSW AA 2.2.7/43). It is an immaterial but vital and animating principle of all or nearly all physical phenomena (DD 1: 36; also see Gabbey 1990 and Henry 1990). More believed that God relies on this "Noble part of his Creation" to carry out his will so that he is not "forced to step out perpetually himself" to set the course of "the great *Automaton* of the Universe" (MG 2.4.4/35).

Insofar as human beings are inspired, they are without a functioning will and thus they are automata organized by God's vicarious power. When inspired, not only is the body an automaton directed by nature's spirit, but the mind is an immaterial automaton directed by divine will and reason. More's term for such a spiritual automaton is "*pure Intellect.*" According to More, our souls "are a middle betwixt the more pure and Intellectual Spirits . . . and the Souls of Beasts." A pure intellect is "uncapable of falling from . . . the participation of Divine Happiness" and "fully incorporate with the *simple Good*" (DD 293–4; also MG 2.11.1/51). It lacks the independence and "self-will" that marks out beings such as us and, in the extreme case, rules the "*perfect*

Beast" (DD 298; MG 2.11.4–5/51–2). When divinely inspired, we are rise above this middle state and become like pure intellects without our own wills and incapable of falling away from God.

Contrast More's view of the human understanding at its best with Locke's view of the mind when it is working well. While More condemns "bottoming a mans self upon himself, a will divided from the will of God" (CP 143), Locke recommends it so that we can find the basic propositions upon which we rest our reasonings and other thoughts (E 1.3.24; WL II: 395).[17] For More, "loving adherence and affectionate cleaving to God" should guide our assent even if it is contrary to the available evidence (CP 8). Right reason is guided by the love of God (Hutton 1984: 185), and inspiration is the highest expression of such love. For Locke, however, guidance by anything other than a love for truth is "a Derogation from the Love of Truth as such," which "should receive no Tincture" from any of our other inclinations (E 4.19.1). Even with respect to religious propositions we should be guided only by love for truth, and hence we should remain indifferent about these propositions until we have sufficient evidence to guide our assent (WL II: 348).

On Locke's view, nothing should trump the propositions we affirm on the basis of evidence we have using our natural faculties, such as intuition and reason (E 4.18.5). Inspiration, no matter what its source, can never trump our natural cognitive capacities. "Light, true Light in the Mind is, or can be nothing else but the Evidence of the Truth of any Proposition," Locke writes (E 4.19.13). If we are not to end up "in the dark, or in the Power of the Prince of Darkness," all our inner impulses and inclinations must be brought "to the Tryal" by reason (E 4.19.13–14). Even the prophet made by God, Locke writes, still has "all his Faculties in their natural State, to enable him to judge his Inspirations, whether they be of divine Original or no" (E 4.19.14). Thus, our voluntary mental activity should have the final say, and not our involuntary impulses, no matter what their source.

Locke believes his view does not preclude the possibility of immediate revelation from God. Either the truths God reveals can also be

---

17. Schouls (1992: 218–19) properly highlights the concept of "bottoming" in Locke. However, it is not clear that for Locke bottoming always involves locating the true propositions. Sometimes it is just the activity of locating the basic assumptions of one's belief structure. The references to the *Essay* and *Conduct* in the text illustrate this ambiguity.

known "by the usual methods of natural Reason" without reliance on revelation or, if not, God "convinces us that it is from him, by some Marks which Reason cannot be mistaken in." In either case, the inspirations are judged by "something extrinsical to the Perswasions themselves" (E 4.19.14). Either the proposition can be known without divine assistance or we have an extraordinary outward sign knowable by natural reason, such as Moses's burning bush, that this proposition is indeed from God (E 4.19.15).

Body and Expression

Although the enthusiastic conception of mind and cognition assigns a minor and mostly negative role to volition in human cognition, enthusiastic conceptions of mind recognize the role the body plays in human thinking. The body's motions were not simply consequences of internal mental life, but typically they are the very expression of mental properties.

The enthusiastic model for understanding the relation between mind and body is the relation between God and creation. As we saw, Boehme's early conception of the relation between God's mind and nature is quite radical in that nature was the body of God and the expression of God's mind. In fact, for Boehme the divine will hungers for self-revelation, and the only way it can do that is with nature. God's wish to reveal itself to itself is the force underlying all of creation, and nature itself becomes a play of divine qualities, particularly, psychological properties of love, anger, pain, and so forth. Thus in Boehme's conception of God we have a clear instance of what has been called "expressivism" (Taylor 1975: 13–25). Boehme makes no use of the model of mirroring and representation, which dominated the 17th and 18th centuries, and focuses instead on the relation of expression. God is not represented but expressed in nature, and for this reason Boehme sees the human mind itself as an expression, and not just a representation, of God.

Since the relation between God and creation is taken to be a model for the relation between the human mind and its body, for Boehme the human mind is expressed, and not just represented, in its bodily actions. Just as natural properties are expression of God's mind, so human beings express with their bodies their inner qualities (Ur I: 58). In fact, the body is required so that the inner human soul can exercise its powers (MM Preface/Bo VII: 1–2). Speech, for example, does not really represent our inner states, but, rather, inner events are externalized and expressed in the movement of the lips and the tongue (Ur I: 192–3 and 208). It is for this reason that Boehme believes that he can read the semantic content of language from the physical features of speech production. To express our inner natures, we have to "acquire the demeanor and make the sound that is appropriate to the object" (Au 19.76–7/Ur I: 208). For example, when pronouncing the German word for earth, "*Erde*," Boehme describes how in the first syllable the tongue quivers at the back of the mouth and in the second syllable it comes sharply forward. The first syllable expresses the fear of God's wrath, while the second syllable expresses courage and passing upward to the mind, the royal seat. This captures not only our own feelings about life on Earth; it also captures God's psychology, namely, that Earth is a product of God's wrath, namely, a punishment for The Fall, but that nevertheless God wishes to draw what is good from Earth, and remake earth again (*wider Neu gebären*) in God's honor and glory (Au 18.69–75/Ur I: 192f).

Henry More censures Boehme's early view that all natural properties such as air, water, light, earth, and heat are part of God and that God is literally everything (PTC 1.11/OO II.1: 538).[18] Nevertheless, More is deeply sympathetic to what in the *Notes upon Psychozoia* he calls the "strange opinion of God being all, and that there is nothing but God" (CP 142). What is right about this view, More writes, is that it expresses the truth that "all things are the mere energie of God, and do as purely depend on him, as the Sun-beams of the Sunne" (CP 142). God is everything in the sense that the sun includes both the source of light as well as the light (*lux* and *lumen*). This Plotinian reading preserves nature's dependence and unity with God without obliterating what More took to be a crucial distinction between God and nature. In the *Censura* of Boehme, More suggests that Boehme's views should be interpreted in terms of this relation between God and the Spirit of Nature (PTC 4.23/OO II.1: 551).

More's commitment to the distinction between God and nature is deep and rises to intemperate anger in his critique of Spinoza. In fact,

---

18. More recognizes that Boehme later changed his mind by adding the *mysterium magnum* (PTC 4.16/OO II.1: 549).

he is willing to forgive Boehme because "he is indeed a simple and sincere man, not an apostate from Moses or from Christ, or a promoter or patron of any principles which tend to bad conduct" who "rises finally to the knowledge of those clearer things, and recognizes the *fixed, tranquil,* and *bright Eternity* as being wholly distinct from *Nature.*" Spinoza, on the other hand, remains "immersed in the faeces of atheism," and More inveighs that Spinoza "expired impenitent in it." More adds that Spinoza is "a sordid and vile atheist who however in that fourteenth Proposition, *Besides God no substance can be nor be conceived,* is seen to wish to inhale the entire Deity not anything else besides, even though that proposition involves the crassest atheism."

What seems to bother More the most is Spinoza's rejection of final cause explanations and what More took to be Spinoza's affirmation of mechanical explanations for matter. Throughout his career, More maintained that a purely mechanical account of matter is inadequate and that bodies themselves need to be animated by nonmechanical and vital principles infused throughout matter. In a letter to Descartes that More wrote in his mid-thirties he maintains that "everything that is called body I hold to be alive in a sottish and drunken way, inasmuch as it is an image and the lowest and basest shadow, though destitute of sense and animadversion, of the Divine Essence" (AT V: 383). A decade later More emphasized a sharp division between mind and matter, in part because he wanted to distance himself from "Behemism" and other forms of enthusiasm (Henry 1986). Instead, he posited the Spirit of Nature, which initially is used to explain only some natural phenomena but which by his seventies is used to explain all natural phenomena (Gabbey 1990).

So More's philosophy is an attempt to hold together dualism with a Plotinian position that makes matter divine and tends to undermine dualism. The tension of these tendencies is evident in his philosophy of mind. Although mind and matter are distinct substances, for More, as for Boehme, mind itself has properties that others, such as Descartes, would ascribe only to matter, and the mind needs the body to fulfill its functions.

Although the human mind is an immaterial spiritual substance, More rejects the Cartesian view that only matter is extended. More believes that all substances, including spirits, are extended (CSP IS 20). In addition to being extended, spirits are capable of motion: they move matter, which in and of itself is passive, and they are capable of moving themselves (CSP IS 25 and 32–3). What distinguishes the human soul from other spirits, such as plant spirits and animal and angelic souls, is that it is a vegetative, perceptive, and rational spirit united with a terrestial body (CSP IS 35).[19]

Although a human mind is an immaterial and immortal spirit, it can never be disembodied. According to More, the soul's body is "the necessary instrument of all her Functions" (CSP IS 103). He writes that "the nature of the Soul is such, as that she cannot act but in dependence on *Matter*, and her Operations are some way or other alwaies modified thereby" (CSP IS 146). Even after death, the human soul "is not released from all *vital union* with all kind of *Matter* whatsoever" (CSP IS 146–7). Not only does the mind need a body to fulfill its functions, which as we saw includes the capacity to reason, the mind is not confined to any one part of its body. The mind is infused throughout the body in such a way that there is a "vital congruity" between the whole mind and the whole body (CSP IS 101–5 and 120). This explains, More believes, why we can walk, sing, or play the lute while consciously thinking about something else (CSP IS 108). It also explains why a body can move about in purposeful ways even after it has been decapitated.

So More is a dualist who believes that human minds must be embodied. This position leads More to speculate about the physical marks – he suggests that they may be dots – that must be found in the brain in order for the soul to be able to remember things (CSP IS 107). Nevertheless, More has little to say about the role of language and other public activities in human cognition. Even his interpretation of the first three chapters of Genesis, which he labels "a Cabbala" (CSP CC 1), barely mentions Adam's naming of the beasts (CSP CC 9, 11–2) and does not address issues concerning the origins of language and Adam's language. This is not surprising given More's denigration of human volition in cognition. Public reasoning, for example, speaking in public or calculating on paper, are voluntary activities, and if the human will is an obstacle rather than a means to knowledge, these activities can be only obstacles for cognition.

---

19. Angelic souls are like human souls except that they have aetherial bodies instead of terrestial bodies.

Conclusion

Involuntary inspiration as an ideal guide of human conduct, including the conduct of the human understanding, is characteristic of enthusiasm, and in the next chapter I argue that this survives in the philosophy of Spinoza. In his accounts, the human understanding is much like a spiritual automaton guided by God, and in this important respect his philosophy of mind can be thought of as enthusiastic and belonging to what Popkin (1983) called the "third force" in 17th-century philosophy.

The idea that the mind is an involuntary automaton survives in contemporary naturalistic accounts of mind. The naturalistic tendency is to view human cognition as a product not of volition guided by an ethics of belief but of internal mechanisms beyond our voluntary control and infused in us by larger, in this case evolutionary, forces. Volition itself is a folk-psychological concept or, at best, an epiphenomenal appearance of underlying causal processes. Thus we are indeed automatons, although not spiritual ones, and cognition from our first-person point of view is more appropriately characterized as contemplation than willful meditation. Conscious awareness is primarily the contemplation of cognitive processes already under way or completed. For these reasons, many contemporary conceptions of mind appear to have enthusiastic features and in key ways are very alien to the model of mind as a product of human artifice we find in the philosophies of Descartes, Hobbes, and Locke.

The idea that the mind is an automaton survives in Leibniz and Kant, but they also preserve the ideal of human beings as makers of their own minds. They are able to combine these apparently incompatible views that the mind is an automaton and a product of its own voluntary actions by elevating the role of public activity in human cognition, but this was possible, it seems, only in light of Spinoza's rationalized conception of involuntary cognition.

6

Spinoza: Resolute Thinking

Becoming a Spiritual Automaton

In 1657 the English Quaker William Ames was proselytizing in the Netherlands and he wrote the following in a letter to Margaret Fell, a fellow member of the Society of Friends:

> Theare is a Jew at amsterdam that by the Jews is Cast out (as he himself and others sayeth) because he owneth no other teacher but the light and he sent for me and I spoke toe him and he was pretty tender and doth owne all that is spoken; and he sayde tow read of moses and the prophets without was nothing tow him except he come toe know it within: . . . I gave order that one of the duch Copyes of thy book should be given toe him and he sent me word he would come toe oure meeting but in the mean time I was Imprisoned. (Hull 1938: 205)

Although Ames does not mention Spinoza by name, it is almost certain that he was referring to him (Popkin 1992: 120–34). What brought Spinoza and the Quakers together was, as Richard Popkin puts it, "the stress on inner light and conviction" (1992: 123).

This inner light, to quote from *The Light on the Candlestick* by Spinoza's friend and translator Pieter Balling, is "a clear and distinct knowledge of the truth within the understanding of every person, which gives rise to such certainty in respect of the being and the quality of things, that it is impossible for him to doubt this" (LK 4). Two important features of inner light can be found in Spinoza's philosophy. First, the inner light was a subjective conviction. It was an inner authority that trumped external authority, specifically, the authority of the established churches. Ames judges Spinoza's language not by how well it conforms to what is said, but by how well it conveyed his inner conviction. Second, the inner light was not an act of will or acquired by human volition. It was divine inspiration that required the renunciation of human will. The inspired soul is not just God's servant, but a slave to God, and "our greatest perfection," Spinoza believes, "is to be such necessarily" (G I: 87).

The stress on inner conviction does not distinguish Spinoza from other early modern thinkers. Descartes, as we saw, also extols inner commitment and resolves "to include nothing more in my judgments than what presented itself to my mind" (AT VI: 18). Locke agrees, and consequently, as Locke points out, although people may be "Professors of, and Combatants for those Opinions they were never convinced of," these opinions really are not their beliefs because belief requires inner conviction (E 4.20.18). A person cannot have a belief simply in virtue of belonging to a group or behaving in a certain manner, for instance, by repeating a creed. Even Hobbes agrees that our inner reason and understanding are a matter of inner conviction that cannot be altered by us at will at the command of an external authority, though he believes that we should make our public behavior conform to established public opinion (L 3.32/410).

What separates Spinoza from Descartes, Hobbes, and Locke is the nature of this inner conviction. While for Descartes, Hobbes, and Locke voluntary deliberation and decision could lead to the inner conviction needed for proper understanding, and the judgments we make in this way are our own achievements, for Spinoza the inner conviction needed for proper understanding involves the renunciation of will and the reliance on the automatic activity of our intellects. For Spinoza, "it is never we who affirm or deny something," but "it is the thing itself that affirms or denies something of itself in us" (G I: 83). It is this feature of Spinoza's theory of mind – this commitment to inspiration – that places Spinoza close to 17th-century religious enthusiasm and makes his theory of mind enthusiastic.

The doctrine of the renunciation of will in cognition is already in place in Spinoza's early treatise on method. Like Descartes and Locke, Spinoza also writes a treatise on how we should properly conduct our understanding, namely, the *Treatise on the Emendation of the Intellect and on the Way by which It Is Best Directed Toward the True Knowledge of Things*. The intellect needs to be purified and emended so that it is capable of the kind of understanding that is needed if one is to attain highest human perfection, namely, being something that loves what is eternal and infinite and knows "of the union that the mind has with the whole of Nature" (G II: 7–10). The reference to the emendation and direction of the intellect toward greater perfection suggests that at least in this early work Spinoza affirms an ethic of belief. Indeed, Spinoza does not deny that the will has a role to play in the project of improving one's understanding. But a closer look shows that the role of the will is limited to getting us into a state where the intellect can proceed on its own without our voluntary and deliberate guidance.

The emendation of the intellect begins with a voluntary mental action, namely, choosing the mode of perception that will allow a person to attain perfection (G II: 12). Spinoza lists four modes of perception or knowledge: by means of a report or hearsay, by means of random or wandering experience (*experientia vaga*), by means of reason (as when a cause is inferred from an effect), and by means of intellectual intuition.[1] By means of intellectual intuition we have an adequate perception of the objective essences of things (G II: 10–11). Reasoning and intellectual intuition are both free of error, but reasoning does not perceive the object adequately because we conceive of the object through something else, as when we conceive of an object on the basis of its causal effects. Only intellectual intuition is both free of error and perceives its object adequately, and hence we should choose this mode of perception if we wish to attain highest human perfection (G II: 12–13).

The aim of Spinoza's method is to turn intellectual intuition toward "a given [*datae*] true idea" and then let the intellect be directed by this true idea (G II: 16; cf. Guéroult 1968: I: 30, n. 42). Since true ideas interact with each other as do the objects the ideas represent, the order generated by true ideas will reflect the order of nature. According to Spinoza, if we proceed in this manner, we will never experience doubt (G II: 17). Doubt, that is, "true doubt in the mind" and not mere verbal professions of doubt, is a function of the lack of our ideas' clarity and distinctness (G II: 29), and our ideas are unclear and indistinct when we investigate without the proper order (G II: 30). If we begin with a given true idea and deduce from it without interruption what can be legitimately deduced from it in the

1. For a detailed discussion of these modes of perception, see Curley (1973).

order determined by the idea itself, we will have only clear and distinct ideas and avoid doubt (G II: 24 and 37).

"Since truth," Spinoza writes, "requires no sign, but it suffices, in order to remove all doubt, to have the objective essences of things, or, what is the same, ideas, it follows that the true Method is not to seek a sign of truth after the acquisition of ideas" (G II: 15). That is, we do not first acquire ideas and then look for the characteristic marks of truth and decide on the basis of the available evidence whether or not an idea is true. Rather, "true Method is the way that truth itself, or the objective essences of things, or the ideas (all those signify the same) should be sought in the proper order" (G II: 15). However, this "seeking in the soul" (G II: 15n) is not an act of will. The unfolding of ideas from a given true idea is determined by the nature of the given idea and how it interacts with other ideas. Consequently, once the mind finds a given true idea and its subsequent thoughts are directed by this idea, the mind will be like a "spiritual automaton" (G II: 33), determined by the "laws of the intellect" (G II: 32) without any influence from the will.[2] So if a person chooses the proper perception, the choice of perception will be the last mental act. After that choice is made, Spinoza's method just consists in the unfolding of true ideas.

The trouble is that one first needs to find a given true idea to get the spiritual automaton going, and turning the intellect toward such an idea is part of the task of Spinoza's method. It could happen that a person happens "by some fate" to light on a true idea and have all his thoughts "flowed to him of its own accord," but this "never or rarely happens" (G II: 17). Therefore, Spinoza writes that he offers a way in which we can come to this way of thinking about things "by a deliberate plan." What deliberate plan does he have in mind to get the mind "to be directed according to the standard of a given true idea" (G II: 17)?

It is not clear what plan for improving the human understanding Spinoza had in mind. For his method to work, a person must already have perceived a true idea: "there will be no Method unless there is

---

2. Cf. Deleuze's discussion of Spinoza's spiritual automaton. Deleuze highlights the causal structure of ideas and what he calls the "unity of form and content" in Spinoza's theory of ideas (1990: 140 and 152–3), but does not discuss the lack of will in the spiritual automaton.

first an idea" and "that Method will be good which shows how the mind is to be directed according the standard of a given true idea" (G II: 16). It seems that what Spinoza intended is that his discussion would lead us to reflect carefully about the nature and powers of our own intellects, and it is the idea acquired by such reflection that will jump-start the spiritual automaton. The activity of this automaton will then eventually lead to an idea that will "reproduce Nature as much as possible" in our minds because "it will have Nature's essence, order, and unity objectively" (G II: 36; also 28–9).

The true idea that will start this investigation is the idea we have of our intellect and the "form of truth," which is a property intrinsic to true ideas and not a relation between ideas and their objects (G II: 37 and 26–7). Since truth is intrinsic to the intellect, the form of truth can be known simply by considering the nature of the intellect without considering anything extrinsic to it. This is not easy and requires effort, but if we attend to the powers of the intellect that we understand clearly, we will come to know the objective essence of our own intellect (G II: 38).

The aim of Spinoza's method, then, is to lead the mind to an intellectual intuition of the intellect so that the intellect can then proceed like a spiritual automaton along the path of truth and to the reproduction of Nature, as far as possible, in our minds. This is not a coherent enterprise, as some have argued (Joachim 1940: 105–11; Koyré 1964). What seems to be problematic about Spinoza's strategy is that, on the one hand, he claims that truth needs no signs and one knows what a true idea is simply by having it, while, on the other hand, he writes that the method involves "understanding what a true idea is by distinguishing it from the rest of perception" (G II: 15). If truth has no signs, then it seems that there can be no method for leading us to truth.

The incoherence vanishes if we recognize that Spinoza's method is not exhausted by the pursuit of truth. It also consists in "restrain[ing] itself from useless pursuits" (G II: 16). The method includes turning the will away from pursuits that distract one from the pursuit of human perfection and choosing this end, and the means for attaining it – reasoning and intuition – over the pursuit of uncertain goals that are or can be mixed with sadness (G II: 5–6). So although the method just is the way of truth once we have chosen this way, we need to choose this way over other ways, such as the pursuit of wealth, honor, or sensual pleasure. Pursuing truth was, at some point, a "new goal" and part of a "new plan of life" that Spinoza adopted after some "deliberation" and "persistent meditation" (G II: 6).

The pursuit of eternal and infinite truths is a source of "joy entirely exempt from sadness," but it is not easy to pursue truth because it is not easy to "put aside all greed, desire for sensual pleasure and love of esteem" (G II: 7). Pursuing truth requires a strength of will and discipline so that one does not fall back on pursuits that can actually lead to sadness. The first step away from the pursuit of money, sensual pleasure, and esteem was to think about the proper goals for a human being: "so long as the mind was turned toward these thoughts, it was turned away from those things [wealth, sensual pleasure, and honor], and was thinking seriously about the new goal."

Moreover, Spinoza's method teaches us to understand what a true idea is and how to distinguish it from other perceptions, not by giving us the marks or signs of truth we can use to identify it but by recommending that we attend to the powers of the intellect and make an effort not to pursue other things. Once we attentively reflect on the intellect, we will intuit a true idea and the nature of truth, and "see" how it differs from false, fictitious, and doubtful ideas. In other words, the method aims to turn the mind's mental gaze, so to speak, in the right direction toward truth and then sustain the mental gaze in the face of the attractions of money, esteem, and pleasure until idea takes over and turns and determines the direction of one's thoughts.

Spinoza's understanding of the role of method can be illustrated in terms of the distinction between meditation and contemplation discussed in the previous chapter. Meditation is voluntary and contemplation is involuntary, but meditation can lead to contemplation. Meditation and deliberation brought him to the pursuit of human perfection and the reflection on the powers of the human intellect, which in turn led him to the involuntary contemplation of the intellect's ideas and their interactions. Once that happens, one is on the intellect's automatic path to perfection. The reader of the *Treatise*, who by following Spinoza's discussion comes to reflect on her own intellectual powers, with enough effort, will find a given true idea of her own intellect that will put her mind on an involuntary pursuit of intellectual ideas.[3]

The Passive Intellect

The evidence that the proper progression of the intellect is involuntary is not unambiguous in the *Treatise on the Emendation of the Intellect*. Spinoza lists the properties of the intellect that we understand clearly and that will lead us to an intuition of the intellect, and one of those properties is that "clear and distinct ideas . . . seem to depend absolutely on our power alone," but "with confused ideas it is quite the contrary – they are often formed against our will" (G II: 39). This may suggest that clear and distinct ideas are the products of human will, and this appears to be corroborated by other remarks about how clear and distinct ideas "are made from the pure mind" (G II: 34) or how true ideas are unlike ideas that have their origins in the imagination and "do not arise from the very power of the mind" (G II: 32).

Perhaps Spinoza in the *Treatise* implicitly assumed that if the idea is a product of the intellect it is a product of the will, and consequently his view on the relation between will and belief is not as clear in the *Treatise* as it becomes in his later writings. In the *Ethics* the intellect has powers to produce ideas on its own without the contribution of volition. This doctrine can already be seen emerging in the *Short Treatise on God, Human Beings, and Their Well-Being*, a work which is much clearer than the *Treatise* on the role of the will in the pursuit of intellectual knowledge.[4]

In the *Short Treatise* Spinoza distinguishes between will and particular volitions. The will is a special capacity or power of the mind that causes particular volitions, and a particular volition is "the par-

---

3. Spinoza's discussion of error in the *Treatise* confirms that for the early Spinoza human volition does not play a role in the actual pursuit of highest human knowledge. Spinoza denies that we can "feign" anything about what is necessary or impossible (G II: 19–21). I can feign only what is not impossible or not necessary, but even that can be accomplished only by remembering that we have made mistakes about contingent matters such as that Earth is round. Of course, I can assert hypotheses that deny what is necessary or affirm what is impossible, but verbally affirming or denying a proposition is not the same thing as really pretending that it is true or false.

4. This is evidence that the unfinished *Treatise on the Emendation of the Intellect* precedes the *Short Treatise* (Mignini 1979).

ticular willing this or that," for example – if Descartes is right – "the particular affirming or denying this or that of a thing" (G I: 81). Spinoza denies that there is a will that causes particular volitions, and consequently the will cannot cause anything because "*nothing comes of nothing*" (G I: 83). Although he grants that there are particular volitions, he denies that beliefs – the affirmations or denials of propositions – are volitions. He writes that he not only denies the existence of a will apart from particular volitions, but also denies "the particular willing this or that, which some have posited in affirmation or denial" (G I: 83). In the *Short Treatise* judgments are not volitions.

Consequently, Spinoza maintains that the intellect is "wholly passive" (G I: 79 and 83). "It is never we who affirm or deny something of the thing," Spinoza goes on to explain, "it is the thing itself that affirms or denies something of itself in us" (G I: 83). Whenever it appears to us that we are the ones who deliberately affirm or deny a proposition, we are really referring to written or spoken discourse, not mental acts. We "shall never bring it about, either by words or by any other means, that we think differently about the things than we do think about them." The perceptions of the intellect, which include judgments, are never voluntary acts, and it is in this sense that the intellect is said to be passive in the *Short Treatise*.

Later in the *Ethics* Spinoza appears to deny that the intellect is passive. There Spinoza maintains that the mind is active insofar as it has adequate ideas, and it is passive insofar as it has inadequate ideas (G II: 140/3P1). However, there really is no conflict on the passivity of the intellect between the *Short Treatise* and the *Ethics*. What Spinoza affirms in the *Ethics* is that the mind has causal powers. He writes in the *Ethics*: "We act when something happens, in us or outside us, of which we are the adequate cause," that is, when what happens "follows from our nature" (G II: 139/3D2). In the *Short Treatise* Spinoza is concerned with whether the activity of the intellect is a voluntary activity, that is, an action produced by a volition. In the *Ethics*, as we see in the next section, the intellect is still passive in that its states are not the products of volition.

Moreover, in the *Short Treatise* Spinoza does not deny that the intellect has causal powers. It is true that in the *Short Treatise* Spinoza highlights the causal contribution of the object at the expense of a discussion of what the intellect contributes. As we saw, he writes that "*the object is the cause of what is affirmed or denied of it, whether it is true or false*" (G I: 84) and that "the Idea proceeds from the existence of the object" (G I: 118). Accordingly, he explains differences of opinion in terms of differences of the way in which an object acts on different people, and not in terms of differences in the intellect (G I: 79). But in his discussion of the causes of the ideas of the intellect he mentions more than the object. He discusses the causes of the ideas of the intellect in connection with desire, which is an appetite for or inclination to pursue an object (G I: 58 and 80).

To have desire, we must have a perception of the object: "*Desire depends on the perception of things*," Spinoza writes, and it is the idea of a thing that "brings with it" desire (G I: 85 and 118; also 58, 80, and 91). For example, the desire one has for the preservation of one's body depends on "the Idea, or the objective essence of such a body, which is in the thinking attribute" (G I: 118). However, "for the existence of an Idea . . . nothing is required other than the thinking attribute and the object" (ibid.). Thus, the idea does not depend just on the object, as Spinoza suggested when he wrote that "the object is *the* cause of what is affirmed or denied" (G I: 84), but it also depends on the attribute of thought.

Spinoza does not elaborate on how ideas depend on our thinking, but it seems fairly clear that he had more in mind than just that an idea needs thought only because it is a mode of thought without supposing that thought makes a causal contribution to the nature of the idea. Spinoza writes explicitly about the powers and effects of the intellect. When we perceive something, "there is a power in us to be aware of it" (G I: 90). We "find . . . in us" not only the effects of extension, but also "the effects of the thinking thing," and the principal effect of thought is "a perception of things," which in turn "generates" desire (G I: 91). Finally, Spinoza describes the freedom of the intellect as something "which our intellect acquires through immediate union with God, so that it can produce ideas in itself" (G I: 112).

But how does the intellect produce ideas in itself? One option is to follow Hobbes and let desire play a role in the generation of ideas, but this does not appear to be an option open to Spinoza in the *Short Treatise*. There Spinoza emphasizes that without perception there could be no desire (G I: 56). For example, the desire to preserve one's own body depends on the idea of such a body (G I: 118). Moreover, after he writes that an idea depends only on "the thinking attribute and the object," he states that "the Idea . . . is the most immediate mode of the attribute [of thought]," and an immediate mode of an attribute is one "that in order to exist, needs no other mode in the same attribute" (ibid.). Desires are modes distinct from ideas, so this means that ideas depend only on objects and the attribute of thought, but no other modes of thought, such as desire. This view is affirmed in the *Ethics*, where Spinoza presents it as an axiom in Part II that modes of thinking such as love and desire depend on an idea, but "there can be an idea, even though there is no other mode of thinking" (G II: 86).

Thus the only role desire can have in generating ideas is as a source of the intellect's perceptions of desire. The intellect, then, is independent of both our volition and desire, and so we cannot be responsible for it. Instead, our intellect, like everything else about us, cannot really be attributed to us, but must be attributed to God. We are "truly God's servants – indeed, his slaves" (G I: 87) and "the only perfection and the final end of a slave and an instrument is to fulfill properly the task imposed on them" (G I: 88). Only when we come to recognize our dependence on God will we become truly happy and free from sadness and other disturbances of the mind, which Spinoza believes are products of error and opinion (G I: 68 and 95). One of the disturbances of mind that will be removed if we follow "true reason" is irresolution (*wankelmoedigheid*) (G I: 70–3). While Descartes proposed volition as a remedy to this state, Spinoza suggests that we need better knowledge.

Later in his exposition and comments on Descartes's *Principles*, Spinoza revises his position slightly. Rather than denying a role for will in the intellect, the will is simply identified with the power of the mind (G I: 279). The will "is a thought, i.e., a power of . . . affirming and denying" and a power is simply a sufficient cause (G I: 280). This is a deflationary view of will. To will is simply to think, and thus Spinoza obliterates the distinction between voluntary thinking and involuntary thinking. On that view of will, even a spiritual automaton has voluntary thoughts because every thought is a volition simply because it affirms something about what is the case. This is the position Spinoza develops in the *Ethics*.

Will and Intellect in the *Ethics*

The discussion of volition and thinking in the *Ethics* is contained mostly in Proposition 49 of Part II. The preceding Proposition 48 states that there is no free will, and that the mind is determined by prior causes, and thus it is orthogonal to the question of whether there are voluntary thoughts because a belief can be voluntary and causally determined. The question at hand is whether or not volition plays a role in determining the intellect.

Strictly speaking, the will can have no role to play in determining the intellect for Spinoza because he does not distinguish between the will and intellect. Proposition 49 states: "*In the Mind there is no volition, or affirmation and negation, except that which the idea involves insofar as it is an idea,*" and, according to Spinoza, a corollary to this proposition is that "the will and the intellect are one and the same" (G II: 130–1). The identity of the will and the intellect is demonstrated as follows:

> The will and the intellect are nothing apart from the singular volitions and ideas themselves. . . . But the singular volitions and ideas are one and the same (by Proposition 49). Therefore the will and the intellect are one and the same, q.e.d.

Spinoza then comments that this means he rejects the "common doctrine" that volition is the cause of error.

Spinoza appears to maintain that a source of the view that a volition is involved in a belief in addition to the intellect is the failure to distinguish between ideas and images (G II: 131–2). This is an odd explanation for Descartes's views because Descartes explicitly distinguished ideas and images (AT VII: 181). Curley (1975: 170–3) suggests that Spinoza's explanation of the Cartesian view is not that ideas are confused with images, but that they are wrongly assumed to be *like* images in important respects. Curley suggests that according to Spinoza, Descartes implicitly assumed that ideas resemble objects in the way pictures or images can resemble objects, and that this is the source of the denial that "*an idea involves insofar as it is an idea*" an affirmation or negation (G II: 130).

Curley does not explain how assuming that ideas resemble their objects is the source of the view that ideas do not involve affirmation or negation.[5] Moreover, Spinoza does not discuss resemblance in his critique of the Cartesian view of the role of will in cognition. Nevertheless, Curley is clearly on the right track in suggesting that the point of Spinoza's critique is not that ideas are confused with images but that ideas are wrongly assumed to be like images in certain respects.

The source of the problem, according to Spinoza, is that ideas are taken to be "mute," like images or pictures on a wall. In the scholium to Proposition 49 Spinoza writes that those who think there is a special role for volition in belief in addition to the idea "look on ideas . . . as mute pictures on a panel, and preoccupied with this prejudice, do not see that an idea, insofar as it is an idea, involves an affirmation or negation" (G II: 132). This echoes an earlier comment in a scholium to Proposition 43. He writes that anyone that doubts that to have a true idea is to have perfect knowledge is someone who "thinks that an idea is something mute, like a picture on a tablet, and not a mode of thinking, viz. the very [act of] understanding [*nempe ipsum intelligere*]" (G II: 124). The prejudice Spinoza rejects is that ideas are mute, not that they are images, and the analogy to a picture on a tablet serves only to clarify muteness.

A picture on a panel or wall is mute in that by itself it does not express or represent a commitment to how things are. The picture is about something, that is, it has content; for example, a painting of a still life represents a wooden bowl on a bench containing grapes, apples, and slices of melon. In one respect even the picture involves an affirmation. The still life represents grapes inside a bowl and a bowl as being wooden and on a bench. Nevertheless, this painting does not represent that in fact there is such a wooden bowl containing such fruit. Consequently, the still life, by itself, is neither true nor false. The viewer may believe that this depicts a real state of affairs or not, but this representation is contributed by the viewer, not the picture.[6]

5. He also asserts without any effort that "it is hard to know what to make of this notion of resemblance between the idea and its object" (Curley 1975: 173). For Descartes, ideas do not resemble their objects in the way pictures resemble their objects. Instead, ideas are representations, and they represent in virtue of a mapping between ideas and their objects in the way numbers and algebraic equations represent geometrical proportions in Descartes's analytic geometry.

6. The painting can become true or false if it involves an affirmation that it depicts a matter of fact. For example, sometimes pictures come with titles that suggest that the picture depicts an event or person, and in this case the picture ceases to be mute.

If ideas are considered mute in the way a painting is usually mute, then it involves no affirmation or negation about what actually is the case, and the affirmation or negation must come from something external to the idea in the way that the affirmation that the picture represents the way things are usually comes from the viewer, not the picture itself. This is indeed how Descartes conceives of ideas in his first discussion of error in the Third Meditations. He writes that if ideas are "considered solely in themselves and I do not refer them to anything else, they cannot strictly speaking be false" (AT VII: 37). Descartes elaborates as follows:

And the chief and most common mistake which is to be found here consists in my judging that the ideas which are in me resemble, or conform to, things located outside me. Of course, if I considered just the ideas themselves simply as modes of my thought without referring them to anything else, they could scarcely give me any material for error. (Ibid.)

For an idea to be true or false, I need to refer the idea to what is the case, that is, I need to affirm it of what is the case. Only when this reference is made, does the idea become a belief or part of a mental assertion.

Being a representation of, say, a red ball already involves a kind of affirmation, namely, that the represented ball has the property of being red. However, on Descartes's view, the representation need not involve an affirmation of what is the case because a person can represent a red ball without affirming anything of what is or is not the case. If the representation is not supposed to be of what is the case, but of what might be the case, then it can be true even if in fact there is no red ball. If the representation is supposed to be of the object I desire, then it is true if a red ball is what I desire, and this again can be true even if there is no red ball. If the representation is simply supposed to be of a red ball, then again it is true even if in fact there is no red ball. All that matters in this case is that there is a representation that represents a red ball.

For Descartes, this additional affirmation is a volition. Given the representation, I decide that the representation is about what is the case or I decide that it is about only what might be the case. In some cases the representation is so clear and distinct that I cannot help but decide that it is about what is the case, but even then volition is involved. As we saw, for Spinoza, an idea already comes with an affirmation and needs no extra volition. Ideas already intrinsically involve an affirmation. Unfortunately, Spinoza does not distinguish between two different kinds of affirmation. In his argument that ideas already involve affirmation, he mentions only the affirmation involved when a property is attributed of an object. He writes that the thought that the idea of a triangle in the thought that three angles of a triangle are equal to two right angles already involves an "affirmation, viz. that its three angles equal two right angles" (G II: 130). He adds that you cannot conceive of a triangle without this affirmation.

A representation can affirm something of an object without affirming anything about what is the case. In Descartes's words, an idea I have can affirm a property of a triangle without this idea being referred to anything outside of me. What Spinoza needs to argue is that the intellect's ideas in and of themselves involve not only an attribution of a property, but an affirmation of what is the case. Only then can Spinoza maintain that ideas are already intrinsically belief-like or assertoric and are in need of no extra faculty or act that refers them to what is the case (Bennett 1984: 162–5). Although Spinoza does not explicitly argue this, it is clear that he had this in mind.

For Spinoza, affirmation about what is the case follows from the affirmation involved in attribution. Spinoza writes that the affirmation involved in attribution "pertains to the essence of the idea of the triangle" (G II: 130). However, for Spinoza everything is in God and nothing can be thought of without God (G II: 56/1P15), and consequently "when we say that the human Mind perceives this or that, we are saying nothing but that God . . . has this or that idea" (G II: 94–5/2P11C). But God's thinking agrees with the order of reality: "*All ideas, insofar as they are related to God, are true*" (G II: 116/2P32). It follows, Spinoza argues, that our "clear and distinct ideas are as true as that God's ideas are," and this is due to the fact that our minds are part of God's infinite intellect (G II: 125/2P43S). It follows for Spinoza that strictly speaking there are no false ideas. What happens is that we are confused because our minds lack some ideas that are in God's mind and that are necessary for clear understanding (G II: 117/2P35S).

For Spinoza it is the very nature of an idea to refer to objects and other entities external to the human mind. So if we have an idea of an object and our idea affirms something of that object, say, that it is red, then we are also affirming something about what is the case because ideas in virtue of their nature represent what is the case. It is part of their content that they are representing what is the case, and this makes all ideas belief-like in the sense of affirming in and of themselves something about what is the case. For Spinoza, ideas on their own "reach right out to reality, articulating it, affirming it" (Lloyd 1990: 121).

The source of this affirmation is God's own thinking. The affirmation and negation of an idea is simply the affirmation and negation of God's own thinking. God is a thinking thing and all individual thoughts are modes of God's thinking (G II: 86/2P1), and as we saw, the order and connection of God's ideas is the same as the order and connection of things. In fact, "a circle existing in nature," Spinoza writes, "and the idea of the existing circle, which is also in God, are one and the same thing" (G II: 90/2P7S). Thus, objects are real and propositions are true simply because God thinks of them (G II: 63/2P16S).[7] So the affirmation that constitutes ideas is, strictly speaking, not our affirmation, but an affirmation of the idea as it is given to us in virtue of the fact that God "constitutes [*constituit*] the essence of the human Mind" (G II: 95/2P11C). The ideas we have are ideas that involve the affirmation produced by God's thinking.

Nevertheless, as was noted in the preceding section, Spinoza argues in the *Ethics* that the mind is active and not passive (G II: 140/3P1). It acts simply in virtue of the fact that it has an essence or nature and some things follow from that nature. The nature of mind is constituted by its ideas, which are modes of God's thinking (G II: 93–96/2P10C–2P13). Some of these ideas are adequate while others are confused, but all of them are causally efficaceous. The adequate ideas of a human's mind are also in God in that God has an idea of that mind and all its ideas. But these adequate ideas in God's mind have effects in God's mind, and therefore, Spinoza maintains, they have effects in the human mind. Consequently, the human mind, insofar as it is constituted by adequate ideas, has causal effects.

The inadequate ideas a person has are also causally efficaceous, but only together with other ideas that the person lacks but that God has (G II: 140/3P1). Therefore, the inadequate ideas a person has

---

7. This is one of the reasons that, strictly speaking, God, as the cause of all things, does not have an intellect. Instead, all intellects are products of God's activity.

are causes only together with the objects of those other ideas God has, that is, objects external to that person's mind. In other words, the person is only a partial cause of these effects, and this, by definition, makes the person passive (G II: 139/3D2).

The crucial step in Spinoza's argument for the human mind's activity is this inference: "But if God, insofar as he is affected by an idea that is adequate in someone's Mind, is the cause of an effect, that same Mind is the effect's adequate cause" (by 2P11C). "Therefore," Spinoza continues, "our Mind (by D2), insofar it has adequate ideas, necessarily acts [*agit*]" (G II: 140). Spinoza argues that the human mind is a cause, and hence is active, in virtue of the fact that the human mind has ideas that God has and that are determined to have an effect by God. So my mind is causally efficaceous because it has an idea that God has and that has been determined by God to have an effect in God's mind. But why should it follow from the fact that an idea is causally efficaceous in God that it is causally efficaceous in my mind?

The answer is in the corollary of Proposition 11 to which Spinoza refers. Proposition 11 states that the human mind is constituted by the idea of an actually existing individual, which turns out to be the body. The corollary states that "the human Mind is part of [*partem*] the infinite intellect of God" (G II: 94/2P11C). The human mind is a proper part of God's intellect, and thus the properties ideas have in God's intellect are properties they have in our minds. God's infinite intellect is not God's attribute of thinking, which is an essence of God and thus *Natura naturans*, but it is nevertheless a mode of God's thinking and as such it is in God as a part is in the whole (G II: 56/1P15).[8] Finite human minds and the ideas that constitute them, in turn, are finite modes that are part of the infinite mode that is God's infinite intellect.

The finite modes that are part of God's infinite intellect are determined by God to have specific causal relations amongst each other. Thus the causal order of the ideas that constitute our minds is determined by God, not by us. On Spinoza's account, "the Mind . . . immediately passes" from one thought to another because the thoughts "are connected with one another, and so ordered that one follows

---

8. On the part/whole relation in Spinoza, see Wolfson (1958: I: 73–6, 323–8) and Sacksteder (1978).

the other" (G II: 191/3P59D4E). He writes that "each of us will pass from one thought to another," but this sequence of thoughts is not driven by us (G II: 107/2P18S). Our minds are detained or driven by our ideas and their causal powers, but this order is determined by God. We only participate, as proper parts, in a divinely determined order.

So, strictly speaking, it is not the case that there is a causal chain in which God produces human minds that in turn cause and order ideas. Spinoza's picture is one in which God is "an infinite logical crust which holds together the crumbs of the infinite number of the finite modes" (Wolfson 1958: 398). The infinite number of finite modes have their causal powers and are ordered causally as a consequence of God's thinking. Our minds do not make a contribution to this order. Our minds are only proper parts of the causally ordered ideas in God's infinite intellect, and the human mind's causal powers are limited to the causal powers of these ideas. The causal powers of these ideas, in turn, rest not on any powers the mind has, but completely on the nature of God's thinking. Thus in the *Ethics* Spinoza preserves and elaborates the view of the *Short Treatise* that "it is never we who affirm or deny something of the thing" (G I: 83).

We do not judge, but the judgments are made for us by God in God's intellect. We participate in this judgment only in virtue of the fact that we are part of God. On this view individual minds are active only in the way that sometimes citizens are said to do things in virtue of what the states do of which they are a part. An individual citizen is said to be at war with a neighbor because her nation is at war simply in virtue of the fact that the citizen is a part of that nation. But strictly speaking it is not the citizen that is at war or peace, but the nation. In the same way, Spinoza was right to maintain that on his view we do not affirm or deny anything, and this remains true of his views in the *Ethics*. In the *Ethics*, to understand is to act (G II: 188/3P58), but understanding is not our achievement. It is something that happens to us simply by virtue of our being proper parts of God.

Vacillation and Resolution

Although Spinoza denies that volition plays a special role in our judgments, it would be false to conclude that for Spinoza cognition proceeds without any contribution from conation. Spinoza's concept of cognition in the *Ethics* is conative (Lloyd 1990). Although for Spinoza the first thing that constitutes a human mind is an idea, and ideas are distinct from and prior to other modes of thinking, such as love and desire, nevertheless the idea necessarily comes with the other modes. When the idea that constitutes a human mind "is given, the other modes (to which the idea is prior in nature) must be in the same individual" (G II: 94/2P11).

In fact, for Spinoza "desire is man's very essence," and desire comprises "any of a man's strivings, impulses, appetites, and volitions" (G II: 190/3P59D1). Since a volition is nothing but the affirmation and denial that is part of an idea, an idea must come with desire.[9] This already follows from Spinoza's claims that *"each thing, as far as it can by its own power, strives [conatur] to persevere in its being"* and that an object's striving is its actual essence (G II: 146/3P6–7). Since minds are constituted by their adequate and inadequate ideas, a mind will strive to persevere by having these ideas (G II: 147/3P9).

Spinoza writes that "the first thing that constitutes the essence of [a human] Mind is the idea of an actually existing Body," and hence the striving must belong to this idea that constitutes the mind. This idea of the body that constitutes the mind strives "to affirm the existence of our Body" (G II: 148/3P10). In other words, the idea that first constitutes, say, my mind is an idea with the propositional content that I have a body, and the affirmation of my body is itself a manifestation of my mind's desire to persevere. As soon as the mind ceases to affirm the present existence of the body, the mind ceases to exist (G II: 149/3P11S). Moreover, the mind's power of thinking is a function of the ideas it has about the power of the body. An idea that enhances or diminishes the body's power enhances or diminishes the mind's power (G II: 148/3P11).

In desiring to persevere, the "Mind strives to imagine only those things that posit its power of acting," and these things bring it joy because they enhance the mind's perfection (G II: 181–2/3P53–54). The mind's desires also determine what it judges to be good, that is,

---

9. This seems to conflict with Spinoza's earlier claim in Part 2 that "there can be an idea, even though there is no other mode of thinking" (G II: 86/2A3). If a volition is a desire and an idea's affirmation or denial is a volition, then there can be no idea without desire unless there can be ideas without affirmation or denial.

useful to us (G II: 209/4D1), and not the other way around (G II: 148/3P9S). Sometimes, however, the mind imagines its own lack of power. It imagines that it is passive in that it is acted upon by something that restrains its power, and this is the cause of sadness (G II: 182/3P55). Since the mind is active only insofar as it has adequate ideas and passive only insofar as it has inadequate ideas, the mind strives to have adequate ideas and the joy that comes with its own activity, and it strives to avoid or destroy inadequate ideas and the sadness that comes with them (G II: 161–2/3P28).

For Spinoza, as for other 17th-century philosophers, irresolution is one of the mind's defects that needs to be treated. He already discussed irresolution in the *Short Treatise*, and in the *Ethics* a key discussion occurs in Spinoza's response to an objection to his identification of will and intellect in the scholium to Proposition 49 of Part 2. Spinoza responds to four objections, and the last one appeals to the apparent fact that through an act of will we can resolve irresolution (G II: 133/2P49S). Sometimes we are in a state of equilibrium between two incompatible ideas and we upset the balance simply by deciding to affirm one of the ideas. Spinoza illustrates the objection with a version of Buridan's ass. The ass, who is thirsty and hungry, must decide between walking to food or walking to water. But the food and water are equally distant from him, and so the ass is infected with indecision. As a result of this indecision, the ass dies of hunger and thirst. If someone were to act like the ass and perish, that would be reason enough to deny that she is rational. But if she resolves the impasse by simply making a decision, then this shows that there is a volition distinct from the intellect, and in fact a person can resolve irresolution by an act of will.

Spinoza's reply is short:

I grant that entirely that a man placed in such an equilibrium . . . will perish of hunger and thirst. If they ask me whether such a man should not be thought an ass, rather than a man, I say that I do not know – just as I do not know how highly we should esteem one who hangs himself, or children, fools, and madmen, etc. (G II: 135/2P49S).

Spinoza's use of Buridan's ass is a bit confusing because the situation Spinoza wishes to illustrate is one in which we are undecided about what to affirm, that is, a case of doubt, while Buridan's ass as described by Spinoza is a case of conflicting desires. However, Spinoza distinguishes between the two situations. Doubt for Spinoza is vacillation of the imagination (*fluctuatio imaginationis*) (G II: 153/3P17S and G II: 125–6/2P44S). A desire, along with joy and sadness, is one of the three primitive or primary affects (G II: 192/3P59D4),[10] and "this *constitution of the Mind which arises from two contrary affects* is called *vacillation of the mind* [*fluctuatio animi*]" (G II: 153/3P17S). The reason Spinoza conflates the two in his example is because for him vacillation of the mind and doubt do not differ except in degree of strength (G II: 153/3P17S).

The crucial feature of Spinoza's response is that he offers no remedy to vacillation. If our minds end in a debilitating logjam of opinions or affects, there is nothing that we can do about it. If the intellect really is in such a state of equilibrium, it will remain in it and perish unless it gets more information or new desires to end the logjam. There is nothing we can do, once in such a debilitating situation, to pull ourselves out of it and reach greater perfection. This also means that Spinoza offers no way to escape the sadness that must come with vacillation, which restrains the mind's power of thinking and as such is a source of sadness (G II: 182/3P55).

In general, for Spinoza "the Mind's knowledge alone" is a remedy for the problematic affects (G II: 280). In the *Ethics* as well as his earlier works, the general remedy Spinoza offers for the mind's defects is reflection and letting one's intellectual powers run their determined course. Spinoza suggests that "*if we separate emotions or affect from the thought of the external cause of the affect, and join them to other thoughts*," we will be able to destroy the affects, including vacillation of the mind (G II: 281–2/5P2). But this is really a preventive measure rather than a cure. Intellectual inquiry depends on us not being torn by the passive affects, which must include vacillation of the mind (G II: 287/5P10). The mind must have "the power of forming clear and distinct ideas, and of deducing some from others" if it is to overcome the mind's defects, but this is precisely the power that vacillation undermines.

---

10. For Spinoza, affects can be actions as well as passions (G II: 139/3D3). If we are the adequate cause of the affect, it is an action. An example of this is joy that is caused by the acquisition of knowledge or desire that arises from reason (G II: 256/4P61). If the cause of joy is external to us, which for Spinoza means that we have an inadequate idea of the joy, it is a passion. So joy caused by the presence of a loved one, for instance, is a passion (G II: 151/3P13S).

For example, Spinoza maintains that the best way to avoid the mind's defects, all of which restrain the mind's activity, is to relate all our ideas to our idea of God (G II: 290/5P14). Our understanding of God will generate the love of God, which promotes the mind's own activity (G II: 290/5P15). But to do this we must already have adequate ideas (G II: 282/5P4), and this is precisely what an irresolute mind lacks. Thus relating our ideas to the idea of God prevents vacillation, but it is not a cure.

Spinoza is fully aware of the fact that he is really not offering any cures in the *Ethics*. Spinoza announces in the introduction to his last section, "*On the Power of the Intellect*, or, *on Human Freedom*," that he will not discuss "*how the intellect must be perfected . . . so that it can perform its function properly*" (G II: 277). His discussion is limited to "the power of the Mind, or of reason" over the affects. In other words, it is not about how to get oneself in such a state that would allow the mind to exercise its power, but simply about the power the mind has. If the problem is that one is in a state in which the power of the mind is restrained by defects, for example, vacillation of mind or doubt, then Spinoza has no remedy to offer.

All that one can do is trust that one's vacillating ideas are such that this vacillation is just a stage in a longer sequence of thoughts that eventually leads to resolution. An example of this would be if we come to have an appetite for one of the contrary alternatives over the other. For Spinoza, this would be a case in which a decision puts an end to irresolution, because for him "decisions of the Mind [*Mentis decreta*] are nothing but appetites themselves" (G II: 143/3P2S).[11] But since appetites are not something over which we have control, this is really not a decision we make. By equating decisions and appetites, for Spinoza there cannot be a decision in favor of one of the alternatives in the absence of an appetite for it.

---

11. An appetite, however, is nothing but the essence of a human being from which "necessarily follow those things which promote his preservation" (G II: 147/3P9S). An appetite, then, just is the striving (*conatus*) for self-preservation that, as we have seen, defines everything. In his Definition of the Affects, Spinoza defines "desire" in very similar terms, but he abstracts desire from self-preservation: "Desire is man's very essence, insofar as it is conceived to be determined, from any given affection of it, to do something" (G II: 190/3P59D1). So for Spinoza any state of an object that determines the object to behave in certain ways, for example, to behave in ways that promote its preservation, is an appetite (Bennett 1984: 222).

Thus Spinoza cannot even admit of a case in which our desire for having a resolute mind makes us decide for one alternative over another even though we are not blessed with an appetite that favors one side over the other. If you are not graced by a resolute mind, there is nothing you can do about it and the sadness that must accompany irresolution. At best you can hope that your present vacillation will lead to mental resolution. However, there is nothing you can do to bring about the realization of this hope. Whether or not this hope will be realized is determined by the nature of the ideas given to you and the laws that determined their order, not by your own voluntary activity.

Conviction and Speech

Spinoza summarizes his doctrine about the will and the intellect as follows: "It teaches that we act only from God's command, that we share in the divine nature, and that we do this the more, the more perfect our actions are, and the more we understand God" (G II: 135/2P49S). This knowledge gives us "complete peace of mind" and it shows us that our "greatest happiness, *or* blessedness" consists in "the knowledge of God alone, by which we are led to do only those things which love and morality advise" (G II: 135–6/2P49S). This doctrine also "teaches how citizens are to be governed and led, not so that they may be slaves, but that they may do freely the things that are best" (G II: 136). By recognizing that through our inner conviction we are God's slaves, we recognize that we are free from bondage to other human beings. Inner conviction, then, sets us free.

This underlies Spinoza's position on freedom of speech. In the *Theologico-Political Treatise* Spinoza announces that he will show that the state authorities have the "right to decide what is just, what unjust, what pious, what impious," but "that they can best retain this right and safeguard dominion if everyone is allowed to think what he wants and say what he thinks" (G III: 11–12). Spinoza's argument is that by our very nature we cannot transfer our right to think and speak to another person, and consequently rulers cannot demand that we speak or think in a certain way.

Nobody "can willingly transfer his natural right of free reason and judgment, or be compelled to do so." A person cannot abdicate his right to accept what is true and reject what is false "even with his own consent" (G III: 239). The reason this right cannot be transferred is that the mental states we have "necessarily follow from the laws of human nature" (G III: 201). You cannot "prevent people from forming judgments according to their intellect, or being influenced by any given emotion" and "every man is by the most highest natural law the master of his own thoughts" (G III: 240). Spinoza's language clearly indicates that this is a psychological fact about human beings, and rulers endanger their ability to rule if they ignore this fact and try to exercise their absolute sovereignty to the point that they try to command what people should think. Although in this context Spinoza does not elaborate on his views about the psychology of judgment, it is obvious that what underlies his views here is his view about the involuntary nature of judgment. The power we have to make judgments cannot be transferred to the control of another, even if we were to consent to do that, because judging is not under our own voluntary control. We are impelled to make judgments according to how the ideas are in our intellect.

Spinoza makes equally strong modal claims about speech in this theological and political treatise. He writes: "it is impossible to deprive people of the liberty of saying what they think" (G III: 246), and "it is far from possible to impose uniformity of speech" (G III: 243). Rulers can enact laws that prohibit people from expressing certain opinions, but "those who hold that the opinions proscribed are sound, cannot possibly obey the law" (G III: 244). For Spinoza, the fact that speech cannot be curtailed follows from his views about belief:

Since, therefore, no one can abdicate his freedom of judgment and emotion, ... it follows that people thinking in diverse and contradictory fashions, cannot, without disasterous perils, be compelled to speak only according to the dictates of the supreme power. Not even the most experienced, to say nothing of the multitude, know how to keep silence. (G III: 240)

Again, this appears to be a psychological fact, and Spinoza does not elaborate on why this is true here.

Fortunately, Spinoza repeats his claim about speech in the preface to Part 3 of the *Ethics*, where Spinoza considers human emotions and actions as facts of nature and treats them "as though [he] were concerned with lines, planes and solids" (G II: 138).

He writes in the *Ethics*: "Experience abundantly shows that men can govern anything more easily than their tongues," and illustrates this a little later:

a drunken man believes that he utters from the free decision of his mind words which, when he is sober, he would willingly have withheld: thus, too, a delirious man, a garrulous woman, a child, and others of like complexion, believe that they speak from the free decision of their mind, when they are in reality unable to restrain their impulse to talk (G II: 143/3P2S).

These comments appear in a note to a proof that aims to show that whatever happens in the body is caused by other bodily states, not by states of the mind, and the note begins with the claim that "mind and body are one and the same individual which is conceived now under the attribute of thought and now under the attribute of extension" (G II: 109/3P2S). Consequently, it is appropriate to understand Spinoza's claims about how we are impelled to speak in terms of his views on the mind-body problem.

As is well known, Spinoza rejects Descartes's dualism and treats the mind and the body in a more unified fashion. Mental and physical properties, that is, in Spinoza's terminology, thought and extension, are different, but they are two different aspects or attributes of the same substance. Unlike Descartes, Spinoza did not believe that there was anything contradictory about supposing that the same thing can think and be extended (G II: 90/2P7S), and in fact, as we just saw, for Spinoza the human mind and body are one and the same thing.

Moreover, according to Spinoza, the mind is constituted by the idea of its body (G II: 96/2P13), and consequently, *"the mind does not know itself, except in so far as it perceives the ideas of the modifications of the body"* (G II: 110/2P23). He further believes that when the mind contemplates itself and its powers, it feels pleasure, and, as he writes in Part 3 of the *Ethics*, it endeavors to contemplate "only such things that assert or affirm its power of activity" (G II: 181–2/3P53 and 54). One of its powers is the power of the understanding to affirm or deny propositions in accordance with the clarity of the intellect's ideas, so this is something that the mind seeks to contemplate. Since it can know itself only by having an idea of its body, this means that the mind's endeavor to know itself must come with ideas of the body that match the mind's contemplation of its power to affirm and deny propositions. Although Spinoza does not make this explicit, an obvious case of this is the mind's perceptions of its body speaking or writing the propositions that the mind affirms or denies.

Of course, for Spinoza, our speaking or writing – bodily actions – are not caused by the mind's convictions. However, "the endeavour of the mind, or the mind's power of thought, is equal to, and simultaneous with, the endeavour of the body's power of action" (G II: 113/3P28D), and "*whatsoever increases or diminishes, helps or hinders the power of activity in our body, the idea thereof increases, diminishes, helps or hinders the power of thought in our mind*" (G II: 94/3P11). This is an elaboration of Spinoza's more general view that the body's states and activities are physical aspects of its mental states and activities. So when the mind endeavors to affirm or deny a proposition, this will be accompanied by a physical aspect, namely, the body's endeavor to make statements. Moreover, whatever will diminish the body's power of speech will diminish the mind's power of thought, and this is the cause of pain (G II: 95/3P11S and G II: 182/3P55).

So we are impelled to speak in accord with our inner convictions, and it is on account of this tight relation between conviction and bodily activity that, it seems to me, Spinoza believed that rulers court disaster when they try to keep people from speaking what they have on their minds.

Spinoza, who not only was a son of former Marranos in exile in Amsterdam but was banished from his synagogue for his convictions, knew first-hand about the conflict between inner beliefs and external authority (Yovel 1989), and he, along with the religious enthusiasts, resolved this conflict in favor of conviction and at the expense of state authority. This commitment to liberty is in stark contrast to Hobbes's authoritarian recommendation that external political authority trump inner conviction not just in religious matters (L 3.32/410), but in other matters as well. In all matters of controversy, including those about "right, policy, and natural sciences," Hobbes writes in *De Cive* (2: 268–9), it is up to the civil authorities to decide who is right according to what is politically expedient (Watkins 1965: 110 and 129–31; Tuck 1987, 1989; Popkin 1992: 9–49).

While Hobbes enslaves the citizen to a human sovereign at the expense of one's service to inner conviction, Spinoza frees the citizen from bondage to human sovereigns by enslaving him to the divinely inspired voice of inner conviction. Unfortunately, Spinoza's liberty is limited to those with resolute minds, and it appears that he has nothing to say for those that have little or no inner conviction. For them Spinoza offers nothing better than the fate of Buridan's ass, and, as we saw in the previous section, the esteem that belongs to "one who hangs himself, or children, fools, and madmen." These people must remain in bondage. Inner conviction, and the liberation that comes with inner conviction, is, for Spinoza, not something we can achieve through our own efforts. If we are fortunate, we already are or eventually will be liberated by the divinely established order of the thoughts we have. But the unlucky rest can do nothing to liberate themselves.

This is especially problematic in light of the fact that disagreement causes vacillation (G II: 164/3P31). Although Spinoza maintains that rulers court disaster when they try to regulate speech, he does not address the fact that by opposing what an individual believes they weaken the mind by causing vacillation. If one's convictions are strong, this vacillation will be overcome, but if not, rulers can successfully impose opinions by limiting speech. Spinoza has nothing to offer that strengthens subjects and gives them the means for overcoming vacillation caused by ruling opinion. We need to turn to Leibniz to find such means to independence and enlightenment for those who lack conviction.

7

Leibniz: Trained Thinking

Will and Judgment

Characteristically, Leibniz finds a way to resolve the difference
between those who maintain that sometimes beliefs can be acquired
at will and those who deny it. In his "animadversions" on Descartes's
Principles (GP IV: 354–406), Leibniz rejects Descartes's view that judgments are a product of will. He writes that "we make judgments not
because we will but because something appears" to the intellect (GP
IV: 361/L 387). Even the care we exercise in our reasoning and our
exhortations to ourselves such as "Watch out what you are doing. Why
are you doing it? Time is passing" are not "in our power or the choice
of our will" (GP IV: 362/L 388). They are neither voluntary nor free,
but simply occur to the intellect without a direct contribution of the
will. More generally, for Leibniz, human ideas are not formed because
human beings will to have them; they form themselves "within us"
and "through us . . . in accordance with our nature and that of things"
(GP VI: 356/Th 364).

Whether or not something will occur to the intellect "depends on
the present degree of perfection," but for Leibniz our present nature
can be a product of earlier voluntary actions. He writes:

It is the business of the will to strive beforehand with all zeal, to prepare the
mind in advance. This can be done usually, partly through the contemplation of the experience of others, . . . partly by the use of our own experience,
. . . and partly also by training the mind to follow a definite series and method
when thinking, so that later the required attitude offers itself spontaneously.
(GP IV: 362/L 388; also see GP III: 400–4/AG 195)

In other words, the will contributes to judgment "obliquely" (GP IV:
357/L 385). A clear case of this is when people accustom "the mind

to attend most strongly to the things which they favor" and thus "come to believe what they will to be true." They willfully "command attention and exertion" toward the evidence that supports the desired belief (GP IV: 356–7/L 385). According to Leibniz, you can even come to believe your own lies and inventions by repeating the story often enough because "strong and oft-repeated impressions may alter considerably our organs, our imagination, our memory, and even our reasoning" (GP VI: 430/Th 435).

The distinction between direct and indirect contributions of the will to cognition appears again in Leibniz's commentary on Locke in the *New Essays Concerning Human Understanding.* In response to Locke's views on the role of volition in judgment, Leibniz denies that it is "within our power or our free will to believe or not to believe" (NE 359). However, even though "we cannot judge what we want to, we can nevertheless act ahead of time in such a way that we shall even-tually judge . . . what we would like to be able to judge . . . today. We attach ourselves to people, reading material and ways of thinking which are favorable to a certain faction; and we ignore whatever come from the opposite faction" (NE 182). By these means "and countless other devices . . . we succeed in deceiving ourselves or at least chang-ing our minds, and so we achieve our own conversion or perversion depending on what our experience has been." Thus for Leibniz, "opinions are voluntary only in an indirect way" and a person "is not responsible for having this or that opinion at the present time," but she "is responsible for taking steps to have it or not have it later on" (NE 456).

If the steps that lead to a certain opinion can be voluntary, then some mental activity will be voluntary and the will is not always "acting at a distance" with respect to cognition.[1] Leibniz endorses this. He believes that volition is a conscious "effort or endeavour [*conatus*] to move towards what one finds good and away from what one finds bad" and this endeavor is produced "immediately" by one's awareness of those things (NE 172). Volition together with power, namely, the ability to do what one wills, results in action, and for Leibniz there can be "voluntary inner acts of our minds which follow from this *conatus*" as well as "outer ones," that is, "voluntary movements of our bodies" (NE 173).

---

1. Cf. Bennett (1984: 160).

In his critical discussion of Descartes's *Principles* Leibniz also maintains that there are voluntary mental acts. He writes that "it is beyond our power to know or to remember all that we will" (G 4: 362/L 388), suggesting that some things are within our power to know or to remember at will. What we know or remember is sometimes a function of how we direct our attention and how hard we try, and as we just saw, for Leibniz these can also be voluntary. He writes: "This one thing we recognize to be within the power of the will – to command attention and exertion" (GP IV: 356–7/L 385). Thus, once it occurs to us spontaneously as a result of prior voluntary mental training to pay attention to what we are doing we still need to act on our own exhortations and exert effort, perhaps to overcome laziness, to pay attention and try harder. For instance, trying to remember a theorem for a deduction and attending to the components of a theorem can be voluntary acts, even when we do not always succeed in remembering or paying attention due to factors beyond our voluntary control.

So although beliefs are not under our direct voluntary control, we can nevertheless voluntarily control our mental attention and effort, and these will play a role in the training of our minds.

The Public Use of Reason

According to Leibniz, one of the ways in which we can indirectly acquire beliefs is "by training [*assuefactione*] the mind to follow a definite series and method when thinking, so that later the required attitude offers itself spontaneously" (GP IV: 362/L 388). A paradigm case of this is the manipulation of physical symbols.

Leibniz is committed to the view that public symbols, including natural languages, play an important role in human reasoning.[2] They are not only used to convey our opinions to other people, but, Leibniz writes, they "aid our own thinking," especially when we are engaged in a complex piece of reasoning (Gu II: 450). In such cases we rely on language in our own internal thinking by thinking about words rather than the objects about which we are reasoning. We can use words as mnemonic devices and we can also use them to draw inferences and discover and verify propositions (NE 335). In fact,

2. See Heinekamp (1972), Dascal (1978, 1987), and Rutherford (1995a).

without symbols difficult reasoning would be impossible (GP VII: 19 and 204), and Leibniz even suggests, echoing Hobbes, that "all our reasoning [*omnis Rationacio nostra*]" is nothing but connecting and substituting characters" (GP VII: 31). Of course, when we rely on symbols without the appropriate internal ideas, our thinking is "*blind or symbolic*" (GP IV: 423). But it is significant that Leibniz calls it a kind of thinking, and that he affirms that this sort of thinking occurs not only in algebra and arithmetic, but "almost everywhere" (GP IV: 423).

Leibniz does not consider all symbol systems to be equally useful. Due to the ambiguity of the symbols of natural language, they are only of limited help to our reasoning (GP VII: 205). Part of the problem is that the simple terms of natural languages signify sensations or perceptions that are both confused and complex (C 360). Thus Leibniz devotes a good part of his adult life, beginning with his dissertation *The Art of Combinations* (written when he was nineteen), to developing a "universal characteristic" or formal symbol system in which "there will be no equivocations or amphibolies, and everything which will be said intelligibly will be said properly" (C 156–7). The underlying idea was that concepts as well as objects are either simple or combinations of simple parts, and the universal characteristic would have the same kind of constituent structure as belongs to ideas. Moreover, the universal characteristic would consist of substitution rules that would govern the transition from expression to expression (C 326).[3]

The use of this characteristic will improve our reasoning because it will improve our capacity to discover truths and justify our judgments. "Truths themselves," Leibniz writes, "would appear successively on paper through the mere analysis of *characters*, that is, through orderly and uninterrupted substitution" (C 352; Dascal 1987: 161). The obvious application for such a calculus is in mathematics, but Leibniz believed such a calculus would have wider applications. He writes:

I necessarily arrived at this remarkable thought, namely, that a kind of alphabet of human thought can be worked out and that everything can be discovered and judged by a comparison of the letters of this alphabet and an analysis of the words made from them. (GP VII: 186/L 222)

---

3. "*Characteristica omnis consistit in formatione Expressionis et transitu ab Expressione ad Expressionem.*"

In this language, errors would manifest themselves as syntactical errors, that is, as violations of the rules governing the formation of the expressions of this language (GP VII: 205).

Such a formal calculus will be a "thread of meditation," namely, a sensible and mechanical direction for the mind so that "even the most stupid will assent to it," Leibniz writes in a letter in 1673 to the secretary of the English Royal Society, Heinrich Oldenburg (A II.1: 241). In a letter to Walter von Tschirnhaus five years later Leibniz again describes the universal characteristic as a "mechanical thread of meditation" (A II.1: 413/GM IV: 453–4/L 193).[4] By means of this calculus our thoughts can be "fixed, abridged, and ordered." Moreover, with the aid of such a mechanical thread of meditation the simpler ideas out of which complex ideas are formed "will at once come to mind." He continues:

Since the analysis of concepts thus corresponds exactly to the analysis of a character, we need merely to see the characters in order to have adequate notions brought to our mind freely and without effort. (A II.1: 413/L 193)

By manipulating an appropriate symbol system we can bring it about that we have before us certain symbols that will "freely and without effort" cause us to have the appropriate thoughts. In this manner we contribute voluntarily, albeit indirectly, to the "perfection of the mind" (A II.1: 413/L 193).

Leibniz recognizes that such a physical guide for improving our thinking is precisely what was missing from Spinoza's *On the Improvement of the Intellect.* According to Leibniz, Spinoza "stopped where I most expected something" (A II.1: 414/L 194). What Leibniz expected is some aid to the human understanding that would allow it to discover truths, justify beliefs, and resolve conflicts of opinion. Leibniz believed that he in fact offers what was missing in Spinoza, namely, his universal characteristic, which he believes will be the greatest aid for improving the human understanding that human beings can hope for (A II.1: 414/L 193). For one thing, such a symbol system will help us resolve conflicting opinions, especially those conflicts where we ourselves cannot decide who is right and "balance the

4. For other places where Leibniz discusses a thread of meditation, see A II.1: 247, 381, 384, and 437.

various inclinations of our own minds" (GP VII: 188/L 224). In short, it will be a remedy for irresolution.[5]

It is noteworthy that Leibniz describes thinking that relies on a mechanical thread as thinking that depends on external circumstances. He does this in connection with a declaration of his "high regard" for problems that can be solved "by mental powers alone" and "without pen and paper." The solutions to these problems "depend as little as possible on external circumstances, being within the power even of a captive who is denied a pen and whose hands are tied" (A II.1: 414/L 194). Accordingly, he recommends that when we have demonstrated propositions with the aid of symbol manipulation, "we ought to try afterward to demonstrate them by meditation alone" (ibid.). Although this cannot always be done, Leibniz writes that he has often been successful at this.

Reason and Divine Illumination

So, for Leibniz, what will truly improve the mind and be a remedy for its problems such as irresolution is a mechanical procedure for manipulating a public symbol system. In this way we will guide our thoughts either in the form of blind thoughts or by using the symbol manipulations to guide our inner thoughts. By applying the mechanical thread of meditation, bodily motion and volition also come to have a rightful place in cognition. We manipulate symbols in order to fix our beliefs and settle our minds on what is true, and we do this by making the bodily motions appropriate to symbol manipulation.

Thus in Leibniz's philosophy of mind we find an alternative to Spinoza's conception of a spiritual automaton. Spinoza's spiritual automaton was driven by inspiration without any input from deliberate voluntary activity. Spinoza's only task was to get into the right frame of mind where the mind is automatically moved from true idea to true idea, but Spinoza had nothing to say about how we get into this frame of mind. Leibniz, on the other hand, suggests that we can make a symbol system that can be a "thread of meditation" so that we

---

5. Tschirnhaus later develops the idea that such a formal calculus is medicine for the mind and all its ailments in his *Medicina Mentis* (1687).

do not have to rely only on inspiration to achieve a resolute mind fixed on truth.

This universal characteristic was supposed to have many of the features that the Enthusiasts were looking for in the divinely inspired language of nature.[6] Leibniz himself writes that his attempt to develop an unambiguous universal language in which some of the physical or formal features of the language (in this case the very structure of its signs) reflect its semantic properties, namely, that they represent essential properties of the things themselves, was an attempt to *construct* what the Enthusiasts thought could be discovered in nature (GP VII: 184–5 and GM IV: 452ff/L 193–4).[7] However, the universal characteristic lacked the essential Enthusiastic feature. It was not inspired, but established by the "wise arbitrary imposition" worthy of human beings (NE 281).

Nevertheless, Leibniz did not leave out inspiration from his picture of the human mind.[8] If we look closer at what is needed for the construction of a universal characteristic, we see that the voluntary making of this artificial characteristic still rests on some divine inspiration.

Jean François Courtine has observed that in the following passage Leibniz distinguishes two ways in which Adam's language of nature could have originated:

Concerning the first-born language used by the first man, some think it was instituted by God's design, others, that it was invented by Adam, a man illuminated by divine inspiration when he gave the names to the animals. (C 151)[9]

Adam's language was either given to Adam by God or it was created by Adam, but with the help of divine illumination. Courtine argues that Leibniz's attempt to develop a universal language was an attempt to create a language as Adam did according to the second view. The universal characteristic was invented, but with divine illumination.

---

6. Couturat (1901: 77), Walker (1972), Coudert (1978), Courtine (1980), Aarsleff (1982: 42–83), and Losonsky (1992).
7. See Courtine (1980: 376).
8. On the role of divine illumination in human cognition, see Adams (1994) and Losonsky (1992).
9. Leibniz's original text is as follows: "*Primigeniam ortam protoplastis usurpatam, quiddam fluxisse putant ab insitituto DEI, alii ab Adamo, viro divinitus illustrato excogitatam, tunc cum nomina animalibus impossuisse traditur.*"

Leibniz indeed locates divine illumination in the human understanding. The universal characteristic was supposed to be constructed by resolving complex ideas into their simple parts, and assigning characters to these simple primitive ideas so that the constitution of the complex ideas would be reflected in the constitution of their complex characters (GP VII: 205ff; and GM IV: 452ff). The success of the construction of the universal characteristic depends on our ability to recognize our ideas, particularly on our ability to clearly distinguish our ideas. But our ideas, which need to be distinguished from our thought about or awareness of them, are produced by God in us even before we think of them, and God determines when we think of them (GP IV: 453 and NE 300). Thus it is not an exaggeration for Leibniz to say that human knowledge just is an emanation of the light of God (GP III: 660 and Gu I: 410–11).

Moreover, not only are our ideas produced by God, but they have something in common with God's ideas: "God has ideas of substances before creating the object of the ideas, and there is nothing to prevent him from passing such ideas to intelligent creatures" (NE 296). However, the ideas in our minds are not identical to the ideas in God's mind (GP IV: 453/sec. 29). Instead, God's ideas are the archetypes for our ideas: "all ideas of the intellect have their archetypes in the eternal possibility of things" (NE 392), namely, the divine understanding. What God's ideas and the ideas in our intellect have in common are patterns or relationships: "although his ideas are infinitely more perfect and extensive than ours they still have the same relationships that ours do" (NE 397). Leibniz has in mind the logical relations ideas have to each other as well as the internal, constituent structure of ideas.[10]

This structure and order of ideas is "common to angels and men and to intelligences in general" (NE 276), and it is "always the same" (NE 412). In fact, "it is something we have in common with God"

---

10. One of the exciting moments in the *New Essays* is Leibniz's criticism of Locke for not recognizing that particles (that is, syncategorematic words such as the copula "is" or the negation "not") "connect not only . . . propositions . . . , and the component ideas of a proposition, *but also the parts of an idea* made up of other ideas variously combined" (NE 330; my emphasis). Leibniz adds, anticipating Kant, that particles should be studied in "greater detail, for nothing would be more apt to reveal the various forms of the understanding" (NE 330). On other anticipations of Kant in Leibniz, see Wilson (1977).

(NE 397). Although our ideas are distinct from God's, they nevertheless exhibit structures or relationships identical to God's ideas.[11] This is why Leibniz can write, "when God displays a truth to us," namely, a relationship of ideas (NE 357, 375 and 396), "we come to possess the truth which is in his understanding" (NE 397).[12]

Consequently, the order of our ideas is a natural order (NE 276; also 85 and 301). Their order is not "instituted or voluntary" but given to human beings (NE 249). The order of our ideas is not subject to our control: "it is not within our discretion to put our ideas together as we see fit" (NE 294). When Locke writes that we choose to make our complex ideas of mixed modes while our simple ideas are given to us, Leibniz responds:

If you take ideas to be actual thoughts, you are right. But I see no need to apply your distinction in connection with the very form or possibility of those thoughts; and that is what we are concerned with when we separate off the ideal world from the existent world. (NE 301)

This ideal world is the realm of ideas, and since for Leibniz "an idea is real . . . if it is possible" (NE 263; also 265, 269 and 398), the realm of ideas is the realm of "possibilities and necessities" (NE 301). However, what is possible is not within our discretion: "possibilities . . . are independent of our thinking" (NE 293). The order of this realm of possibility, which is ultimately subject only to the laws of

---

11. To Arnauld, Leibniz writes that created substances are made "according to the same designs [*desseins*]" (GP II: 57). These "designs" are not simply God's plans or intentions, but "laws of the general order of [a] possible world . . . as well as the concepts of all the individual substances which must enter into this same universe" (GP II: 51). That our thoughts share a structure with reality is also suggested by Leibniz (1677) in the "Dialogue on the Connection between Things and Words" (GP VII: 190–3/L 182–5).

12. I reject the received view that Leibniz was a nominalist; e.g., see Martin (1964), Mates (1986), and Jolley (1990). Jolley claims that "divine illumination is out of place in Leibniz's system, for it has no real work to do within the nominalist framework" (10). Suffice it to say here that when Jolley maintains that for Leibniz "ideas are psychological items, not abstract or logical entities" (135), he is saying something true, but only partly true. Ideas are psychological entities with abstract properties: structure and order, and this is what we share with God's ideas. Moreover, neither Leibniz's denial of the independent existence of abstract entities (Gr II: 547) nor his claim that individuals are fundamentally real (e.g., GP IV: 147, 158; or NE 323), entails the denial of the reality of universals properly understood, namely, as common structures that cannot exist apart from individual substances.

identity and noncontradiction, is something that human beings cannot make but can only discover, exhibit by formal demonstration, and express with a universal characteristic.[13] So, Leibniz's universal characteristic rests on a naturally ordered and innate realm of ideas, and this is the divine inspiration that allows human beings to construct a universal characteristic that can in turn be used to guide our thinking with these ideas.

Mind and Endeavour

The inspired ideas of the human mind are not passive; they are striving entities that produce activity. Leibniz writes that "in the case of souls everything is to be explained in vital terms" (C 12), and consequently Leibniz's picture shares with Hobbes and Locke the view that thinking itself is a dynamic process driven by a kind of desire.[14]

For Leibniz, ideas are dispositions to produce perceptions or thoughts in the appropriate circumstances. He writes:

That the ideas of things are in us means therefore nothing but that God, the author alike of things and of mind, has impressed a power of thinking upon the mind so that it can by its own operations derive what corresponds perfectly to the nature of things. (GP VII: 264/L 208)

Of course, we do not have the power to have a particular thought at any time whatsoever; rather, we have the power to think of it in the appropriate circumstances (GP VII: 263/L 207). Leibniz makes this point in many places, especially in his defense of innate ideas in the New Essays (NE 52 and 80; Kulstad 1983). However, Leibniz also rejects pure dispositions and bare powers: "True powers are never simple possibilities; there is always endeavour and action" (NE 112).[15] Ideas as dispositions must belong to something active.

This dynamic conception of the mental pervades Leibniz's whole philosophy. Consider his account of basic substances or monads in the Monadology (GP VI: 607–23). Monads must change, and these changes must proceed from an internal principle (principe interne).

---

13. Heinekamp (1976: 536 and 560). Also see M. Wilson (1967).
14. Already in 1676 Leibniz compares ideas to the velocity and direction of motion (L 155).
15. See NE 61, 79, 110, 140, and 379. C. Wilson (1989: 262–3) and Jolley (1990: 159–61).

This internal principle that determines these changes is appetition (sec. 11). It is important to keep in mind that these appetites are active (sec. 15). In the manuscript of the *Monadology* Leibniz also calls this internal principle an "active force," and this reflects the way Leibniz earlier in his life discussed the internal endeavors of substances. This is developed most clearly in Leibniz's important essay *De Ipsa Natura* (1698).[16] The nature of a substance is not simply the concept of its development.[17] The nature, essence, or substantial form of a substance is a "primitive motive force which . . . always acts," and this "primitive force of action . . . is itself the inherent law impressed upon it by divine command" (GP IV: 511–2/L 503–4). God's command or decree that an object exist, Leibniz writes, leaves an "impression," "vestige," or "subsistent effect" on the object, and this vestige or impression left by God's command is the primitive active force "residing in things" and "from which the series of phenomena follow according to the prescription of the first command" (GP IV: 507/L 500–1). A substance's nature, then, is a primitive active force in the substance, and that force is a law that determines all the changes of states that constitute a substance.[18]

The states of a monad that unfold as a result of the monad's strivings are called "perceptions" by Leibniz because they are expressions or representations of the external world (sec. 14). Although Leibniz has little to say about expression in the *Monadology*, he is explicit about it in other places. For Leibniz, "[t]hat is said to express a thing in which there are relations [*habitudines*] which correspond to the relations of the thing expressed" (GP VII: 263–4/L 207). This correspondence, moreover, must be lawlike. In the *New Essays* he writes that expression involves an "orderly," "precise and natural" relationship between the properties of the expression and those of what it

16. Also see Leibniz's remarks on endeavors and primitive active forces in the *Nouveaux Essais* (NE 169 and 172f). For a full treatment of this essay, see C. Wilson (1987).

17. See Mann (1987) for a critique of the view that a nature is nothing but a complete concept of its successive stages of development. An example of this view is Woolhouse (1982: 45–64). However, it should be pointed out that in Woolhouse (1985) he explicitly acknowledges the importance of the concept/nature distinction in Leibniz's philosophy.

18. To the Dutch Cartesian de Volder, Leibniz writes: "But that which persists . . . contains primitive force, so that primitive force is the law of the series, as it were" (GP II: 262/L 533). See Gale (1970: 123).

expresses (NE 131; also see GP II: 112).[19] This relationship is either one of similarity or a mapping such as there is between a circle and an ellipse in which "any point whatever on the ellipse corresponds to some point on the circle according to a definite law" (GP VII: 264/L 208).[20] Consequently, our ideas can express God's ideas as well as the external world insofar as there is an appropriate one-to-one mapping between our ideas, God's ideas, and the external world.[21]

The basics perceptions of a monad should not be confused with sensation or consciousness. These are complex perceptions that include memory in the case of sensation (sec. 26), and consciousness includes memory, apperception – perception of one's perception – as well as a high degree of clarity (secs. 19 and 23–24). Nevertheless, the fundamental dynamic properties of a monad apply to higher-order monads such as conscious minds. For Leibniz, human "thought consists of conation, as body consists in motion" (GP I: 72–3), and "the state of the soul, like that of the atom, is a state of change, a tendency. The atom tends to change its place, the soul to change its thoughts" (GP IV: 562/L 579). In fact, Leibniz's only model for substance has to be the mind because he denies that the basic ontological units can be material and governed by mechanical principles (GP IV: 562/L 579). Leibniz believes that the basic units of reality must be simple and hence without parts and material objects always have parts (secs. 3 and 17). For this reason Leibniz is quite happy to call a monad a "soul [ame]" as long as we keep in mind that perception is not confused with sentience or consciousness. Leibniz believes that when we are unconscious or when we have an "altogether dreamless sleep" our mind "does not differ noticeably from a simple monad" (sec. 20).

Accordingly, Leibniz appeals to mental phenomena in his account of substance. He argues that there are unconscious or what he calls "minute perceptions" (sec. 21) because in order for us to become

19. This seems to differ from his earlier characterization of expression in "What is an Idea?" in which he allows for arbitrary as well as natural correspondence (GP VII: 264/L 208). In the *Theodicy* it also seems that mental representations must have a "natural relation" to what they represent (GP VI: 326/sec. 356).
20. Also NE 131 and GP VI: 327/sec. 357.
21. This is why Leibniz can maintain that the universal character "will lead us into the interior of things" (GM IV: 453) and argue against Locke that words signify things as well as ideas, and that words can signify more than we know (NE 256, 287, and 354; also see Gu II: 450/sec. 5).

aware of a perception, the perception already had to have been present (sec. 23). In the *New Essays* he supports this with some well-known examples of how one's consciousness of the roaring noise of the sea must be made up of unconscious perceptions of individual crashing waves and how after we become accustomed to a certain sound – for example, the sound of a machine – we cease to be conscious of it, although our sense organs are still responding to it (NE 54–55; also GP IV: 459).

In Leibniz's very early *Paris Notes* (1676) he argues that the mind's nature consists in the continuous capacity to reflect on its own thoughts, and he supports this with an example of how after he lies awake at night thinking obsessively about the same thing for nearly an hour he begins "then to think of this difficulty in thinking and stupefy myself into reflections through perpetual reflections" (Jag 94–99/L 161). This reflective ability makes the mind indestructible and a true unity. In fact, minds are the only "true unities," and thus, Leibniz writes, "solidity or unity of body comes from the mind" (Jag 94–99/L 162).

The active nature of substances is also explained by Leibniz in terms of the mind's activity. In the *Paris Notes* Leibniz not only notices that he has a persistent capacity to be self-conscious, but also notices the "succession of spurts of his mind" and the "direction of the mind" as it moves from one thought to another (Jag 94–99/L 161). Much later in Leibniz's account of how he arrived at his "New System of the Nature and Communication of Substances" (1695) he writes that we must think of substances "in terms similar to the concept which we have of *souls*" because their nature consists of force, which means that they have something "analogous to sense and appetite" (GP IV: 479/L 454). Still later in his correspondence with the Dutch physicist and mathematician Burcher de Volder, Leibniz maintains that monads have active and passive powers "like the ego" (GP II: 251/L 530) and urges on the puzzled de Volder that Leibniz's conception of substantial activity is "most intelligible because there is something in it analogous to what is in us, namely, perception and appetite" (GP II: 270/L 537). He repeats this in the *New Essays*, completed in 1704, where he agrees with Locke that "the clearest idea of active power comes from us from the mind. So active power occurs only in things which are analogous to minds, that is, entelechies; for strictly matter exhibits only passive power" (NE 172).

Nowhere is the dynamism of Leibniz's philosophy of mind clearer than in his attempt to show the affinity between his philosophy and contemporary Enthusiasm. In his "True *Theologica Mystica*," Leibniz writes that the essential light of God is the eternal word of God, which contains the archetypes of all things, and that we have such an inner light that God ignites (*anzündet*) in us (Gu I: 410). This inner light is described as having the force (*Kraft*) to give us the right knowledge of God. Later he writes that in our substance there is a "footprint" of God's omniscience and power (Gu I: 411). As a result, all things have something of everything else, but with a varying force of clarity (*Kraft der Klarheit*) (Gu I: 412).

Much of this mystico-theological terminology has equivalents in Leibniz's rationalized logico-metaphysical terminology.[22] However, the dynamism of the mystico-theological terminology must not be cut out from the content of the rational terminology. For example, it is true that "radiation [*Bestrahlung*]" is equivalent to "the operation of ideas through the law of the best possible" or the "essential light" as "the region of ideas or possibilities," but the dynamism of the mystical terminology must be included in Leibniz's rationalized terminology. What is unique about Leibniz is that he is able to incorporate significant features of contemporary enthusiasm without giving up on his conception of the mind as something that can be under our voluntary control.

Body and Soul

As we saw, the most important way we can control our minds is by using our bodies, as is the case when we calculate. That all minds come with bodies is a central feature of Leibniz's philosophy and it is through their physical bodies that minds can represent themselves as well as the rest of the universe (Deleuze 1993: 85–6; Rutherford 1995b: 193–4). One reason Leibniz gives for this is that human minds cannot reason without using physical symbols (NE 212). Since this is the case, Leibniz believes that this must be a designed feature of this world, which he believes is the best of all possible worlds. "It is an admirable arrangement on the part of nature," Leibniz writes, "that we cannot have abstract thoughts which have no need of something

---

22. As Leroy Loemker shows in a footnote to this piece in L 369.

sensible, even if merely symbols such as the shape of letters, or sounds" (NE 77).

Although minds need physical bodies, they do not causally inter-act because there is not real interaction in the created universe, according to Leibniz. Instead, God creates substances in such a way that although all their states "arise from its own nature [*fonds*]," they are in "perfect *conformity* to things without" (GP IV: 484/L 457). For instance, the soul represents the world around it not in virtue of causal interaction, but in virtue of a preestablished harmony that determines that the soul has states that express the states of the exter-nal world (NE 440). This also holds for the relation between the human mind and its organic body. The states of the soul correspond to states of the body so perfectly that there is even a state of the mind "corresponding to the circulation of the blood and to every internal movement of the viscera, although one is unaware of such happenings" (NE 116).

An important feature of Leibniz's conception of mind and body is that both are automata. While the body is a natural automaton that follows the "laws of the corporeal mechanism," or what Leibniz in the *Monadology* calls the "laws of efficient causes or the laws of motion" (sec. 78), the mind "is an *automaton that is spiritual or formal*" (GP IV: 485/L 458; also see sec. 18). Although a spiritual automaton is not mechanical, "it contains in the highest degree all that is beautiful in mechanism" (GP VI: 356/Th 365). The sequences of movements of bodies, which are governed by the laws of efficient causality, are expressed in souls by sequences of representations regulated by the laws of final cause, that is, principles of good and evil, so that "every present perception leads to a new perception, just as every movement that it represents leads to another movement" (GP VI: 356–7/Th 365; also see GP VI: 599/AG 207). In Leibniz's famous analogy, mind and body are like two clocks constructed "from the start with such skill and accuracy that one can be assured of their subsequent agreement" (GP IV: 498/L 460).

It should be noticed that in describing the mind Leibniz uses Spinoza's phrase "spiritual automaton" (Friedmann 1946: 149). As we saw earlier, Spinoza used the term in his *Treatise on the Emendation of the Intellect* (GP II: 33), and late in life Leibniz commented on this passage in his response to Johann George Watchtower, who attempted to show that there is significant "accord between the Cabala and Spinoza" (Friedmann 1946: 134).

Watchtower believed that Spinoza's comment that the soul is a spiritual automaton applied only to souls, and not the mind, and Leibniz comments on Spinoza and Watchtower as follows: "Both are wrong, for I say that the soul acts spontaneously and yet as a spiritual automaton, and that this is also true of the mind" (AG 279). Minds and souls are exempt from the "impulses of external things," and both are spontaneous in that they are driven by "effort [*conatus*], that is, through desires in accordance with the laws of the good." However, this spontaneity does not mean that all of a soul's or mind's activities can be explained without referring to external objects. For example, a mind depends on other created external objects, but this dependency is "moral," not physical. In "creating the mind, God took things other than the mind itself into consideration" (AG 279), and this God would have to do to ensure that there is harmony among all of creation.

To illustrate this point in the *Theodicy*, Leibniz borrows an example from M. Jacquelot's *Conformity of Faith and Reason* in which there is an automaton made in such a way that it fulfills the master's orders all day long at the right moment when the master issues the order (GP VI: 137/Th 157). When the automaton fulfills the master's order, what it does is not causally or physically dependent on the master, but the master's influence is "ideal" or "objective" because what it does depends on the knowledge the automaton's maker has of what the master will command (GP VI: 138/Th 159).[23]

In the same manner, Leibniz writes, "God has accommodated the body to the soul and has arranged beforehand that the body is impelled to execute its commands" (GP VI: 138/Th 159). A crucial feature of this arrangement is that in imperfect souls such as ours, not only does the soul appear to command the body, but "the soul is swayed [*incliner*] by the passions arising out of corporeal representations" (GP VI: 139/Th 159). These passions of the soul are not really brought about by the soul's body or any other physical body in the soul's environment. Instead, in such a case the soul has confused and

---

23. Leibniz is assuming that this knowledge is not causally dependent on what the master does.

indistinct perceptions that are responsible for its states. We need to examine passion and action in Leibniz more closely, but first let us turn to his conception of freedom.

Automation and Freedom

Leibniz believes that the conception of mind as a spiritual automaton does not preclude that the mind's actions are free. Leibniz writes in his *Theodicy* that "All is . . . certain and determined beforehand in man, as everywhere else, and the human soul is a kind of *spiritual automaton*" in which freedom and necessity are combined (GP VI: 131/Th 151).

Freedom, for Leibniz, involves both spontaneity and choice or volition (Parkinson 1970: 57–8). A mind's inner force that determines its development (instead of external forces) gives the mind spontaneity (GP IV: 484/L 457). But spontaneity and volition are not the same thing. "Everything voluntary is spontaneous," Leibniz write, "but there are spontaneous actions which are not chosen and therefore are not voluntary" (GP IV: 519/L 494). For instance, a moving tennis ball set in motion along a smooth trajectory is behaving spontaneously, but it is not free. Referring to Aristotle, Leibniz writes that in addition to being unconstrained, a free action needs to be deliberate (NE 176), and what Leibniz has in mind is that the action must be "accompanied by choice" and "considerations of good and bad" (NE 177).

Without choice, a substance's succession of states, including a mind's ordered succession of representations, would be spontaneous, but not free. A mind without choice is as spontaneous (on Leibniz's view) but unfree as a moving tennis ball. But volition is compatible with determination. As we just saw, a will is always determined by reasons and never indifferent with respect to its given alternatives. Unfortunately, Leibniz's view is complicated by the fact that although he believes that reasons and other motives always determine the will, he also writes on many occasions that they "incline without necessitating" (NE 116 and 179 and GP VII: 390/L 697).

What Leibniz had in mind is that given "all the internal or external circumstances, motives, perceptions, dispositions, impressions, passions, inclinations taken together," the choice I make in those circumstances, say, to leave for Italy, is not necessary because the denial does not imply a contradiction (GP III: 401/AG 194). Leibniz does not simply mean that it is possible that I did not choose to leave, but that the proposition that *in all these circumstances taken together, I will choose to leave* is not necessary. It is not necessary because it can be denied without contradiction (GP III: 401/AG 194). Consequently, for Leibniz the truth of the proposition that *in all these circumstances taken together, I will choose to leave* depends on God's free choice in creation to make the best of all possible worlds. As is well known, Leibniz believes that there is an infinite number of possible worlds conceived of in God's mind, and God has good reasons to choose one over the rest and create it. The reason God has is the principle of fitness or perfection: The possible worlds are ordered in terms of degrees of perfection – their degree of variety and order – and the best one has a maximum degree of variety combined with order.[24] In the case of volition, the principle of fitness requires that God create the world in which it is true "that the prevailing inclination always triumphs" (GP VI: 132/Th 152).

Although the proposition that *in all these circumstances taken together, I will choose to leave* is not necessary in an absolute sense because its denial does not entail a contradiction, it has what Leibniz calls "*hypothetical* or *consequential*" necessity (GP III: 400/AG 193). While a proposition that cannot be denied without contradiction is absolutely necessary, a proposition is hypothetically necessary if what is necessary is that proposition *given* some other fact, and what Leibniz specifically has in mind is God's choice in creation. So in the case of my choice to leave, what is necessary is this: *given God's choice, in all these circumstances taken together, I will choose to leave*. This hypothetical necessity is compatible with the fact that it is not necessary that in all these circumstances taken together, I will choose to leave.[25]

Another important feature of Leibniz's view of freedom is that although volition is essential to freedom, it will always be determined. Leibniz rejects the notion that the will can be completely indifferent with respect to several alternatives. The idea that there is such "*absolute indifference* or *indifference of equilibrium*" is a "chimera which

---

24. See *Monadology*, secs. 53–5 (GP VI: 603/L 639) and GP IV: 430–1/L 306.

25. It may seem that if it is necessary that given God's choice, I will choose to leave, then if God's choice is necessary, it will also be necessary that I choose to leave (Curley 1974: 243). For a discussion of this issue, see Adams (1994: 16–22).

shocks the principles of good sense" (GP III: 401/AG 194). Every action has a reason that motivates it even when we are not aware of those reasons (AG 280). "*Reason* in the mind of a wise being," Leibniz writes, "and *motives* in any mind whatsoever do that which answers to the effect produced by weights in a balance" (GP VII: 389/L 696). That is, "*choice follows the greatest inclination*," by which Leibniz understands "both passions and reasons, true or apparent" (GP III: 401/ AG 194).

Since the will must be directed by the understanding, judgments and volitions are distinct for Leibniz. While for Spinoza, as we saw, judgments – that is, the mind's affirmations and negations – were volitions and there was no need for willpower in addition to the mind's judgments, for Leibniz the mind's affirmations and negations are not volitions (AG 280). Leibniz believes that the will must not be confused with understanding (GP VI: 423/Th 428), and an important reason for distinguishing the two is that it preserves freedom.

The will is determined in every mind: "In every intelligent being," Leibniz writes, "the acts of will are of their nature posterior to the acts of the understanding" (Du V: 386). Consequently, Leibniz rejects divine volitionalism, a view shared by Cartesians as well as Enthusiasts such as Boehme and his followers. One of these disciples was Pierre Poiret,[26] whom Leibniz mentions in the same breath as Descartes when in the *Monadology* Leibniz rejects divine volitionalism:

We must not imagine as do some, however, that since the eternal truths are dependent on God, they are arbitrary and dependent on God's will, as Descartes and later Monsieur Poiret seem to have held (sec. 46).

In the discussion of Boehme in Leibniz's correspondence with another Boehme disciple, André Morell, Leibniz rejects the enthusiastic view that God's will or even "hunger" is primary and produces reason (Gr I: 133f):

The primitive essence of every substance consists of force; it is this force in God that makes it that God necessarily is, and that all which is must emanate from him. Next comes light or wisdom, which includes all possible ideas and all eternal truths. The last complement is love or will, which chooses among the possibilities that which is best, and it is the origin of contingent truths or of the actual world. Thus the will is born when the force is determined by the light. (Gr I: 139)

26. On Poiret, see Meyer (1985: 74).

God wills what is good and just, and things are good and just independently of God's will (sec. 56). If God's will were without a motive, it would be blind and arbitrary (GP VII: 408/L 708 and GP VI: 423–4/Th 428–9). The difference between God's will and human will is that God is moved only by true and good reasons, while we can be moved by apparently true and good reasons, as well as our passions.

Passion and Action

As we just saw, for Leibniz freedom involves not only spontaneity, but volition as well. Unfortunately, Leibniz has a notion of volition which is broad enough to apply to all substances. On Leibniz's view, all substances act voluntarily in the sense that they are driven by appetition. To be a substance is to have perceptions and appetites that determine a substance's perceptions and their order. So this notion of volition does not help us to distinguish the voluntary action of a conscious being from those actions of nonconscious substances. Fortunately, Leibniz recognizes this and distinguishes between the broad class of appetites or endeavors that all substances have and the volitions of a conscious mind.

In the *New Essays* a mind's volition is an appetite of a certain sort. While every appetite is the effort or endeavor toward what is perceived as good and away from what is perceived as bad, a volition, strictly speaking, involves apperception or self-awareness. An action is voluntary in this narrower sense, when "one can be aware of and reflect upon when they arise from some consideration of good and bad," and there are "also appetitions of which one can be aware" (NE 173; also 192). So here in the *New Essays* volition is to will as understanding is to perception. Understanding is a perception combined with reflection, while volition is the endeavor of an appetite combined with reflection.

In his *Theodicy* Leibniz introduces another feature to distinguish freedom from bondage in a system in which "all that passes in the soul depends . . . only upon the soul, and its subsequent state is derived only from it and from its present state" (GP VI: 137/Th 157). Here Leibniz refers to the distinctness of perceptions. He writes that God is fully free because God has only distinct perceptions, while a human being not only has distinct perceptions "forming its dominion," but also "a series of confused perceptions or passions, forming its bondage" (GP VI: 137/Th 158; also *Monadology*, sec. 49).

The distinctness of perceptions is not to be confused with the distinctness for ideas (McRae 1976: 36). We have a distinct idea of an object if we can enumerate the features of the object that are sufficient for distinguishing it from other objects (GP IV: 422/L 291). The distinctness of perceptions is a matter of degree and it should be understood in terms of the force or vivacity of the perception. A distinct perception is one that is sufficiently forceful or "heightened [*relevé*]," as Leibniz writes in the *Monadology* (secs. 24 and 25), so that we can become aware of it. With only indistinct perceptions we would not be conscious, but in a state akin to a swoon or a dreamless sleep (sec. 20). Indistinct perceptions do not command our attention, and to be motivated by them is to be under the sway of our passions. When moved by passion, what we do is still caused by our own perceptions, but they are not perceptions of which we have any awareness and thus it seems to us as if we are motivated by forces external to us.

When the perceptions that motivate us are distinct and we are aware of them, we act. However, only God is capable of pure action because, as we saw, only "a Divinity . . . [has] none but distinct perceptions" (GP VI: 137/Th 158). According to Leibniz, human action is a product of many perceptions and appetites, including conflicting and indistinct ones, and the volition of which we are aware in a voluntary action is only partially responsible for the action (NE 192; GP VI: 427/Th 432). It is the presence of indistinct, that is, unconscious, perceptions that keeps us from having full direct voluntary control over anything we do. The conscious volition is only one factor that plays a role in determining the next state, and the other unconscious factors are not under our direct control.

Nevertheless, we have "some power over these confused perceptions also, even if in an indirect manner." Leibniz writes that although the mind "cannot change its passions forthwith, it can work from afar towards that end with enough success, and endue itself with new passions and even habits" (GP VI: 137–8/Th 158; also GP III: 403/ AG 195).

We are now in a position to see how for Leibniz we can voluntarily, albeit indirectly, acquire beliefs. As we saw in the beginning of this chapter, for Leibniz beliefs are not in our direct control, but can be controlled indirectly. They cannot be controlled directly because we do not have immediate control over all the confused perceptions that are responsible for beliefs, but the mind can indirectly control beliefs. Immediately following the claim that the mind has power over confused perceptions, Leibniz writes:

It even has a like power over the more distinct perceptions, being able to endue itself indirectly with opinions and intentions, and to hinder itself from having this one or that, and stay or hasten its judgment. For we can seek means beforehand to arrest ourselves, when occasion arises, on the sliding step of a rash judgment; we can find some incident to justify postponement of our resolution even at the moment when the matter appears ready to be judged. Although our opinion and our act of willing be not directly objects of our will (as I have already observed), one sometimes, takes measures nevertheless, to will and even believe in due time, that which one does not will, or believe, now. So great is the profundity of the spirit of man. (GP VI: 137–8/Th 158; also see GP III: 403/AG 195)

What makes this profundity of the human mind possible is that it can change the minute and indistinct perceptions that are responsible for a mind's future states. But how can this be possible on Leibniz's view of mind? The confused perceptions cannot be changed directly because we are not aware of them or we have a confused awareness of them as passions of the mind that are due to actions of other bodies (*Monadology*, sec. 52). Moreover, the mind cannot come to know all of its minute perceptions because to know all of them it would have "know completely the whole universe which is embraced by them, that is, it must needs be a God" (GP VI: 357/Th 365).

What makes this possible for Leibniz is the fact that the mind is embodied and that mind and body are in preestablished harmony. The mind can use its body to change its minute perceptions. Insofar as the mind has distinct perceptions, it is active and the body is created by God in such a way that "the body is impelled to execute [the mind's] orders" (GP VI: 138/Th 159). Of course, the body is not literally caused to move by the mind's will, but preestablished harmony ensures that "the body must have been so formed in advance that it would do in time and place that which responds to the volitions of the soul" (GP VI: 354/Th 400).

But the relationship between mind and body is reciprocal. When the body moves on account of its mind's volitions, harmony guarantees that there will be corresponding changes in the mind. The mind perceives these bodily changes in a confused and passive manner, but nevertheless "the movements which are developed in bodies are concentrated in the soul by representation" and these confused representations include an "innumerable number of small perceptions" that in fact are regulated by our particular natures (GP VI: 356/Th 365). In sum, our confused and minute internal mental states over which we have no direct voluntary control and which are in part responsible for our mental states, including the beliefs and desires we have, can be influenced indirectly via our distinct perceptions. Our distinct perceptions that constitute voluntary activity correspond to appropriate changes in our bodies and their physical environments. These changes in our bodies and their physical environments in turn are accompanied by confused perceptions in us, and these new, confused perceptions that accompany bodily changes are responsible for new internal mental states, because "every present perception leads to a new perception" (GP VI: 356–7/Th 365). Among those new perceptions can be new beliefs, including ones that we initially wanted to have.

So we can bring about new beliefs in us indirectly through appropriate behavior. Sometimes this kind of belief formation is rational, for instance, when a person desires to believe a theorem and seeks to prove it. The voluntary manipulation of appropriate symbols causes new perceptions, and when the proof is successful, I fix on a belief that I wanted to have. Here the "thread of meditation" is, as Leibniz believed, an aid to the rational improvement of our understanding. Of course, acquiring a belief can also be suspect. I can choose to ignore relevant information or decide to include information that I have not fully examined but that helps me to reach the desired conclusion. Then when I reach the conclusion, I can conveniently forget or choose to ignore that the conclusion depended on an unexamined and perhaps doubtful proposition, and firmly believe in the conclusion and believe that it is justified.

The Enlightened Mind

Leibniz's conception of the enlightened mind as a trained mind, where training involves our bodies and the world around us, has practical consequences. This is especially clear in his "Memoir for the Enlightened Persons of Good Intention," a sketch of the enlightened mind and a handbook on how enlightened people with good intentions can avoid being "carried away by the torrent of general corruption" and "do some good" (Kl X: 8/PW 103).

Leibniz writes that even when one has good intentions, the "want of attention or application, and the want of intelligence or information" are the causes of being carried away by corruption, and Leibniz's aim in this memoir, written in his mature years, is to "demonstrate how one could remedy these two defects of attention and application" (Kl X: 8/PW 104). How to remedy the abuses and defects of the human understanding is a common 17th-century theme, but the significance of Leibniz's handling of it is that it has explicitly public and political dimensions. It is this aspect of Leibniz's philosophy of mind that, I believe, at least helps to set the intellectual stage for Kant's conception of the enlightened mind as escaping tutelage through the public exercise of reason.

It is noteworthy that right from the start of the *Memoir* Leibniz writes that part of the problem is that even when one has good intentions and "enough skill or enough mental energy to see what he ought to do, *one finds only rarely people with whom one dares to be open*" (Kl X: 8/PW 104; my emphasis). In fact, the success of his remedy for the two defects of application and of information depends on "the good fortune of meeting persons who took what is most important and most solid to heart" (Kl X: 8/PW 104).

Leibniz then proceeds to express his optimism about the happiness that can be obtained if we improve our understanding, but again it is significant that here he does not write just about individual happiness, but about the happiness of "men" and that "they" could make great progress "if they were willing to set about it as they should," and that we have the means to accomplish in a decade what would take centuries without them (Kl X: 8/PW 104).

Of course, an individual alone can contribute to general progress: "One need only will" (Kl X: 8/PW 104). Nevertheless, "to achieve this it would be best that this will exist in several [persons] with whom one deals. Nothing is stronger than association." One advantage of cooperation is that "a thousand things can be done by two or three or by several [people] who understand each other, which will never be done, or never be well done, if they work without communicating" (Kl X: 17/PW 109).

The importance of association is not a minor feature of Leibniz's political opinions, but a central feature of his metaphysics. Leibniz's "great principle of metaphysics as well as of morality" is that the universe is governed by the most perfect intelligence which is possible, and for Leibniz this means that all minds constitute a divine society or city (Kl X: 9–10/PW 105; see *Monadology*, secs. 85–6). Consequently, individual happiness depends on the common good (Kl X: 10/PW 105). Leibniz writes:

Every enlightened person must judge that the true means of guaranteeing forever his own individual happiness is to seek his satisfaction in occupations which tend toward the general good; for the love of God, above all else, and the necessary enlightenment, will not be denied to a mind which is animated in this way. (Kl X: 10–11/PW 105)

The general good is advanced by three things: (1) enlightening people's understanding, (2) strengthening people's "will in the exercise of virtues, that is, in the habit of acting according to reason," and (3) "try[ing] to remove the obstacles which keep them from finding truth and following true goods" (Kl X: 11/PW 105).

The understanding is enlightened by, among other things, perfecting "the art of reasoning, that is, the method of judging and inventing which is that true logic that is the source of all objects of knowledge" (Kl X: 11/PW 106). As we know, for Leibniz this means perfecting a universal characteristic so that we all can have a stable thread of meditation.

The will is improved with the guidance of a "public authority" that will reform education so that virtuous activity is agreeable and becomes people's second nature. Those whose education while young did not provide them with the proper training will have to depend on a mixture of a variety of influences: good company, good representations of good and evil, frequent self-reflection and self-examination, "saying often to oneself: *dic cur hic; hoc age; respice finem* [state why here; do this; watch the end]," and finally a system of punishments and rewards that enforces virtuous behavior (Kl X: 12/PW 106).

By enlightening the understanding and strengthening the will Leibniz believes that the obstacles to happiness that are internal to the mind will be removed. The obstacles that are external to people's minds – the obstacles due to the body and its social and natural environment – will be removed as much as possible if we "seek the means of preserving [people's] health, and of giving them the conveniences of life" (Kl X: 12/PW 106–7). To this end, we must advance the natural as well as the social sciences, Leibniz believes. Not only must we "inquire into the nature of bodies in the universe," but we must know "human history, and the arts and sciences that depend on it" (Kl X: 13/PW 107). For Leibniz this includes the study of languages, archeology, literary and legal history, as well as what we would today consider to be political science.

To achieve all this, "great princes and principal ministers" must be persuaded to advance these ends (Kl X: 14/PW 107). Leibniz had no conception of a democratic or representative government: for Leibniz one of the benefits to rulers of the enlightenment of the general populace is that they will serve them better. However, Leibniz did not share Hobbes's absolutist conception of sovereignty. Leibniz was a federalist in the sense that the sovereignty of individual states, including their right to maintain armies, was not abrogated when alliances and federations, such as the Swiss Federation or the so-called Holy Roman Empire, were formed (Kl IV: 57/PW 117). This was especially relevant to the German Empire because Leibniz recognized that on Hobbes's conception of sovereignty, "there will be nothing in our land but out-and-out anarchy" (Kl IV: 58/PW 118). For Hobbes, government must be unitary or nothing at all, but Leibniz defends the federation where "supreme power is divided" (Kl IV: 59/PW 119). True, in such unions the probability of dissension is increased, but this is outweighed by the benefits of such a union. "Hobbes' fallacy lies in this," Leibniz writes, "that he thinks things which entail inconvenience should not be borne at all – which is foreign to the nature of human affairs" (Kl IV: 59/PW 119).

More important, Leibniz believes that people will follow their own wills and rely on their own judgment about their welfare if "they are not persuaded of the supreme wisdom and capability of their rulers, which is necessary for perfect resignation of the will" (Kl IV: 60/PW 120). Such rulers do not exist on Earth, and consequently states that do not require such resignation will be more effective. So in politics, as in cognition, human volition plays a central and positive role, and should not be wholly submitted to the authority of another.

In fact, it seems that for Leibniz, the task of government is to enhance individual volition, and not to subjugate it: as we saw, we should promote the common good, which means enlightenment and "freeing [people] from annoying inconveniences, in so far as this is feasible" (Kl X: 14/PW 107). Of course, Leibniz has intellectuals, scholars, and scientists in mind, who need the freedom to pursue their projects, which means that scholarly and scientific societies need to be given public support (Kl X: 19–21/PW 110). But Leibniz's attention is not limited to the needs of his own class when he is concerned about freeing people from annoying inconveniences. Elsewhere Leibniz writes that "above everything else one must seek means of obviating public misery." The poor must be given "the means of earning their livelihood," and this must be done not only in the form of charity, but by "taking an interest in agriculture, by furnishing to artisans materials and a market, by educating them to make their productions better, and finally by putting an end to idleness and to abusive practices in manufactures and in commerce" (F IV: 150–1/PW 106n2).

So Leibniz not only uses behavior to synthesize the conception of the mind as an involuntary automaton and the conception of the mind as the product of voluntary activity, but he understands that how we behave is a function of social and political factors. If enlightenment requires the improvement of our understanding, and we can try to improve our understanding only indirectly through our behavior, for instance, by how we direct our inquiry and how we use our language, then the social and political context must not stand in the way of such improvement. Enlightenment requires an enlightened social and political order. By connecting the improvement of the human understanding to public behavior, and seeing that behavior that improves the mind requires social and political conditions that support or at least do not stand in the way of such improvement, Leibniz concludes the 17th-century dialectic about the role of volition in human cognition and prepares the ground for Kant's philosophy of enlightenment.

8

Conclusion: The Public Mind

We saw that for Leibniz, progress toward enlightenment is tied to action: through appropriate voluntary behavior human beings can change their minds. But human behavior is tied to community, and if human beings are to improve their minds, they need a proper social and political context that makes such improvement possible. How human beings move their bodies has many constraints, and some of these constraints are of a social and political nature. Consequently, Leibniz turned to the question about what rulers should do to promote enlightenment, and one of the things they must promote, at least to some degree, is human freedom, namely, "freedom from annoying inconveniences, in so far as this is feasible." Thus Leibniz comes to see how inner enlightenment depends on human action, which in turn is at least partly shaped by external social and political conditions.

Leibniz could appreciate the dependence of inner enlightenment on human action in part because of the philosophical discussion about cognition and volition in 17th-century Europe. The whole century is marked by the quest, made prominent by Descartes, to find ways of improving the human understanding and trying to free it as much as possible from debilitating influences. Moreover, Leibniz's predecessors believed that the improvement of the human under- standing required some voluntary human effort. We have to want to improve our minds, guide our thinking in a proper manner, avoid cognitive pitfalls, withhold judgment when appropriate, and hazard judgments when we have sufficient evidence. Leibniz's philosophy is also marked by this quest for cognitive reform – he searches for ways of making our ideas clear and for better languages that will help us in both discovery and justification – and he understands the pursuit of knowledge as a human activity that involves human volition.

Although Leibniz, like Descartes, is a proponent of cognitive reform, he pushes this reform beyond the reform of how we think. Leibniz, unlike Descartes, recognized that the human mind is embodied. While Descartes recognizes the cognitive role of the body and bodily movement only for a very brief moment (in his description of a lute-player's knowledge), Leibniz follows Hobbes and assigns an important role to the human body. Of course, Leibniz is not a materialist, but as we saw, he believes that all created minds must have organic bodies, and he explicitly acknowledges and endorses Hobbes's idea that public symbols – whether the symbols of ordinary language, logic, algebra, or geometry – are needed in long trains of reasoning, as we find in the sciences and law. For Hobbes and Leibniz, this use of symbols, which both understand to be a voluntary human action, is not just a symptom of reasoning, but part of the reasoning process itself.

The idea that language is constitutive of certain mental processes can also be found in Locke when he maintains that words play a role in the making of some of our complex ideas. Moreover, Hobbes and Locke agree that desire has a key role to play in human cognition. However, Locke pays much more attention to what might be thought of as the phenomenology or folk psychology of cognition and belief formation. While Hobbes focuses on the mind as a complex process that involves gross behavior as well as what today we might refer to as neural processes, Locke is not interested in the physiological details of cognition. Locke reaffirms Descartes's first-person perspective; he wants to describe the processes and elements of the human understanding as they appear to us in careful reflection. In fact, Locke is skeptical about what we can know about the physical processes that underpin human understanding.

Consequently, Locke's discussion of the role of volition in human cognition has very little to say about bodily action. Locke returns to the Cartesian focus on internal mental action and pays attention to what Locke takes to be the intellectual labor that goes into the making of the human mind. Not only do we sometimes exercise for better or worse the will to believe, but many of our ideas that we use to form our beliefs are the products of the workmanship of the understanding. In this latter respect, Locke departs significantly from Descartes.

By highlighting the degree to which our basic ideas themselves are products of mental activity, Locke sets the stage for Kant's philosophy of cognition.

Although Locke highlights the areas of the human understanding that are subject to our control, he does not deny that there are necessary and involuntary operations of the understanding. However, he does not see it as his job to discuss these features at length because for Locke both the crowning achievements of the human understanding and its dismal errors are due to human volition. The job of highlighting the involuntary features of the mind fell to 17th-century Enthusiasts and Spinoza. These philosophers turned to the involuntary dimensions in part because they did not share Descartes's, Hobbes's, and Locke's optimism about the role the will can play in the human understanding. Instead, they saw the will as ineffective at best or a roadblock to knowledge at worst. Human understanding will be improved, they maintained, only if the will is suppressed and the mind's automatic operations are unlocked or released. When they are released, the mind is opened to either divine inspiration or natural infusion. The role of the will was only to keep itself under control and to jump-start the spiritual automaton that all human beings have.

Leibniz incorporates this notion that we are spiritual automatons without denying or denigrating the role of volition in cognition. The human mind has a structure that it shares with all intelligent beings, and this mental structure is not constructed by us, but it is given to us at creation. Although we do not create our ideas, we do control how we think with them, and this is where our minds are subject to our own training. Training the mind, however, is not a mere mental affair involving only intellectual effort. According to Leibniz, the mind can be trained only by using the body and its environment, for instance, when a person learns to do algebra by calculating with pencil and paper.

These, then, are the threads – reforming the human understanding, liberating it from external authority, making it more self-reliant, using the mind's automatic processes, and guiding it through voluntary physical behavior – that Leibniz weaves together in his philosophy, and this is the cloth that Kant uses to fashion his Enlightenment essay in 1784.

The major link between Kant and Leibniz, and more generally the 17th century, is Christian Wolff (1679–1754), who was the philosophical symbol if not the philosopher laureate of the Prussian Enlightenment. The motto of the Enlightenment, as Kant declares in his essay, is *"Sapere aude!* Have the courage to use your *own* understanding!"* and prior to Kant no public figure in Prussia exemplified this motto better than Wolff. Wolff himself begins his *Logic,* published in 1713, with the injunction that "everyone . . . should . . . strive to find how to use the powers of their understanding with as much agility and swiftness as possible" (GW I.1: 105). The *Logic* together with two other volumes on *Ethics* (1720) and *Politics* (1721) are the core of Wolff's German writings that were responsible for Wolff's reputation throughout the German lands.

One striking feature of these books is their argumentative styles. Wolff explains his approach by referring to Locke's injunction in *Of the Conduct of the Human Understanding* that the best aid to the human understanding is mathematical reasoning because it seeks distinct ideas that are tied together in perspicuous demonstrations (ibid.).[1] Accordingly, Wolff tries to define all his technical terms and lay out the reasoning he uses to reach his conclusions. It is on account of this style of philosophizing that Kant later observes in the *Critique of Pure Reason* that the "celebrated Wolff" became "the author of that spirit of thoroughness which is still not extinct in Germany" and that he showed "how the secure progress of a science is to be attained only though orderly establishment of principles, clear determination of concepts, insistence upon strictness of proof, and avoidance of venturesome, non-consecutive steps in our inference" (Ak III: 22).

But there is more to Wolff's method than seeking well-defined and deductive reasoning in all areas of philosophy. What distinguishes Wolff's quasideductive philosophizing from Spinoza's work, for instance, is that Wolff attempts to combine mathematical rigor with simple and even folksy writing that made him popular beyond academia (Mühlpfordt 1983: 239). Wolff wrote in German because he wanted to reach "beginners," and he wanted to write in a manner that would not strike lay readers as strange or fancy (GW I.1: 107). He wanted his work to be useful not only in the sciences and higher academic circles but in ordinary human life, and it is for this reason that he calls his writings "pragmatic" (GW I.3: 70; also see 5). His

---

1. Wolff not only refers to Locke in the Preface to Wolff's *Logic,* but in 1708 reviewed *Of the Conduct of the Human Understanding* in *Acta Euruditorum* (GW I.1: 18 and 253).

writings are indeed easy to read and they give the reader a sense of why Wolff was already a popular lecturer when he turned to writing philosophy in German.

In his lectures and sermons Wolff recommended the use of one's own reason in an intellectual climate where reference to scripture was thought to be the best way of resolving theological disputes (Hinske 1983: 314–15). This recommendation was a refreshing, undogmatic alternative to orthodoxy, particularly for the younger generation of students, many of whom would apply Wolff's method and ask for definitions and arguments in other seminars and lectures, to the chagrin of Wolff's colleagues (Birke 1966: 1–2; GW I.10: 146–7 and 189–90). His students came armed with a new standard for teaching that we can see at work in this passage: "I do not force my teachings on anyone," Wolff writes, adding that he is also a willing student, as long as he is not being ordered to agree with something because an authority said so while "holding a knife to my throat" (GW I.3: 97).

Wolff paid a price for his enlightened teaching and writing, and his reference to a knife at his throat is not hyperbole. On November 13, 1723, Frederick William I, King of Prussia and Frederick the Great's authoritarian father, ordered Wolff to leave Prussia and his professorship of mathematics and natural science at the University of Halle within forty-eight hours or face death by hanging.[2] The immediate cause of this expulsion was a lecture he gave arguing that the content of Confucian morality shows that reason by itself, without the help of revealed religion, can discover moral truth. Wolff drew the obvious conclusion that because morality rests on universal reason instead of special religious knowledge, atheists also can be moral. This upset the leading Pietists of Halle, who began the campaign against Wolff that led to his forced exile. The official reason for banishment was that Wolff taught determinism and atheism.

Thus Wolff became a symbol for the Prussian Enlightenment, and it was appropriate for the Prussian Wolffians gathered in the Society of the Friends of Truth (Société des Aléthophiles) to mint a medal in 1736 with the motto *Sapere Aude* (Venturi 1971: 39–42). More important, when Frederick the Great, who was an enthusiastic reader of Wolff in the 1730s, ascended to the Prussian throne in 1740, one of his first acts was to invite Wolff to return to Halle, where he became

---

2. Wolff's wife was pregnant at the time and he also had a young son.

chancellor in 1743. This was an important act intended to express Frederick the Great's commitment to the enlightened rule he described for the reading public in *Antimachiavell,* a treatise critical of despotism and published by Voltaire. Recalling Wolff was part of several enlightened royal acts that shifted the political climate in Prussia, including relaxing Prussia's rigid censorship laws and abolishing judicial torture.

By the time of the Berlin Enlightenment debate in the 1780s, Wolff had been dead for almost thirty years and his influence had declined sharply, but his name was still invoked as a symbol of the Enlightenment. Several months before Kant published his Enlightenment essay, the important Prussian legal reformer Ernst Ferdinand Klein published an essay in the *Berlinische Monatsschrift* defending the freedom of thought and press (Schmidt 1996: 87–96). In this essay, Klein, who was trained in the Wolffian natural law tradition at Halle, has the reader imagine a soliloquy by Frederick the Great that ends with the words:

Errors, even the most dangerous, will never gain fame through my persecution, but as they deserve, will be detested and forgotten.

By contrast, the beneficial influence of philosophy shall not be limited by any coercive laws. Wolff shall come back to my state, and whatever does not plainly contradict the state, good morals, and the universal religion shall be taught freely and publicly. (Ibid.: 90)

Klein then continues in his own voice to extoll princes, kings, and other "guardians of immature children" to follow Frederick's example and give people "the freedom to which they have an inalienable right from birth, the freedom to think and share their thoughts" (Ibid.: 91).

Klein had very good reasons for invoking Wolff in this discussion of freedom. Not only was Wolff punished for what he professed in his teaching and his publications, but the key ideas in this short passage – the freedom to philosophize and, more generally, think; the tolerance for error, publicity, and immaturity – were well developed by Wolff's philosophy. Even before his expulsion, Wolff defended academic freedom on the grounds that it was required by the fundamental principle of civil society, namely, to promote the welfare of society. Human beings need institutions devoted to the pursuit of truth and new inventions, and to that end, civil societies should have academies devoted to the sciences (GW I.4: secs. 299–300).[3] But in order to pursue truth, members of these academies need to have the freedom to examine, critique, and publish their findings. No views should be foisted on the academy and they should not be tied to the teachings of some authority; instead, they should be given "complete freedom" (GW I.4, para. 304). Worries about the dire consequences of such freedom are unnecessary because the pursuit of truth, guided by proper methods, is never harmful even when it leads to error.

False beliefs, Wolff maintains, can never harm society, and thus nobody should be punished merely for having certain opinions (GW I.5: 307–8/sec. 359). Even the teaching of false views should not be punished unless they really endanger the security and welfare of society. When they do pose a danger, it is not the erroneous belief that requires punishing, but the actions that are the consequences of those beliefs. Wolff adds that even in such cases where errors do lead to acts that threaten society, punishment should be mild because the effects of opinions are slow and easily corrected (GW I.5: 311/ sec. 361).

Wolff's justification for academic freedom is ultimately tied to his metaphysics. Human beings have perfections, which are based on the Leibnizian idea of harmony (GW I.2: sec. 152), and it is their nature to strive for perfection. Morality requires that we maximize our perfection, which includes maximizing the perfection of others (GW I.4: 11–2 and 539/secs. 12 and 767).[4] Maximizing human perfection requires a society (GW I.5: 1–2/sec. 1), and thus people contractually agree to form civil societies or states, which are one and the same for Wolff. The key concept in Wolff's politics is welfare, and the basic principle of human beings in civil society is, "Do what promotes the welfare of society and refrain from doing what hinders it or is in some other way detrimental to it" (GW I.5: 3 and 7/secs. 3 and 11). For

---

3. The scope of investigation is set very broadly by Wolff. They should study theoretical as well as practical subjects, including political institutions and police departments (GW I.5: 249/sec. 306).

4. Perfection is a real property, is something God has to an infinite degree, is discoverable by reason, and is independent of either human or divine will. God does not define or construct perfection; instead, God examines the realm of possibility and chooses to create what is perfect (GW I.4: 7/sec. 5). Hence Beiser (1992: 31) is wrong to maintain that the main difference between Kant's and Wolff's ethic is that Kant locates moral value in the will while Wolff locates it in God's intentions.

Wolff, social welfare is tied to human perfection, which is essentially tied to human happiness because attaining greater perfection is a source of happiness (GW I.4: 16, 35, and 38/secs. 19, 53, and 57). To promote human welfare, societies need to promote human happiness (GW I.5: 171–2/sec. 227), and this requires knowledge. Consequently, Wolff argues, we need schools and academies that are devoted to gathering, organizing, and disseminating knowledge (GW I.5: 215/sec. 284).[5] We need academies of science in particular devoted to the pursuit of truth unhindered by political and financial concerns (GW I.5: 241–5/secs. 299–302) and free to pursue truth for truth's sake (GW I.5: 245–7/secs. 303–4). In short, for Wolff the pursuit of human perfection requires academic freedom.

Wolff had defined this position by 1721, a few years before his expulsion, and it is not a surprise that after his forced exile, his commitment to freedom of thought and public expression became stronger and broader in scope. In 1728 he published the *Preliminary Discourse on Philosophy in General* with a section devoted to "The Freedom to Philosophize," in which he defends freedom for all who philosophize, and not just those who belong to an academy of science. This discussion is also notable because he explicitly connects freedom and publicity: "the freedom to philosophize is the permission to state publicly our own opinion on philosophical issues," and "philosophical servitude" is when "one is not permitted to state openly one's own opinions on philosophical issues" (PD secs. 151–2).

Philosophy requires freedom because, when done properly, it uses philosophical method, which demands that one use only concepts that one can define accurately and arguments that one can recognize as sound (PD sec. 156). A person that follows the philosophical method will not repeat the opinions of others without proper evaluation and inner conviction. A person that must repeat the views and arguments of others and is censured from openly providing one's own assessment of these views "groans under the yoke of servitude" (PD sec. 151).

Exactly why the philosophical method requires the ability to reason *in public* is not explicitly addressed by Wolff. But it seems clear why

5. It is clear in this discussion that when Wolff uses the term "academy of science" he is referring to all institutions of higher learning devoted to scientific instruction and research (GW I.5: 214–17/secs. 284–5).

he begins to focus on publicity. As we saw, human beings need to cooperate if they are to improve themselves. This applies to the pursuit of knowledge. The philosopher, Wolff writes, "loves and works for truth for its own sake." Thus the philosopher pursues truth no matter where or when it is discovered, and this means that it does not matter if it was discovered by others or by oneself (PD sec. 155).[6] Moreover, the pursuit of truth requires systematizing known truths, that is, recognizing the connections or relations between various truths, and this requires cooperation between scientists working in different areas (GW I.5: 250–1/sec. 307).

The means for such cooperation is language, of course, because it is by means of language that we communicate our thoughts (GW I.1: 151). But the need for language runs even deeper for Wolff and gives him another reason why thinking, even apart from communication, has a public component. Wolff writes in the preface to his *Logic* (GW I.1: 109) that he was profoundly influenced by Leibniz's *Meditation on Knowledge, Truth and Ideas*, where, as we saw in Chapter 7, Leibniz identifies "blind or symbolic" thinking, which Leibniz says we use "in algebra and in arithmetic, and indeed almost everywhere" (GP IV: 423). Accordingly, Wolff believes that although intuitive knowledge without the help of public symbols is superior, we often need words not just to communicate with other people but to think on our own (GW I.1: 152 and 157). Wolff believes that symbolic knowledge magnifies the extent and depth of the human intellect and that usually symbolic thinking is preferred to intuitive thinking because symbolic thought is more distinct (Ungeheuer 1983: 111). So by its very nature thought relies on public activity, namely, the use of language.[7]

In sum, Klein's reference to Wolff in connection with the freedom to philosophize, to teach freely and publicly, and to tolerate error was carefully chosen not only because Wolff's exile and return were significant to the cause of freedom in Prussia, but because his teachings

---

6. Needless to say, it also means that philosophical method requires that truth is not subordinated "to fame, or to power, or to the favor of others" (PD sec. 155).

7. Wolff makes the interesting comment that words have meanings even if the user does not have concepts associated with the word. For example, the word "lynx" refers to an animal that hunters know very well, but that most people use without having "neither a clear, let alone a distinct concept of it" (GW I.1: 154). Thus Wolff would be a counterexample to the claim that all traditional philosophers believe that reference is a function of what speakers have in mind (Putnam 1975).

and writings developed and defended freedom of thought. It should also be noted that the reference to immaturity in Klein's passage also has the marks of Wolff. In his political philosophy, Wolff devotes some effort to defining the nature of immaturity, maturity, and guardianship (GW I.5: 90–3 and 109–13/secs. 119–23 and 145–57), and the same is true of his legal writings (Schmidt 1996: 63). Also, Klein echoes Wolff's paternalism when he writes that those "whom God has made . . . guardians of his immature children" should in their role as guardians preserve their subject's inalienable freedom to think and to share their thoughts.[8] Although Wolff has what was an enlightened understanding of what it is to be a parent,[9] his political philosophy is thoroughly colored by the assumption that rulers stand to their subjects as fathers to their children (GW I.5: 200/sec. 264).

Since the leading problem of Kant's enlightenment essay is how to "exit from self-incurred immaturity" and throw off "the yoke of immaturity" (Ak VIII: 35–6), it has been suggested that Kant's use of "immaturity" in the Enlightenment essay was stimulated by Klein's discussion (Laursen 1996: 256; Schmidt 1996: 63). This seems very plausible. Kant wrote the Enlightenment essay for the December 1784 issue of the bimonthly *Berlinische Monatsschrift* and he dates his short essay September 30, 1784. Klein's essay appeared anonymously in the same journal in April 1784, and it is likely that Kant read this essay. After all, Kant's Enlightenment essay is a response to a footnote in this periodical[10] and Kant during this period was a frequent contributor to the *Berlinische Monatsschrift*. Moreover, there are other striking similarities between Kant's and Klein's essays. For instance, Kant

8. Moreover, we saw that Wolff's discussion of the freedom to philosophize refers to the "yoke of philosophical servitude" (PD §153). While servitude and immaturity are distinct states, they are both states in which a people are required to subject their wills to a superior (GW I.5: 90–1/§§119–120 and 184).

9. For instance, parents are bound to command only what accords with morality, and children are not bound to obey to commands that are immoral (GW I.5: 93/sec. 125). Moreover, parental power over children ceases when children "can care for and govern themselves [*sich selbst versorgen und regieren können*]" (GW I.5: 92–3/sec. 123).

10. In December 1783 the *Berlinische Monatsschrift* published an essay by one Johann Friedrich Zöllner criticizing purely civil marriage ceremonies. In the essay he maintains that the word "enlightenment" confuses people and in a footnote asks "What is enlightenment? This question, which is almost as important as what is truth, should indeed be answered before one begins enlightening. And still I have never found it answered" (Schmidt 1996: 2).

echoes Klein's discussion of the worry that freedom will allow officers to question the commands of their superiors (Schmidt 1996: 92; Ak VIII: 37). Also, Klein declares that sometimes one needs to "obey the command, not to consent to it; to do, not to judge; to follow, not to agree," and Kant similarly writes that in those situations "one is certainly not allowed to argue; rather, one must obey" (ibid.).

Although the evidence is circumstantial, it strongly suggests that Klein's essay, especially the passage that brings together freedom, publicity, and immaturity, played a role in stimulating Kant's own thinking about the connection between enlightenment, freedom, and publicity, and his central thesis that enlightenment – "removing the yoke of immaturity" – requires the freedom to reason in public. If this is the case, then Klein's essay is a place where Kant's thinking about enlightenment is fastened to the philosophy of Wolff. This essay brought together the key the elements of Wolff's philosophy of freedom that Kant then develops and molds together into a new vision of human enlightenment. Since Wolff himself was working with key ideas he located in Leibniz's philosophy, it appears that Kant inherited from Wolff the significant insight achieved by 17th-century philosophy that enlightenment depends on the ability to use one's own understanding in public.[11]

What is new in Kant's vision is, first, that he drops the paternalist framework. While for Klein and Wolff, rulers were guardians who in their role as guardians should preserve their subject's right to think in public, for Kant the political task is to escape immaturity altogether. He is ironic about the guardians "who have graciously taken up oversight of mankind" and who have "made their domestic animals stupid and carefully prevented these placid creatures from daring to take even one step" on their own. The role of the guardian now is to free human beings from immaturity, not to give them more freedom within the confines of their immaturity (Ak VIII: 40). Of course, this accords with Kant's larger political vision that civil

---

11. Of course, much of Kant's philosophy can be seen as a reaction to Wolffian philosophy. It is quite correct to think of Kant "as a powerful mind struggling to rethink the philosophy of another," namely, Leibnizian philosophy as interpreted by Wolff, "from its foundation and, so to speak, to disrupt it from within" (Paton 1969: 73). But a consequence of such working from within the system is that Kant's work is shaped in distinct ways by this Wolffian context (Engfer 1983: 48–9; also see Vleeschauer 1962).

society must preserve the autonomy and dignity that characterizes human maturity.[12]

Second, Kant places a distinct emphasis on publicity.[13] He explicitly draws a distinction between public and private domains and he emphasizes the phrase "public use [*öffentlichen Gebrauch*]" when he writes that enlightenment requires nothing more than the most harmless kind of freedom, namely, "the freedom to make a *public use* of one's reason in all matters" (Ak VIII: 36). This distinct emphasis on publicity distinguishes Kant not only from Klein and Wolff but from Moses Mendelssohn's contemporary answer to the question, "What is Enlightenment?" (GSJ VI.1: 115–19). Mendelssohn distinguishes enlightenment from culture, and while the latter is tied to sociality, "man *as man* needs no culture, but he needs enlightenment."

Although Kant is special in that he has an explicit concept of publicity and connects enlightenment and publicity, the theme that human enlightenment depends on the freedom of thought, and that this is tied to public activity, particularly speech and writing, is not unique to Kant and can be found throughout the debate to which Kant's essay was a contribution. The other root of the debate – besides Zöllner's footnote – is a short lecture given in December 1783 to the Berlin Wednesday Society, or the secret Society of the Friends of Enlightenment, to which Klein, Mendelssohn, and other eminent writers and reformers belonged (Birtsch 1987). The prominent physician J. K. W. Möhsen asks "[t]hat it be determined precisely: What is enlightenment?" and then goes on not only to mention the "freedom to think, to speak and also to publish" in one breath, but also recommends that we examine the role human language plays in hindering or furthering human enlightenment (Schmidt 1996: 49–50).

In 1787 the radical theologian Carl Friedrich Bahrdt (who was imprisoned for publishing a book depicting Jesus Christ as an

---

12. As the late Lewis White Beck has pointed out, a crucial aspect of Kant's philosophy is the "Rousseaustic Revolution." Rousseau maintained that human beings are obligated to obey only the laws that they helped to establish, and this is the essence of human freedom: obeying your own laws. While Rousseau works this out for politics, "the doctrine of autonomous government by free citizens of a republic is deepened by Kant into a moral, metaphysical, and even religious conception" (Beck 1965: 223–4).

13. On Kant and publicity, see O'Neill (1989: 28–50) and Laursen (1996).

ordinary good man) exhorted: "People! Freedom to think and to judge independently from authority . . . is the holiest, most important, most inviolable right of a person (ibid.: 99). He then adds that "the freedom to speak and to write is no less a universal human right," and he argues that the right to speak and to think are so inseparably bound in their employment "that whoever takes away the one takes away the other." The reason for this is that "the right to speak in itself is the only means, the only way of using the right to think" (ibid.: 101). Somewhat later in 1793, the young Fichte also connects the freedom of thought to the freedom to use language in public (ibid.: 121 and 146).

Although the connection between enlightenment, freedom, and publicity was clearly established by the end of the 18th century, the connection Leibniz draws between enlightenment and physical well-being was much less developed. Nevertheless, this issue was not lost to the Enlightenment debate. In an essay published a few months before Kant's "What Is Enlightenment?," the philosopher Karl Leonhard Reinhold argued that enlightenment was not just something for the elite, but that the masses (*Pöbel*) had the capacity for enlightenment as well. He argues that the ignorant state of most people is due not to nature but to their social circumstances. He writes that "the ordinary fool is . . . not born but bred, and under better circumstances would have become what the happy few are who partake of these circumstances." Moreover, "the deeper one descends into the lowest classes, the more obvious becomes the cause of ignorance and errors, the more salient becomes the lack of opportunity and means, as well as the number of obstacles to rational culture" (ibid.: 70). Thus in order to develop rational culture, these deficiencies and obstacles would have to be treated and removed.

The idea that material conditions are relevant to enlightenment is expressed with characteristic vigor by Hamann in a letter written in 1784 in response to Kant's essay. Hamann mocks the idea that it is laziness or cowardice that is a hindrance to enlightenment. Hamann blames the "guardians," who see human beings as less than machines – as "mere shadows of [their] grandeur" – and who order people to "believe, march, pay." An "army of priests" is as detrimental to enlightenment as an "army of thugs, henchmen and purse-snatchers." What keeps people unenlightened is "the financial exploitation of immature persons, till they have paid their last penny" (ibid.: 147).

Kant's Enlightenment essay is open to Hamann's criticism because there Kant ignores the material conditions for or obstacles to human enlightenment. Similarly, when he discusses "popular enlightenment" in another essay, he discusses only education, and not material welfare. However, Kant does not altogether ignore the ties between enlightenment and human welfare in his writings (Kneller 1998: 2–3). As Allen Wood has pointed out, in the essay "Conjectural Beginnings of Human History" Kant argues that it is only in a society that has developed technology and enough wealth to sustain some form of a market that "the systematic and well-rounded cultivation of human faculties can first begin" (Wood 1998: 25; also see Ak VIII: 119–20). However, there is a price to pay for this new, wealthier stage of development, namely, intense inequality and oppression, and the unhappiness and vice that come with it. Although Kant feels with Rousseau the pain of this situation, he sees it as unavoidable and as the development of a fundamental trait of human beings, namely, their "unsocial sociability" (Wood 1998: 28). Human beings are essentially social beings who need to cooperate to live and flourish, but at the same time they live in antagonism and conflict with each other. Although this is a trait human beings cannot escape, modern civilization intensifies it over earlier stages of human social development.

The connection between enlightenment and material conditions is also made in Kant's *Pedagogy*. In this short work on education, "true enlightenment" is not just a matter of education, but it is a "real upbringing [*Erziehung*]," which includes maintenance or care as well as education (Ak IX: 450 and 441). While education consists of discipline and instruction, maintenance consists of proper nourishment, housing, and clothing. Kant devotes a section to the "physical upbringing" of a child, where he discusses proper nursing, among other things, and recommends that toddlers have as much freedom of movement as possible without endangering their safety (Ak IX: 454). Physical upbringing also includes learning how to control voluntary bodily movements and sense organs (Ak IX: 966). To this end, Kant recommends various exercises, including throwing objects, because these will train the senses and the body. In fact, he urges that children learn how to walk on narrow footpaths and steep ledges because "if a person cannot do these things, he is not fully what he is capable of being" (Ak IX: 467).

For Kant, physical education also includes what he calls the "physical education of the mind" (Ak IX: 469). He distinguishes it from moral education and it involves cultivating or improving the natural operations of the understanding, such as memory. Kant believes that these operations can be cultivated with physical activity. For example, reading, writing, and learning languages improve memory, which is necessary for good judgment (Ak IX: 474). Moreover, the instruction of a child should combine knowledge and know-how (*Wissen* and *Können*), as is the case in mathematics. Kant adds that, in general, knowledge and our ability to speak effectively should be combined, and it is clear that he believes that this enhances not only our speaking abilities but our knowledge as well (Ak IX: 474).

Although physical education of mind and body is necessary for developing the human capacity for freedom, it needs to be complemented with moral education, which teaches children moral maxims and rules and how to follow them. Part of moral education includes teaching how to follow rules, and for Kant this involves physical activity. Children should have specific rules about bedtime, chores, play, and so forth, and they need to follow these without exception. This will help them to learn how to follow their own rules and thus become autonomous individuals (Ak IX: 481).

So for Kant there is a pedagogical dimension to autonomy that ties mind and body together. For human beings to become what they are capable of being, which first and foremost are autonomous beings who dare to follow their own minds, they need to raise their children properly (Ak IX: 445). Enlightenment cannot focus on the individual, but must look to the parents and how they raise their children, and in fact pertains to the whole species. We need to care about what they eat and how they are clothed and sheltered, and we need to train their bodies and minds. From the beginning we need to give children freedom of movement while training their minds and their bodies.

Kant's views on the moral requirements of community and mutual aid complement his pedagogy. As several recent commentators have argued, Kant saw a connection between morality, political autonomy, justice, and mutual aid (Van der Linden 1988; Herman 1993; Rossi 1998; Wolff 1998). Morality is essential to rationality, and rationality in morals means that the principles of our actions do not preclude others from acting on the same principle. We must consider ourselves to be lawgivers in a rational community where all rational beings are treated as ends and not as means only. When we consider ourselves in that way, we will recognize that we have a duty of beneficence because we, by our very nature, depend on the help we get from others (Ak IV: 423). This is captured in Kant's notion of an ethical commonwealth, a community of free citizens following the dictates of their own reason and caring for the conditions that make the public use of reason possible, which includes mutual respect for the dignity of all its members.

An ethical commonwealth is a community that maximizes freedom, rationality, and mutual aid; it is a community of world citizens where people use their own reason and speak with their own voices. The idea of such a community exerts a powerful influence in later centuries. It plays a significant role in various successful and unsuccessful attempts at social reform and revolution. If human beings will continue to hope for enlightenment, the idea of such a community will continue to flourish. Unfortunately, how to actually build such a community, or come even reasonably close, remains at the turn of this millennium an unsolved problem for human beings. Still, it is clear that as long as the insight achieved by late 17th-century philosophers and developed in the 18th century, namely, that human enlightenment depends on the public exercise of reason and the material conditions that make this possible, does not become common knowledge, this will remain an unsolved problem in the 21st century.

Bibliography

Aarsleff, H. 1982. *From Locke to Saussure.* Minneapolis: University of Minnesota Press.

Adams. R. M. 1994. *Leibniz: Determinist, Theist, Idealist.* New York: Oxford University Press.

Alexander, P. 1985. *Ideas, Qualities and Corpuscles: Locke and Boyle on the External World.* Cambridge, UK: Cambridge University Press.

Anscombe, G. E. M. 1975. "The First Person." In *Mind and Language: Wolfson College Lectures 1974.* Ed. S. Guttenplan, pp. 45–65. Oxford: Clarendon Press.

Armstrong, D. M. 1968. *A Materialist Theory of Mind.* New York: Humanities Press.

Ashworth, E. J. 1981. "'Do Words Signify Ideas or Things?' The Scholastic Sources of Lockes's Theory of Language." *Journal of the History of Philosophy* 19: 299–326.

Ashworth, E. J. 1984. "Locke on Language." *Canadian Journal of Philosophy* 14: 45–73.

Ayers, M. 1991. *Locke.* 2 vols. London: Routledge.

Baier, A. 1986. "The Idea of the True God in Descartes." In Rorty 1986: 359–87.

Barnouw, J. 1980. "Hobbes's Causal Account of Sensation." *Journal of the History of Philosophy* 18: 115–30.

Barnouw, J. 1989. "Hobbes's Psychology of Thought: Endeavours, Purpose and Curiosity." *History of European Ideas* 10: 519–45.

Bechtel, W., and A. Abrahamsen. 1991. *Connectionism and the Mind.* Oxford: Basil Blackwell.

Beck, L. W. 1965. *Studies in the Philosophy of Kant.* Bobbs-Merrill: Indianapolis.

Beck, L. W. 1969. *Kant Studies Today.* La Salle, IL: Open Court.

Beilin, H. 1989. "Piagetian Theory." *Annals of Child Development* 6: 85–131.

Beiser, F. C. 1992. *Enlightenment, Revolution, and Romanticism.* Cambridge, MA: Harvard University Press.

Bennett, J. 1984. *A Study of Spinoza's Ethics*. Indianapolis: Hackett.

Bennett, J. 1990. "Why Is Belief Involuntary?" *Analysis* 50: 87–107.

Benz, E. 1936. "Zur Metaphysischen Begründung der Sprache bei J. Boehme." *Euphorion* 37: 340–54.

Benz, E. 1970. "Die Schöpferische Bedeutung des Wortes bei Jacob Boehme." In *Mensch und Wort. Eranos Jahrbuch 1970*. Leiden: Brill.

Bertman, M., and M. Malherbe. 1989. *Thomas Hobbes: De la Métaphysique a la Politique*. Paris: J. Vrin.

Birke, J. 1966. *Christian Wolff und die Zeitgenössische Literatur-und Musiktheorie*. Berlin: de Gruyter.

Birtsch, G. 1987. "Die Berliner Mittwochsgesellschaft." In *Über den Prozess der Aufklärung in Deutschland im 18. Jahrhundert*. Eds. H. E. Bödeker and U. Hermann. Göttingen: Vandenhoeck & Ruprecht. Translated in Schmidt 1996: 235–52.

Brandt, F. 1928. *Thomas Hobbes' Mechanical Conception of Nature*. Copenhagen: Levin and Munksgaard.

Burge, T. 1986. "Cartesian Error and the Objectivity of Perception." In *Subject, Thought and Context*. Eds. P. Pettit and J. McDowell, pp. 117–36. Oxford: Oxford University Press.

Chappell, V. 1986. "The Theory of Ideas." In Rorty 1986: 177–98.

Chisholm, R. 1968. "Lewis's Ethics of Belief." In *The Philosophy of C. I. Lewis*. Ed. P. A. Schilpp, pp. 223–42. La Salle: Open Court.

Chomsky, N. 1966. *Cartesian Linguistics*. New York: Harper and Row.

Christensen, S. M., and R. W. Turner, eds. 1993. *Folk Psychology and the Philosophy of Mind*. Hillsdale, NJ: Lawrence Erlbaum.

Churchland, P. S., and T. J. Sejnowski. 1992. *The Computative Brain*. Cambridge, MA: MIT Press.

Clark, A. 1989. *Microcognition*. Cambridge, MA: MIT Press.

Clifford, W. K. 1947. *The Ethics of Belief and Other Essays*. London: Watts.

Cohen, J. L. 1992. *An Essay on Belief and Acceptance*. New York: Oxford University Press.

Cottingham, J. 1986. *Descartes*. Oxford: Basil Blackwell.

Cottingham, J., ed. 1992. *Cambridge Companion to Decartes*. Cambridge, UK: Cambridge University Press.

Coudert, A. 1978. "Some Theories of Natural Language from the Renaissance to the Seventeenth Century." *Studia Leibnitiana. Sonderheft* 7: 106–14.

Courtine, J.-F. 1980. "Leibniz et la Langue Adamic." *Revue des science philosophiques et théologiques* 64: 373–91.

Couturat, L. 1901. *La logique de Leibniz d'aprés documents inédits*. Paris: J. Vrin.

Crocker, R. 1990. "Mysticism and Enthusiasm in Henry More." In Hutton 1990b: 137–56.

Cummins, R. 1989. *Meaning and Mental Representation*. Cambridge, MA: MIT Press.

Cummins, R. 1991. "The Role of Representation in Connectionist Explanations of Cognitive Capacities." In *Connectionism and Philosophy*. Eds. W.

Ramsey, S. Stich, and D. Rumelhart, pp. 91–114. Hillsdale: Lawrence Erlbaum.

Curley, E. M. 1973. "Experience in Spinoza's Theory of Knowledge." In Grene 1973: 25–59.

Curley, E. M. 1974. "Recent Work on 17th Century Continental Philosophy." *American Philosophical Quarterly* 11: 235–55.

Curley, E. 1975. "Descartes, Spinoza and the Ethics of Belief." In *Spinoza: Essays in Interpretation*. Eds. E. Freeman and M. Mandelbaum, pp. 159–89. La Salle: Open Court.

Dascal, M. 1978. *La Sémiologie de Leibniz.* Paris: Aubier-Montaigne.

Dascal, M. 1987. *Leibniz: Language, Signs and Thought.* Amsterdam: John Benjamins.

Dascal, M. 1992. "Why Does Language Matter to Artificial Intelligence." *Minds and Machines* 2: 145–74.

Dawkins, R. 1976. *The Selfish Gene.* Oxford: Oxford University Press.

Debus, A. G. 1970. *Science and Education in the Seventeenth Century: The Webster–Ward Debate.* New York: Elsevier.

Deleuze, G. 1990. *Expressionism in Philosophy: Spinoza.* New York: Zone Books.

Deleuze, G. 1993. *The Fold: Leibniz and the Baroque.* Trans. T. Conley. Minneapolis: University of Minnesota Press.

Dennett, D. 1991. *Consciousness Explained.* Boston: Little, Brown.

Devitt, M. 1990. "A Narrow Representational Theory of Mind." In Lycan 1990: 371–98.

Dewey, J. 1931. "The Unit of Behavior." In *Philosophy and Civilization.* New York: Minton.

Dreyfus, H., and S. Dreyfus. 1986. *Mind over Machine.* New York: Free Press.

Elert, W. 1973. *Die Voluntaristische Mystik Jacob Böhmes: Eine Psychologische Studie.* Aalen: Scientia.

Engfer, H. J. 1983. "Zur Bedeutung Wolffs für die Methodendiskussion der deutschen Aufklärungsphilosophie: Analytische und synthetische Methode bei Wolff und beim vorkritischen Kant." In Schneiders 1983: 48–65.

Fodor, J. 1980. "Methodological Solipsism Considered as a Research Strategy in Cognitive Psychology." *Behavioral and Brain Sciences* 3: 63–73.

Fodor, J. 1987. *Psychosemantics.* Cambridge, MA: MIT Press.

Foellesdal, D. 1982. "Husserl's Notion of Noema." In *Husserl, Intentionality and Cognitive Science.* Ed. H. Dreyfus, pp. 73–80. Cambridge, MA: MIT Press.

Formigari, L. 1988. *Language and Experience in 17th Century British Philosophy.* Philadelphia: John Benjamins.

Frankfurt, H. G. 1971. "Freedom and the Concept of a Person." *Journal of Philosophy* 68: 5–20.

Frege, G. 1892. "Über Begriff und Gegenstand." In Frege 1962: 66–80.

Frege, G. 1962. *Funktion, Begriff, Gegenstand.* Ed. G. Patzig. Göttingen: Vandenhoeck & Ruprecht.

Frege, G. 1967. "The Thought: A Logical Inquiry." In *Philosophical Logic.* Ed. P. F. Strawson, pp. 17–38. Oxford: Oxford University Press. First published in 1910 as "Der Gedanke. Eine logische Untersuching," in *Beiträge zur Philosophie des deutschen Idealismus* 1: 143–57.

Frege, G. 1980. *Philosophical and Mathematical Correspondence.* Eds. G. Gabriel, H. Hermes, F. Kambartel, C. Thiel, and A. Veraart. Chicago: University of Chicago Press.

Friedmann, G. 1946. *Leibniz et Spinoza.* Paris: Librairie Gallimard.

Gabbey, A. 1982. "Philosophia Cartesiana Triumphata: Henry More, 1646–71." In *Problems of Cartesianism.* Eds. T. M. Lennon, J. M. Nicholas, and J. W. Davis, pp. 171–250. Kingston and Montreal: McGill-Queens University Press.

Gabbey, A. 1990. "Henry More and the Limits of Mechanism." In Hutton 1990b: 19–35.

Gale, G. 1970. "The Physical Theory of Leibniz." *Studia Leibnitiana* 2: 114–27.

Garber, D., and M. Ayers. 1998. *The Cambridge History of Seventeenth-Century Philosophy.* 2 vols. Cambridge: Cambridge University Press.

Gert, B. 1989. "Hobbes's Account of Reason and the Passions." In Bertman and Malherbe 1989: 83–92.

Gibson, J. 1917. *Locke's Theory of Knowledge and Its Historical Relations.* Cambridge, UK: Cambridge University Press.

Gibson, J. J. 1979. *The Ecological Approach to Visual Perception.* Boston: Houghton Mifflin.

Gilbert, N. 1963. "Resolution and the *School of Padua." Journal of the History of Philosophy* 1: 223–31.

Goldman, A. 1970. *A Theory of Human Action.* Englewood Cliffs: Prentice Hall.

Grene, M., ed. 1973. *Spinoza: A Collection of Critical Essays.* Garden City, NY: Anchor Books.

Gründer, K., and W. Schmidt-Biggeman, eds. 1984. *Spinoza in der Frühzeti seiner Religiösen Wirkung, vol. 12: Wolfenbütteler Studien zur Aufklärung.* Heidelberg: Lambert Schneider.

Guéroult, M. 1968. *Spinoza.* 2 vols. Paris: Aubier.

Guéroult, M. 1984. *Descartes' Philosophy Interpreted According to the Order of Reasons.* 2 vols. Trans. R. Ariew. Minneapolis: University of Minnesota Press. Translation of *Descartes Selon L'ordre des raisons.* 2 vols. Paris: Aubier.

Hampshire, S. 1959. *Thought and Action.* London: Chatto and Windus.

Haugeland, J. 1978. "The Nature and Plausibility of Cognitivism." In *Mind Design.* Ed. J. Haugeland, pp. 243–81. Cambridge, MA: MIT Press.

Haugeland, J. 1985. *Artificial Intelligence: The Very Idea.* Cambridge, MA: MIT Press.

Heinekamp, A. 1972. "*Ars Characteristica* und Natürliche Sprache bei Leibniz." *Tijdschrift Voor Filosofie* 34: 446–88.

Heinekamp, A. 1976. "Sprache und Wirklichkeit nach Leibniz." In *History of Linguistic Thought,* Ed. H. Parrett, pp. 518–70. Berlin: de Gruyter.

Henry, J. C. 1986. "Occult Qualities and the Experimental Philosophy: Active Principles in Pre-Newtonian Matter Theory." *History of Science* 24: 335–81.

Henry, J. C. 1990. "Henry More versus Robert Boyle: The Spirit of Nature and the Value of Providence." In Hutton 1990: 55–76.

Henry, M. 1993. "The Soul According to Descartes." Trans. S. Voss. In Voss 1993: 40–51.

Herman, B. 1993. *The Practice of Moral Judgment.* Cambridge, MA: Harvard University Press.

Heyd, M. 1981. "The Reaction to Enthusiasm in the Seventeenth Century: Towards an Integrative Approach." *Journal of the History of Modern Philosophy* 53: 258–80.

Hinchman, L. 1996. "Autonomy, Individuality and Self-Determination." In Schmidt 1996: 488–512.

Hinske, N. 1983. "Wolffs Stellung in der deutschen Aufklärung." In Schneiders 1983: 306–20.

Hubbeling, H. G. 1984. "Zur frühen Spinozarezeption in den Niederlanden." In Gründer and Schmidt-Biggeman 1984: 149–80.

Hull, W. I. 1938. *The Rise of Quakerism in Amsterdam, 1655–1665.* Swarthmore College Monographs on Quaker History, no. 4. Philadelphia: Swarthmore College.

Hutin, S. 1960. *Les disciples anglais de Jacob Boehme au XVIIe et XVIIIe siècles.* Paris: Denoël.

Hutton, S. 1984. "Reason and Revelation in the Cambridge Platonists and Their Reception of Spinoza." In Gründer and Schmidt-Biggeman 1984: 181–99.

Hutton, S. 1990a. "Henry More and Jacob Boehme." In Hutton 1990b: 157–68.

Hutton, S., ed. 1990b. *Henry More (1614–1687): Tercentenary Studies.* Dordrecht: Kluwer.

James, S. 1997. *Passion and Action: The Emotions in 17th-Century Philosophy.* Oxford: Clarendon Press.

James, W. 1956. *The Will to Believe.* New York: Dover.

Joachim, H. H. 1940. *Spinoza's Tractatus de Intellectus Emendatione.* Oxford: Clarendon Press.

Jolley, N. 1990. *The Light of the Soul.* Oxford: Clarendon Press.

Jolley, N., ed. 1995. *The Cambridge Companion to Leibniz.* Cambridge, UK: Cambridge University Press.

Jolley, N. 1999. *Locke: His Philosophical Thought.* Oxford: Oxford University Press.

Kaplan, D. 1989. *Demonstratives.* In *Themes from Kaplan.* Eds. J. Almog, J. Perry, and H. Wettstein, pp. 481–630. Oxford: Oxford University Press. This was first circulated as a typescript in 1977.

Karmiloff-Smith, A. 1992. *Beyond Modularity: A Developmental Perspective on Cognitve Science.* Cambridge, MA: MIT Press.

Kayser, Wolfgang. 1930. "Boehmes Natursprachlehre und ihre Grundlagen." *Euphorion* 31: 521–62.

Kenny, A. 1968. *Descartes: A Study of His Philosophy.* New York: Random House.

Kenny, A. 1972. "Descartes on the Will." In *Cartesian Studies.* Ed. R. J. Butler, pp. 1–31. New York: Bobbs-Merrill.

Klibansky, R., E. Panofsky, and F. Saxl. 1964. *Saturn and Melancholy: Studies in the History of Natural Philosophy, Religion and Art.* New York: Basic Books.

Kneale, M., and W. Kneale. 1962. *The Development of Logic.* Oxford: Clarendon Press.

Kneller, J. 1998. "Introducing Kantian Social Theory." In Kneller and Axinn 1998: 1–14.

Kneller, J., and S. Axinn. 1998. *Autonomy and Community.* Albany: State University of New York Press.

Knowlson, J. 1975. *Universal Language Schemes in England and France: 1600–1800.* Toronto and Buffalo: University of Toronto Press.

Knox, R. A. 1950. *Enthusiasm: A Chapter in the History of Religion.* Oxford: Oxford University Press.

Koyré, A. 1964. *Traité de la réforme de l'entendement.* Paris: Vrin.

Koyré, A. 1968. *La philosophie de Jacob Boehme.* New York: Burt Franklin.

Kretzmann, N. 1968. "The Main Thesis of Locke's Semantic Theory." *Philosophical Review* 77: 175–96.

Kretzmann, N. 1975. "Transformationalism and the Port-Royal Grammar." In Antoine Arnauld and Claude Lancelot, *General and Rational Grammar: The Port-Royal Grammar.* Trans. J. Rieux and B. Rollin, pp. 176–95. The Hague: Mouton.

Kulstad, M. 1983. "Leibniz's Theory of Innateness in the *New Essays.*" *Proceedings. IV. Internationaler Leibniz-Kongress,* pp. 410–17. Hannover: G.-W. Leibniz Gesellschaft.

Laird, J. 1934. *Hobbes.* London: Ernest Benn.

Larmore, C. 1998. "Scepticism." In Garber and Ayers 1998: 1145–92.

Laursen, J. C. 1996. "The Subversive Kant: The Vocabulary of 'Public' and 'Publicity.'" In Schmidt 1996: 253–69.

Lewis, C. I. 1955. *The Grounds and Nature of the Right.* New York: Columbia University Press.

Lloyd, G. 1984. *The Man of Reason: "Male" and "Female" in Western Philosophy.* Minneapolis: University of Minnesota Press.

Lloyd, G. 1990. "Spinoza on the Distinction between Will and Intellect." In *Spinoza: Issues and Directions: Proceedings of the Chicago Spinoza Conference.* Eds. E. Curley and P.-F. Moreau, pp. 113–23. Leiden: E. J. Brill.

Llull, R. 1985. *Selected Works of Rámon Llull.* Vol 1. Ed. and trans. A. Bonner. Princeton: Princeton University Press.

Losonsky, M. 1989. "Locke on the Making of Complex Ideas." *Locke Newsletter* 20: 35–46.

Losonsky, M. 1990. "Locke on Meaning and Signification." Presented at the Clarendon Locke Conference, Christ Church, Oxford. In Rogers 1994: 123–41.

Losonsky, M. 1992. "Leibniz's Adamic Language of Thought." *Journal of the History of Philosophy* 30: 523–43.

Losonsky, M. 1993. "Passionate Thought: Computation, Thought, and Action in Hobbes." *Pragmatics and Cognition* 1: 245–66.

Losonsky, M. 1996. "John Locke on Passion, Will and Belief." *British Journal for the History of Philosophy* 4: 267–83.

Losonsky, M. 2000. "On Wanting to Believe." In *Essays on Belief and Acceptance.* Ed. P. Engel, pp. 101–31. Dordrecht: Kluwer Press.

Lott, T. L. 1982. "Hobbes's Mechanistic Psychology." In *Thomas Hobbes: His View of Man.* Ed. J. G. van der Bend, pp. 63–75. Amsterdam: Rodopoi.

Lycan, W., ed. 1990. *Mind and Cognition.* Oxford: Basil Blackwell.

Lyons, J. 1981. *Language and Linguistics.* Cambridge, UK: Cambridge University Press.

McRae, R. 1976. *Leibniz: Perception, Apperception and Thought.* Toronto: University of Toronto Press.

Mann, J. 1987. "The Nature of a Nature in Leibniz." *Studia Leibnitiana* 19: 173–81.

Marion, J.-L. 1993. "Generosity and Phenomenology: Remarks on Michel Henry's Interpretation of the Cartesian *Cogito.* Trans. S. Voss. In Voss 1993: 52–74.

Markie, P. M. 1986. *Descartes' Gambit.* Ithaca: Cornell University Press.

Markie, P. M. 1992. "The Cogito and Its Importance." In Cottingham 1992: 140–73.

Marr, D. 1982. *Vision.* New York: W. H. Freeman.

Martin, G. 1964. *Leibniz: Logic and Metaphysics.* Trans. K. J. Northcott and P. G. Lucas. Manchester: Manchester University Press.

Mates, B. 1986. *The Philosophy of Leibniz.* Oxford: Oxford University Press.

Meyer, R. W. 1985. *Leibniz and the Seventeenth-Century Revolution.* Trans. J. P. Stern. New York: Garland.

Mignini, F. 1979. "Per la datazione e l'interpretazione del *Tractatus de Intellectus Emendatione* di B. Spinoza." *La Cultura* 17: 87–160.

Millikan, R. G. 1984. *Language, Thought, and Other Biological Categories.* Cambridge, MA: MIT Press.

Montmarquet, J. 1986. "The Voluntariness of Belief." *Analysis* 46: 49–53.

Mühlpfordt, G. 1983. "Radikaler Wollffianismus: Zur Differenzierung und Wirkung der Wolffschen Schule ab 1735." In Schneiders 1983: 237–53.

Nagel. T. 1969. "The Boundaries of Inner Space." *Journal of Philosophy* 66: 452–58.

Naylor, M. B. 1985. "Voluntary Belief." *Philosophy and Phenomenological Research* 45: 427–36.

O'Neill, O. 1989. *Constructions of Reason: Explorations of Kant's Practical Philosophy.* Cambridge: Cambridge University Press.

Parkinson, G. H. R. 1970. *Leibniz on Human Freedom. Studia Leibnitiana, Sonderheft* 2. Wiesbaden: Franz Steiner.

Passmore, J. A. 1986. "Locke and the Ethics of Belief." In *Rationalism, Empiricism, and Idealism: British Academy Lectures on the History of Philosophy.* Ed. A. Kenny, pp. 23–46. Oxford: Clarendon.

Paton, H. J. 1969. "Kant on the Errors of Leibniz." In Beck 1969: 72–87.

Pécharman, M. 1990. "Philosophie Première et Théorie de l'Action selon Hobbes." In *Thomas Hobbes: Philosophie Prèmiere, Théorie de la Science et Politique*. Ed. Y. C. Zarka and J. Bernhardt, pp. 47–66. Paris: Presses Universitaires de France.

Pécharman, M. 1992. "Le Discourse Mental Selon Hobbes." *Archives de philosophie* 55: 553–73.

Peirce, C. S. 1955. *Philosophical Writings of Peirce*. Ed. J. Buchler. New York: Dover.

Peters, R. S. 1956. *Hobbes*. Hammondsworth: Penguin Books.

Peters, R. S., and H. Tajfel. 1957. "Hobbes and Hull – Metaphysicians of Behavior." *British Journal for the Philosophy of Science* 8: 30–44. Reprinted in *Hobbes and Rousseau*, pp. 165–83. Eds. M. Cranston and R. S. Peters. Garden City: Anchor Books.

Petry, M. J. 1984. "Behmenism and Spinozism in the Religious Culture of the Netherlands, 1660–1730." In Gründer and Schmidt-Biggeman 1984: 111–48.

Piaget, J. 1952. *The Origins of Intelligence in Children*. Trans. M. Cook. New York: International University Press.

Pojman, L. P. 1985. "Believing and Willing." *Canadian Journal of Philosophy* 15: 37–55.

Pombo, O. 1987. *Leibniz and the Problem of a Universal Language*. Münster: Nodus.

Popkin, R. H. 1979. *The History of Scepticism from Erasmus to Spinoza*. 4th ed. Berkeley: University of California Press.

Popkin, R. H. 1983. "The Third Force in Seventeenth-Century Philosophy: Scepticism, Science and Biblical Prophecy." *Nouvelles de la République de Lettres* 1: 35–63. Reprinted in Popkin 1992.

Popkin, R. H. 1992. *The Third Force in Seventeenth-Century Thought*. Leiden: E. J. Brill.

Popkin, R. H. 1998. "The Religious Background of Seventeenth-Century Philosophy." In Garber and Ayers 1998: 1: 393–422.

Price, H. H. 1954. "Belief and Will." In *Proceedings of the Aristotelian Society* 28: 1–26.

Putnam, H. 1975. "The Meaning of 'Meaning.'" In *Mind, Language and Reality: Philosophical Papers*. Vol. 2, pp. 215–71. Cambridge, UK: Cambridge University Press.

Rodis-Lewis, G. 1992. "Descartes' Life and the Development of His Philosophy." In Cottingham 1992: 21–57.

Rogers, G. A. J., ed. 1994. *Locke's Philosophy: Content and Context*. Oxford: Oxford University Press.

Rorty, A. O. 1992. "Descartes on Thinking with the Body." In Cottingham 1992: 371–92.

Rorty, A. O., ed. 1986. *Essays on Descartes' Meditations*. Berkeley: University of California Press.

Rosenthal, D. M. 1986. "Will and the Theory of Judgment." In Rorty 1986: 405–34.

Rossi, Philip J. 1998. "Public Argument and Social Responsibility: The Moral Dimensions of Citizenship in Kant's Ethical Commonwealth." In Kneller 1998: 63–86.

Rudderman, D. B. 1988. *Kabbalah, Magic and Science.* Cambridge, MA: Harvard University Press.

Rudolph, R. 1989. "Hobbes and His Critics: The Implications of Deliberation." In Bertman and Malherbe 1989: 63–82.

Rumelhart, D., P. Smolensky, J. McClelland, and G. Hinton. 1986. "Schemata and Sequential Thought Processes in PDP Models." In *Parallel Distributed Processing: Explorations in the Microstructure of Cognition.* Vol. 2. Eds. J. McClelland, D. Rumelhart, and the PDP Research Group, pp. 7–57. Cambridge, MA: MIT Press.

Russell, B. 1945. *A History of Western Philosophy.* New York: Simon and Schuster.

Rutherford, D. 1995a. "Philosophy and Language in Leibniz." In Jolley 1995: 224–69.

Rutherford, D. 1995b. *Leibniz and the Rational Order of Nature.* Cambridge, UK: Cambridge University Press.

Rutkowska, J. C. 1993. *The Computational Infant.* London: Harvester Press.

Ryle, G. 1949. *The Concept of Mind.* New York: Barnes and Noble.

Ryle, G. 1971. "John Locke." In *Collected Papers.* London: Hutchinson.

Sacksteder, W. 1978. "Spinoza on Part and Whole: The Worm's Eye View." In *Spinoza: New Perspectives.* Eds. R. W. Shahan and J. I. Biro, pp. 139–59. Norman: University of Oklahoma Press.

Sacksteder, W. 1982. "Hobbes: Man the Maker." In *Thomas Hobbes: His View of Man.* Ed. J. G. van der Bend, pp. 77–88. Amsterdam: Rodopoi.

Salmon, N., and S. Soames, eds. 1988. *Propositions and Propositional Attitudes.* New York: Oxford University Press.

Salmon, V. 1966. "Language-Planning in Seventeenth-Century England: Its Context and Aims." In *In Memory of J. R. Firth.* Ed. C. E. Bazell, pp. 370–97. London: Longmans.

Schmidt, J., ed. 1996. *"What Is Enlightenment?": Texts and Interpretations.* Berkeley: University of California Press.

Schneiders, W., ed. 1983. *Christian Wolff 1679–1754: Interpretationen zu seiner Philosophie und deren Wirkung.* Hamburg: Felix Meiner Verlag.

Schouls, P. A. 1989. *Descartes and the Enlightenment.* Kingston: McGill-Queen's University Press.

Schouls, P. A. 1992. *Reasoned Freedom: John Locke and the Enlightenment.* Ithaca: Cornell University Press.

Segal, G. 1991. "Defence of a Reasonable Individualism." *Mind* 100: 485–94.

Shapiro, B. 1969. *John Wilkins, 1614–1672.* Berkeley: University of California Press.

Sorell, T. 1986. *Hobbes.* New York: Routledge and Kegan Paul.

Spragens, T. A. 1973. *The Politics of Motion.* Lexington: University of Kentucky Press.

Stoudt, J. 1957. *Sunrise to Eternity*. Philadelphia: University of Pennsylvania Press.

Struck, W. 1936. *Der Einfluss Jakob Böhmes auf die englische Literatur des 17. Jahrhunderts*. Berlin: Junker und Dünnhaupt.

Styazhkin, N. I. 1969. *History of Mathematical Logic from Leibniz to Peano*. Cambridge, MA: MIT Press.

Sutton, J. 1998. *Philosophy and Memory Traces: Descartes to Connectionism*. Cambridge: Cambridge University Press.

Taylor, C. 1975. *Hegel*. Cambridge: Cambridge University Press.

Tuck, R. 1987. "The 'Modern' Theory of Natural Law." In *The Language of Political Theory in Early Modern Europe*. Ed. A. Pagden, pp. 99–119. Cambridge: Cambridge University Press.

Tuck, R. 1989. *Hobbes*. Oxford: Oxford University Press.

Ungeheuer, G. 1983. "Sprache und symbolische Erkenntnis bei Wolff." In Schneiders 1983: 89–112.

Van der Linden, Harry. 1988. *Kantian Ethics and Socialism*. Indianapolis: Hackett.

Van Fraassen, B. 1984. "Belief and the Will." *Journal of Philosophy* 81: 235–55.

Venturi, F. 1971. *Europe des Lumières: Recherches sur le 18e siècle*. Paris: Mouton.

Vleeschauer, H. J. de. 1962. "Wie ich jetzt die Kritik der reinen Vernunft entwicklungsgeschichtlich lese." *Kant Studien* 54: 351–68.

Völker, L. 1972. "Gelassenheit. Zur Entstehung des Wortes in der Sprache Meister Eckharts und seiner Überlieferung in der nacheckhartischen Mystik bis Jacob Böhme." In *Getempert und Gemischet*. Eds. F. Hundsnurscher and U. Müller, pp. 281–312. Göttingen: Kümmerle.

Voss, S., ed. 1993. *Essays on the Philosophy and Science of René Descartes*. Oxford: Oxford University Press.

Walker, D. P. 1972. "Leibniz and Language." *Journal of the Warburg and Courtauld Institutes* 35: 294–307.

Ward, R. 1710. *The Life of the Learned and Pious Dr. Henry More*. London: Downing and Close.

Watkins, J. 1965. *Hobbes's System of Ideas*. London: Hutchinson.

Watson, J. B. 1930. *Behaviorism*. New York: W. W. Norton.

Webster, C. 1975. *The Great Instauration: Science, Medicine and Reform: 1626–1660*. London: Duckworth.

Webster, C. 1982. *From Paracelsus to Newton*. Cambridge: Cambridge University Press.

Weeks, A. 1991. *Boehme: An Intellectual Biography of the Seventeenth-Century Philosopher and Mystic*. Albany: State University of New York Press.

Williams, B. 1973. "Deciding to Believe." In *Problems of the Self: Philosophical Papers*, pp. 136–51. Cambridge, UK: Cambridge University Press.

Wilson, C. 1987. "*De Ipsa Natura*." *Studia Leibnitiana* 19: 148–72.

Wilson, C. 1989. *Leibniz's Metaphysics: A Comparative and Historical Study*. Princeton: Princeton University Press.

Wilson, M. 1967. "Leibniz and Locke on 'First Truths.'" *Journal of the History of Ideas* 28: 347–60.

Wilson, M. 1977. "Confused Ideas." In *Essays on the Philosophy of Leibniz.* Ed. M. Kulstad, pp. 123–37. *Rice University Studies in Philosophy* 63. Houston: Rice University.

Wilson, M. 1978. *Descartes.* London: Routledge.

Wittgenstein, L. 1953. *Philosophical Investigations.* New York: Macmillan.

Wolff, R. P. 1998. "The Completion of Kant's Moral Theory." In Kneller 1998: 39–61.

Wolfson, H. A. 1958. *The Philosophy of Spinoza.* 2 vols. New York: Meridian Books.

Wood, A. W. 1998. "Kant's Historical Materialism." In Kneller 1998: 15–37.

Woolhouse, R. S. 1982. "The Nature of an Individual Substance." In *Leibniz: Critical and Interpretive Essays.* Ed. M. Hooker, pp. 45–64. Minneapolis: University of Minneapolis Press.

Woolhouse, R. S. 1983. *Locke.* Minneapolis: University of Minneapolis Press.

Woolhouse, R. S. 1985. "Pre-Established Harmony Returned: Ishiguro versus the Tradition." *Studia Leibnitiana* 17: 204–19.

Yolton, J. 1970. *Locke and the Compass of Human Understanding: A Selective Commentary on the "Essay."* Cambridge: Cambridge University Press.

Yolton, J. 1985. *Locke: An Introduction.* Oxford: Basil Blackwell.

Yovel, Y. 1989. *Spinoza and Other Heretics: The Marrano of Reason.* Princeton: Princeton University Press.

Zemach, E. 1985. "*De Se* and Descartes: A New Semantics for Indexicals." *Nous* 19: 181–204.

Index

Printed in the United States
85691LV00004B/286-303/A